Design and
Aesthetics in Wood

Design and Aesthetics in Wood

Edited by

Eric A. Anderson, Professor of
Wood Products Engineering

George F. Earle, Professor of Art

State University of New York
College of Environmental Science
and Forestry

Sponsored Jointly by   State University of New York
College of Environmental Science
and Forestry
Syracuse University School of Art
New York State Science and
Technology Foundation
under a grant from the
New York State Science and
Technology Foundation

Design and Aesthetics in Wood
First Edition
Published by the State University of New York
College of Environmental Science and Foresty,
Syracuse, New York
Distributed by State University of New York
Press, 99 Washington Avenue, Albany,
New York 12210
© 1972 State University of New York
All rights reserved
Printed in the United States of America
Library of Congress Cataloging in
Publication Data
Design and aesthetics in wood.

A symposium sponsored by the State
University College of Forestry, Syracuse
University School of Art, and the New
York State Science and Technology
Foundation, and held at the State
University College of Forestry at Syracuse
University, Nov. 7–9, 1967.
Bibliography: p.
1. Wood—Congresses. 2. Woodwork
—Congresses. 3. Design, Industrial—
Congresses. I. Anderson, Eric A., 1907–
ed. II. Earle, George F., ed. III. New York
(State). College of Forestry, Syracuse.
IV. Syracuse University. School of Art.
V. New York State Science and
Technology Foundation.
TA419.D47   624'.184   75-171186
ISBN 0-87395-216-2

Dedicated to   Edwin C. Jahn,
who gave so freely of his wisdom,
counsel and encouragement in the
course of this symposium.

Contents

Preface

This symposium on "Design and Aesthetics in Wood" was held at the State University of New York College of Environmental Science and Forestry on 7–9 November 1967. Concurrent with the conference was an exhibition, sponsored by the College of Environmental Science and Forestry and the School of Art of Syracuse University, in which the art objects and industrial products illustrated here were a part.

This symposium brings together for mutual stimulation the vision and imagination of the designer and architect and the knowledge of the engineer and technologist. To provide a certain perspective, there is added the analytic insight of the philosopher defining aesthetics and design. We hope that these various viewpoints will together come alive and ultimately produce from their interpenetration of disciplined thought and creative vision new concepts and possibilities of design in wood—forms richer in aesthetic value and more elegantly efficient in usefulness than current wooden forms, which are now in retreat before new materials. It is hoped, too, that this symposium will generate greater understanding of man's long and intimate association with wood and of how he may still wish to remain dependent on wood products for his well-being and happiness in a world of new materials and unfamiliar forms—in other words there may truly be some kind of ecological relationship between man and wood.

The idea behind the symposium was a belief that the forests of the world—a great ever-renewable natural resource—can be made to do much for all mankind if wood products can be freed from the exhausted forms of present use. This belief holds that the very length and pervasiveness of man's association with wood is based on deep-seated affinities that extend in depth and complexity far beyond wood's actual usefulness to man. These affinities call for a new shaping of this old material rather than either abandoning it for more "obedient" or novel materials, on the one hand, or stubbornly defending its use in an ever-smaller number of traditional forms on the other.

The spirit of the symposium is not a blindly partisan or a traditional defense of wood, for it notes both the unconventional restructuring of wood and the superiority of other materials for certain uses. Rather a main thrust of the symposium is against our culture's blind rejection of wood just because wood lacks novelty, inventiveness, and imagination—qualities associated with new materials because they are new and have attracted design effort. The symposium speaks repeatedly to the point that wood, by its very richness of variety—by the very omnifarious quality that allows other substances to surpass it for specific uses—offers design opportunities, especially when combined with new techniques and materials, of novel freshness, inventiveness, and imagination, that can make other materials appear sterile and mean. In a world of vanishing natural resources, however, no justification is required for any attempt to obtain the greatest possible contribution, aesthetic and utilitarian, from the one great resource that is not disappearing, our forests.

We wish to express our appreciation to the New York State Science and Technology Foundation for its generous support which made possible the conference and the preparation of this book.

We wish also to express our deep appreciation to D. Lee DuSell, who, assisted by Jerome J. Malinowsky, designed and assembled the Exhibition; Jean Fisher, with whom the idea of the conference originated; Edwin C. Jahn and Richard E. Pentoney, who were responsible for so much of the College's support; Laurence Schmeckebier, whose advice and guidance were invaluable; and Arthur J. Pulos, William J. Wasserstrom, Frank J. Hanrahan, D. Kenneth Sargent, Willard Gullicksen, John I. Zerbe, and Aubrey Wylie, all of whom acted as discussion leaders at the conference. To the many, many dedicated people on the faculty and staff and to the students of the College of Environmental Science and Forestry and School of Art who helped with the various tasks associated both with the conference and this symposium, we express our sincere thanks.

The Editors

Introduction

This symposium was inspired by a desire to make the artist, the architect, the wood-products manufacturer, the engineer, the wood scientist and the wood technologist more aware of the contributions each of the others make to the design, both functional and aesthetic, of a wood object, whether it is a toy or a home, a figure or an arch. This objective implies a cross-fertilization of creativity and knowledge that can bring to wood the same sensitivity of thought and concentrated effort, the same excitement of understanding, the same recognition of usefulness and versatility that now exists for the newer and less traditional materials. The old stereotyped attitudes toward wood—a kind of dull tunnel vision with little or no recognition of wood's true character—can never recognize potential new usage, adaptability, and fresh expression that can expand horizons of wood utility and aesthetic value. Such a new viewpoint might enable the architect to see wood as a truly versatile material that can be fabricated to meet his requirements. Perhaps the manufacturer will look to the real needs of the architect and fabricate his wood products to meet these needs. The designer can contribute better design of the product and the wood technologist might alter wood to suit the manufacturer's and architect's needs.

The contributors were asked to consider wood and its design in the context of social needs—this implies creative design, both functional and aesthetic. Accordingly, they write in terms of community as well as individual needs, of economic and manufacturing requirements, of design as it affects efficiency and utility and as it affects people psychologically; they write of safety, of the successes and failures they have had in bringing out the beauty and human appeal of wood, and of wood as an element in the essential awareness of man.

They even discuss the place of wood design in our political and economic systems, both its historical role in the power structure of nations and its contemporary role given the limitations of our raw materials reservoirs.

Seldom has so diverse a group of people from such a wide range of professions been asked to contribute their particular expertise to the consideration of a problem such as design and aesthetics in wood. Their interest varied from a direct, professional involvement with wood and wood design to a concern for design or aesthetics of a wide range of materials. The different viewpoints within their broad common interest—their sometimes amusing contradictions—serve to strengthen the mix with resolvable tension. The editors hope that the reader will consider each writer's viewpoint as contributing to the whole rather than being totally significant in itself, so that the contributors, speaking from their various convictions and fields of knowledge, will together help stimulate an awareness of the rich, still untapped resource that wood represents in our environment and thereby allow this ancient, yet modern material to achieve a fuller measure of its potential.

It seems inevitable that certain sectors of this broad subject area, design and aesthetics in wood, must be less thoroughly treated than others, however we hope that a variety of viewpoint rather than a carefully balanced range of professional representation would not only offer a more stimulating result but also might come closer to covering all sectors of interest. Thus, while architecture is represented possibly even more than its economically predominant use of wood might justify, its representatives range critically over man's fascination for and use of wood, past and present, and from large, exterior structure to small, interior form. Some may feel the symposium should have a specific spokesman for the

designer of the smaller industrial and domestic objects, such as comprise the photographic section on the Exhibition, but the editors feel that the Exhibition itself presents this viewpoint with unique effectiveness; that it says much about wood in domestic interior and industrial use that could be said in no other way.

From the symposium as a whole comes the idea of "living" wood as "friendly" to man, as a material of warmth, as a material loaded with meaning for man. This theme emerges as more than sentimentalism or nostalgia for the days before the instant forms of plastic or the shiny coldness of metallic finishes. It speaks rather for the innate, instinctive, sensory reactions to certain materials that attract and away from others that repel. It describes curious counterfeits in which the appeal of wood is forged upon some other less appealing material. The papers contrast the meaning and symbolism of wood with stone and masonry forms, and note in passing the curious reversals of treating wood to look like stone or painting masonry to look like wood.

The papers do not attempt to present wood as universally the best material— rather there is an honest recognition that each material has its suitable use. As Carl Koch says, technology can find a substitute to perform *any one* of wood's many functions better and cheaper. However, there is common recognition that wood is not now being used to its greatest potential and that it has certain very unique characteristics that can contribute significantly to aesthetic experience and enriched living in ways that the narrow aims of technology turn away from.

Implied by the papers is the need for a revised philosophy among wood-products industrialists—a change from a pure marketing philosophy to one showing respect for and recognition of the merits wood has because of its relation to people and their needs—from a shortsighted utilitarian view to an understanding of the part aesthetic design of wood products can play in human happiness. Such a change will bring a more secure place for all manner of objects in wood. Examples are drawn upon from Japan and Scandinavia to show the importance wood can have, the near reverence it can inspire. There does not seem to be a question of whether wood is useful or inherently aesthetic; rather, there is the question of how to give wood design the freshness but absolute "rightness" that characterizes so many of the objects of the Exhibition—both a captivating presentation of wood as substance and an almost seductive invitation to use.

In forming this symposium, it was felt that there were things about wood—in both its aesthetic and design potential—that were not being said and that needed saying. Wood should continue to be recognized as man's most useful natural material and its special meanings to man should be validated. It was held that part of wood's interest and fascination lies in the print of its growth that it carries on its fiber and texture, part in the infinite variety wood has, which gives it a warm, human quality as compared to the cold artificiality of synthetic materials. For the material of man himself is as infinitely irregular as wood, although man strives to produce regularity. And perhaps a third attraction that wood has is the moderate resistance it puts up against man's attempt to work it and against nature's forces of decay. Again, wood is of human scale in this respect. As the papers bring out, man monumentalizes stone, the monarch of natural material, but wood he feels to be more intimate and democratic. One paper even defends the decay process in wood and speaks against automatic efforts to prevent rot.

Overall, it is felt that wood can play a greater role now than it does—that the speed and narrow directionality of technology is unbalanced in its thrust for efficient production and synthetic regularity. By reexamining wood's quality as a material, so long taken for granted, it is possible to counter this unbalanced drive of production. Man today seems especially ready to reassess and reevaluate wood, for he is eager to bring certain rich, human qualities back into his life. We believe that with a true understanding of wood's unique qualities, designers can release imaginative forms that are fresh and new and expressive of contemporary human needs and ideals.

The editors hope that this volume will contribute to the fulfillment of such a goal.

The Editors

PART I
Wood as Art and Artifact

Wood is a material whose wide variety is perhaps the root of its fascination for us. This diversity is also found in the views expressed regarding wood. Among these papers there is no straight-line progression from A to Z as in a well-organized scientific treatise. Rather, there is an interplay of design aesthetics, material technology, and social ecology, not only between but within papers. In spite of this diversity, however, four general categories of ideas and thought are visible and the papers have been grouped within them.

The first of these has been titled "Wood as Art and Artifact." Here the orientation is generally toward questions of aesthetics, questions of wood and its philosophic meanings to man, as well as the relation of wood to man's social needs, both in art and craftsmanship. Opening the section is Reyner Banham, who gives background and insight into the subject of wood in furniture, architecture, and other usage and establishes, often wittily, many issues and questions that come up again and again in other papers. The question of the integrity of false wood veneers and grain forgeries of various kinds—over baser wood or over nonwood materials—is well exposed and even turned around. He sketches in some origins of the concept of "wood as fine art," and of wood as psychologically "friendly to man," and examines with great penetration the "mystique of wood," its quality of being "loaded with meanings," and its symbolism for life styles. Finally he states the paradox of man and wood well—a paradox that reappears throughout the book—that man is forced to somehow doctor wood to perform with the precision he has taught himself to require, but at the same time, in his heart he can truly love only the "unreliable" living wood which he must desiccate, mummify, or otherwise kill to use.

Banham's critical viewpoint as an architectural scholar is followed by that of a practicing architect, Carl Koch. His paper reflects a career-long interest and emphasis on the total design of structure from furnishings and furniture to multiple-dwelling concepts and exposes his concerns for the aesthetic, social, and philosophical aspects of the subject. Koch, unlike other contributors, speaks strongly of wood conservation—he would develop this natural product only for purposes for which it is especially and even uniquely suited. Like Banham he traces man's traditional associations with and affinities for wood and forests. But he is deeply concerned and anxious about overuse and depletion of the nation's forests. He takes a somewhat different approach to wood imitations than Banham's amused tolerance and bitterly condemns the use of wood for structures where it is concealed by metal and plastic surfaces—real wood should be available to the eye and hand and not hidden. In a more philosophic vein he describes eloquently the value of personal involvement in the crafting of wood, its virtues for the individual in its resistance to the precision molds of machine production. He cites Japanese reverence for wood and relates wood-working to a growing hunger for the complete or whole-man experience of craftsmanship. He concludes with a harsh dismissal of museum art in favor of a "real involvement with life" through craftsmanship. To him the carpenter has a potentially more effective art than the painter, because the carpenter can introduce beauty into the useful as well as create utility by itself. "Art," he says, "is nothing but the process of doing anything well."

This sets the stage for Paul Weiss, whose radical position that craftsmanship and art are mutually exclusive sharply contradicts not only Koch but the entire traditional viewpoint of the design profession—architecture, furniture design, industrial design, and especially designers in wood —because, as Banham brings out, for over fifty years since the early collages of modern art, wood and wood grain have generated an art cult that has spread from easel painting to sculpture and to product design. For many, the Exhibition itself, which follows Weiss in this volume, contradicts Weiss's definition that usefulness rules out art, that there can be no craftsman in the artist and no artist in the craftsman. However Weiss speaks as a philosopher whose critical analysis of aesthetics starts from a more absolute base—he presents aesthetic experience as occurring almost without concept or object, and the artist as making something only to *be,* not something to function. Perhaps Weiss's opinion is best made understandable by his comment that architecture is a business, a craft, and an art; so far as the architect is an artist his objective has nothing to do with profit or utility. In any case Weiss is quite clearly in opposition to other contributors when he flatly separates craftsmanship—the enhancing of material by skillfully combining graceful form and harmony of parts with function—from art.

On the other hand, Weiss establishes a theme common to the symposium contributors when he speaks of the "vitality and vibrance of wood which we get, not by touch or mere sight, but by a kind of organic interplay with it, particularly when it is alive . . . that an aesthetic appreciation penetrates below the surface and allows for a vital participation in what is alive."

The philosopher's approach, with its astringent sharpness of terminology, its shift in semantic arrangements, its contradiction of the familiar, forces us to rethink accustomed positions but offers the reward of fresh insight and a new sense of reality.

The final sections of "Wood as Art and Artifact," the introduction to the Exhibition by Laurence Schmeckebier and the photographic presentation of these wood objects by D. Lee DuSell, together represent the position of the artist-designer, with his shaping, sculpting, constructing, and fabricating of small objects, in contrast to the architect with his larger constructions and the technician with his concern for wood as a material. It can be safely assumed that Schmeckebier feels no mutual exclusion between art and craftsmanship and that the Exhibition objects are offered without exception as both art and craft. Schmeckebier notes that the characteristic common to all the objects is a respect for the nature of the material. Here he refers to Brancusi "whose devotion to the medium often determined the content: the craftsman's thinking hand discovering the thoughts of the material." Weiss, by a perhaps forced fineness of discrimination, isolates craftsmanship from art and the ingenious functional use of wood from creative expressions wholly free of function. The photographic Exhibition offers substantive rebuttal to this position.

Is There a Substitute for Wood Grain Plastic?

REYNER BANHAM
Reader in Architecture
University College, London

Reyner Banham received his doctorate at London, where he studied history of art. World War II saw him in the Engines Division, Experimental Department of Bristol Aeroplane Company. Since then he has served on the editorial staff of Architectural Review, *done independent research for the Graham Foundation in Chicago, and has been architectural correspondent for* New Society *and for the* New Statesman. *He was chairman of the Working Commission on Definition and Doctrine of the International Council of Societies for Industrial Design. He has written several books and is a frequent contributor to professional journals.*

In the remote and picturesque ghost-city of Port Townsend in the state of Washington, I lunched at the Bartlett House, possibly the most westerly example of the Hudson River Bracketed style, a handsome double-fronted mansion, built entirely of wood, full of ingenious and crafty carpenter's details, warmed and serviced by wood-burning stoves. From its front garden one could look out across the still waters of the Sound and see islands apparently still covered in aboriginal forest, except where thin horizontal wisps of wood smoke lay across the scene as neat and pretty as those in a Japanese wood engraving. And the smell of that smoke hung sharp and dramatic on the still afternoon air.

For a visitor like myself, born and brought up in a culture and a part of the world where a wood fire is a demonstrative luxury, where aboriginal forest must be preserved as jealously as rare birds or ancient buildings and where timber is a commodity that often has to be rationed in times of national stringency—with such a background I was bound to be somewhat impressed not only by the sheer abundance of trees, wood, and timber, but also by the sense of a whole way of life, a civilization almost, carved out of that abundance.

Then a neighbor looked in to ask for help in unloading the week's shopping from the station wagon. Almost the first commodity to be loaded into my arms from the tailgate of the wagon—which had plastic panels of simulated wood on its sides—was something I had never seen before: perfectly regular cylindrical logs of reconstructed wood, identical in length and diameter and packaged in standard bundles of eight.

"Where shall I put these?" I inquired.

"By the stove in the living room!"

I did so, but in the process I underwent what anthropologists call culture-shock— the sheet-steel jacket of the neighbor's stove was handsomely adorned with enameled wood graining!

The whole experience was culture-shock too in the contrast between past and present; a past in which tree-wood was a substance to burn and to build and to look upon, but was always one and indivisible, the same substance. And a present in which the real substance and fictive appearance of wood had drifted so far apart that not only was the appearance of woodgrain to be found on substances that had never at any stage of their history been tree products, but also that the substance of wood for burning had to be re-created in its own image, that fictional logs had to be made from the waste products of processes whose raw material had once been logs.

You may regard such a situation as farcical, derisory, hysterical, sinister, or schizophrenic, but you cannot fail to regard it if you observe the life of North America as it is lived at present. Nor can you fail to reflect it on the rest of the world, for in every nation and people that traditionally employed wood for construction and furnishing, this dichotomy between form and substance may be observed—there is hardly a modern hotel from Oslo to Osaka

to Ottawa where you will not discover that seemingly wooden surfaces are in fact plastic or metal. But before we damn the whole situation out-of-hand as a modern aberration, we should remember that it does have historical antecedents.

In the ancient English fishing port of Whitby, from which Captain Cook sailed to discover most of what we know of the South Pacific, there is a spectacular church, roofed in with a structure like ship's wooden deck and lit by skylights identical with the glazed hatch of the local fishing cobbles. The internal space of the church contains about the maximum amount of woodwork compatible with human occupation and religious ceremony —the floor space is entirely subdivided by chest-high partitions into private pews with locking doors; galleries—also subdivided— bracket off every piece of solid wall, and a complex three-decker pulpit rises in carpenter-baroque fantasy to a height of perhaps eighteen feet in the center of the church. You would think it was carpentry rather than the Trinity that was worshipped there—especially as most of this wood has artificial wood graining painted on it!

In practice, this wood-grained paint has perfectly reasonable justifications. The wood must be painted to preserve it, especially in that corrosive seaside atmosphere, and the graining of the paint serves to reassert the nature of the material beneath it. Or even enhance its nature, for quite often on top of wood one knows to be perfectly ordinary, boring, straight-grain yellow pine, appears such an efflorescence of figuring and knots as never grew on any tree in heaven or earth. Indeed, the grainer's art became quite independent of the wood beneath in the nineteenth century in England, and expressive figuring spread from the woodwork of exposed window frames and door cases to the cheap stucco that commonly surfaced extremely common brickwork, much as the imitation sanded stone-painting spread over the wooden carcasses of many buildings of the same period in the U.S.A.

In both cases, the primary need is to give some form of weather-protection to a common constructional material, but in both cases artifice seizes the opportunity to make the material appear less common; to disguise stucco as wood and wood as stone. Stern moralists from Ruskin onwards have found either subterfuge intolerable, have damned stucco, and insisted that wood look like the wood it really is, and brick like brick. So, the generation of architects—Le Corbusier, Mies Van der Rohe—who in the 1920s covered concrete in stucco and white paint to make it look more like concrete and waxed indignant at Frank Lloyd Wright's use of steel to help seemingly wooden cantilevers carry well beyond the possibilities of wooden construction—such men, when they used wood in their interiors as a visual relief from the austerities of steel and glass, frequently finished up using woods as expensive as they were impractical in order to get figurings strong enough to register visually.

So, if Le Corbusier hoped to make these "materials friendly to man" available to all mankind with his common universal generosity, he was going to need exotic woods, or at least exotic veneer, on the cheap. And they were to become available, sure enough—though somewhat later—printed by the yard on paper and either pasted on to the wall or bonded into the surface of plastic laminates. Which he, and most architects, now profess to find disgusting.

It quite often happens that, in discussion with architects or interior decorators of my acquaintance, we argue this way and that over the ideal qualities required of a kitchen work-surface or something similar and in the end, when all aspects of durability, cleaning, heat resistance, and appearance have been totted up, I have to say "admit it, the answer to your problem is wood-grain, Formica-faced block board—but you haven't got the guts to use it!"

In my turn, I should admit that "guts" is an unkind way of putting the matter. Most architects would say that they have a moral scruple against employing such a deception on the public. But I think we should notice that this has now become a very *nice* scruple, in the Shakesperian use of *nice,* and the morality involved has to be sliced very fine. For these same architects would probably accept, without moral difficulty, such a material as exterior grade, mahogany-faced plywood, in which the face veneer is apt to be a misrepresentation of the substance of the plies behind, and in which there may be quite as much miscellaneous plastics for bonding and weathering purposes as there is in avowedly plastic-faced block boards or chipboards.

The difference between the morally intolerable and the morally tolerable may only be the difference between paper (made from wood) with a grain printed on it and wood (paper-thin) with a grain grown in it. I wouldn't like to try and explain this situation to an intelligent Martian or even an intelligent four-year-old human being. Both would certainly find more interest and more profit in discussing what is behind the paper-thin surface graining.

For what does lie behind is an avowal of the uselessness of wood as nature provides it. Plywood, laminates, block board, chipboard and, indeed, paper too—are all ways of remoulding wood nearer to heart's desire, structural need, or green-backed profit. The pressing up of veneer into plies and laminates has grown from a way of making expensive figures cover more dull grain—the original use of veneers—into a way of making a continuous, wooden, thin sheet-material with better performance, utility, and range of sizes than regular match-boarding could ever offer. And the materials rolled out from chips and assembled from blocks seem to have started as ways of reusing the vast quantities of fairly homogeneous offcuts that arise from the mechanical working of raw wood—but grew into a way of producing wood substitutes with better strength-weight ratios, stiffness-weight ratios, or better dimensional stability.

Technical historians of the wood-processing industries may want to quarrel with me about the intentions or outcomes of these developments—and I must admit myself a layman in the history of such techniques—but any observant layman must see that these are the effective practical outcomes of the transformation of wood. It emerges as a material at last freed from the immemorial faults of shake, split, warp, shrink, and the rest of it. The layman who "does it himself" knows that any normal tree wood he uses is apt to do any of these things and that he will rarely buy a parcel of lumber that does not contain some pieces too faulty to be used. But if he buys ply, "compo," or other made-up boards, he can at least be sure of avoiding any of these traditional faults critical to his structural intentions.

And if he talks to friends in, say, the furniture industry, he will hear that their very economic survival depends on their not using wood as nature provides it. There can be no mass production, they point out, without interchangeability of parts, and there can be no interchangeability of parts that are not dimensionally stable. Terence Conran, English furniture manufacturer, once said to me, "What is the use of my making up stocks of wooden components if they come out of stock a different size to what they went in, just because the weather has changed? We would love to mass-produce and mechanize, but as

things are we always finish up with so much hand fitting to pay for, that we never accumulate the capital to buy a mechanical plant, even if we could use it." Part of his trouble, indeed, is that he makes "well-designed" furniture and sells it therefore to a restricted and educated clientele who feel —like architects—that the use of chip-board and such are dishonest practices, without realizing that without such practices they could never afford well-designed furniture at all.

Or to put it another way, without such practices we might, in a true mass-producing society, have to give up using wood altogether. On the other hand, for quasi-mass-producing industries and ones where the required dimensional tolerances are fairly sloppy, and the housebuilding industry fulfills both requirements, wood obviously has a long future. In the most sophisticated of architectural housing practice the ultimate production process and the ultimate arbiter of dimensional tolerances is he whom Serge Chermayeff once described as "the same old eighteenth-century carpenter with his mouth full of nails." And a house structure, once up, is allowed to settle, shift, take up, creak, and go bang in the night, in a manner that would be intolerable in a yacht hull, an aircraft propellor, or a normally jointed chair or table.

For each of these more specialized uses, Mother Nature's tree-wood is a "non-starter," or nearly so, and we all of us increasingly know it. And as natural tree-wood has increasingly faded from our tangible and structural environment, so we have come increasingly to value its appearance, real or fictitious. And it is not only the ignorant and allegedly cultureless with their fake wood-grain station wagons and knotty-pine wallpaper and embossed-grain aluminum roll-away garage doors who hunger after the sight of wood. Many a cultured household is proud to display upon its coffee table a wooden bowl by Prestini's (or some other less cunning) hand. So this is real wood, not applied graining, but it is wood used in a context that would have been rare a generation ago, and unknown three generations since—our grandfathers would have relegated a wooden bowl to the kitchen, if they had possessed them at all.

Along side such semi-fine-art objects, the fine arts too have developed a new passion for wood and its grainy structure. But, by a splendid irony, the tremendous revival of interest in wood—as a carver's material in the generation of Henry Moore, and as a printmaker's material in the sense of changing from end-grain boxwood, which is neutral in the finished print, to side-grain softwood which registers its grain—in both these cases the revaluation of wood was preceded by George Braque's joking use of wood-grain paper in Cubist collages from 1911 onwards. In historical fact, those wood-grain decorator's papers are the almost exact halfway stage between the hand-painted grainer's art of the nineteenth century and the applied-printed grains of today, so this was an extremely suitable point for modern art to join the cult.

I do not use the word *cult* rashly—I mean it to be taken seriously, with those religious overtones that the word retains, say, in French, even if they are largely lost in English. What is rash here is that I propose to change from historical exposition to psychological speculation. Obviously, though, it is a fact that we regret the passing of something valuable in the disappearance of natural tree-wood from our practical surroundings and wish it back in simulation and in art. What is it that we feel we have lost?

Le Corbusier, I think, was not kidding when he listed wood among those "materials friendly to man." We actively like wood. We pick up and handle wooden objects in a way in which we rarely do with other materials. Indeed we expect the handle-end of a tool or weapon to be of wood and regard other materials as poor substitutes. He that "set his hand to the plow, and looked not back," expected his hand to touch wood—and so does the man who gets into a racing car and puts his hand to the wheel. The butt of a gun and the grip of a screwdriver, the baseball bat and haft of an axe are all, in our expectation, wooden. And for good reasons—many of the qualities possessed by wood make it a natural for handles; the ease with which it can be shaped, its resilience under impact and its poor conductivity of heat, which brings it to comfortable hand temperature almost as soon as it is grasped.

And so our hands become immemorially conditioned to the grasp of wood and it has acquired for us an ancient familiarity which may encourage us to sentimentality, but depends on an objective human need—to grasp only that which may comfortably be grasped. Notice how wooden-handled cutlery has come back in the last ten years, in defiance of the unrelenting rituals of modern hygiene. The grasp of wood is probably as basic to human culture as the making of fire and the writing of language—a Viking marauder in the tenth century might have brained an Irish chieftain with a lump of wood that came to hand and then added it to the fire, without knowing that some valued historical record was notched in its edge in Ogham script.

But, in general practice within the culture we inhabit, valuable records have been carved in stone, not wood. Partly because stone is more durable, but more perhaps, because stone is the dominant material of the Mediterranean basin—poor in wood in all historic time—from which our conscious culture derives. Masonry, statuary, Latinate languages, Greek philosophy, Roman law —these are the cultural concepts we have consciously cultivated in universities, the courts of princes and judges, and have illuminated with that Christian religion which is in so many ways the distilled wisdom of settled Mediterranean peasant communities. This is our superculture, so to speak, so that for both the king of England and the president of the United States we built imitations of the masonry mansions of Mediterranean noblemen and we regard the progress of Abraham Lincoln from wooden log cabin to the stone White House as an *upward* movement.

Maybe it was, but if a wooden building represents, in economic fact, the bottom end of the scale, why does the top end have to be a stone one? The Norwegian royal family have a sizeable masonry palace in Oslo and an equally impressive one in wood in Trondheim. But this is rare; wood is generally the symbolic material of our underculture and disregarded so. But it is nonetheless symbolic of very valuable parts of our culture. It is the material of tools and trade; until recently it was the material of transportation and movement in boats and carts and early aeroplanes; it was—and is—the material of the dwellings of the humble, the pioneers, the adventurers. Above all, it was and is the material of the northern forests where most of us come from, the original environment of our human stock and many of our most valued social concepts, such as practical equality and universal democracy.

I know that for many cultured people, talk about the forests of Northern Europe conjures embarrassing or downright sinister visions of Nazis capering about in torchlit Walpurgisnacht orgies. The point is well taken, the forests and democracy are not inevitably linked. And on the other hand, the vain and inhumane pomposities of Mussolini's regime were acceptable to a number of cultured people just because they seemed to sustain the traditions of masonry architecture, marble statuary, and Roman law. It should also be added however that the democratic Scandinavians caper about in torchlit orgies from time to time and this leads to nothing more ominous than a lot of harmless jollity and new scenarios for Ingmar Bergmann.

I will refrain from generalizing too extensively from what may be a unique personal experience, but I must testify that the most sustainedly and deafeningly good-natured party I was ever at was conducted in full Viking vigor in a wooden ski hut in a Norwegian forest to celebrate the broaching of the spring beer. Merry peasants come in all flavours and many different kinds of party gear. You can have innocent fun in a forest clearing or a paved piazza, by the harvest moon or the midnight sun. But we do not seem to concede that one can have a valid higher culture in the context of a forested landscape and a wooden-built environment.

And whether this exclusive preference for a Mediterranean culture is right or wrong, the fact remains that most of us Anglo-Saxon or Nordic peoples came from a wooden environment and originally steered around the world in wooden ships and largely lived in wooden houses. We speak a language full of wood-words or wooden-type meanings even when the words are ultimately Latin. What, for instance, do we do with our proudest contribution to human justice, the jury of twelve good men and true? We *empanel* them. Where do we (or did we until recently) cast our universal democratic vote? In a wooden *box* (whereas the vote of the more limited democracy of Athens was cast in a pottery urn). Hospitably, we offer bed and *board,* and for both justice and refreshment we are called to an originally wooden *bar*. And there is probably some good reason why *bastard* means "son of a wooden bench!"

The Germans, Norwegians, Ukrainians, Danes, Swedes, Finns, Russians, Poles, and English (if not Irish and Welsh) who came to colonize North America came mostly from wood-built farms and wood-built towns. They had, in some cases, worshipped in wooden churches and wooden synagogues, they had in nearly all cases cooked at wood fires and eaten from wooden bowls and even wooden spoons. They came from a landscape that had been cleared of forests since the middle ages, or even awaited clearing, or is still not cleared today, and on arriving in North America found themselves frequently in another forested landscape that still awaited clearing. They looked out upon America's trees and enjoyed an incredible abundance of wood, and some very old and atavistic instincts—or at least, *ingrained* habits—were fulfilled in overplus. Until recently the life and economy of North America has enjoyed an orgy of wooden self-indulgence which is probably without precedent or previous equal, and I believe this has created a culture which is, unknowingly, "hooked" on wood.

What I am suggesting is less that North America as a culture is suffering from wooden withdrawal symptoms, than that it is now in the condition of the drinker who discovers that the bottle he thought nearly half full is nearly three-quarters empty. With natural woodland fast disappearing from the areas within the reach of the ordinary citizen, and with natural wood fast vanishing from his built environment, he overreacts and begins to fight desperately to keep every scenic drive through the redwood country or to ornament every non-wooden object with simulated wood grain.

Perhaps the situation should be phrased even more mildly than that. I would settle for something like the following summary of what I have been hinting at so far: that the use and experience of wood is an essential and basic part of the cultural inheritance of all northern, non-Mediterranean peoples.

Though they have cultivated Mediterranean arts, architecture, and design, the constant presence of wood in their working environment, both indoors and out, satisfied whatever cultural needs they had for contact with this material. *As long as the wood was there.* Once the real presence of natural tree-wood began to be withdrawn, then their cultural situation began to be thrown off balance and overcompensations began to appear—men began to exaggerate the nature of natural wood, invent wood where none was, refabricate wood products to look more like wood, cultivate a mystique of carpentry, wood-carving and do-it-yourself, and finally, to prepare symposia on aesthetics and design in wood.

For it is inconceivable to me that a culture that was at home with wood and comfortable with it, would ever feel any need to discuss wood at this high intellectual level. It was this thought that prompted me to approach the matter in the way I have done. I am sure many writers will address themselves to the topic under discussion in a bluff and practical way, explaining how they use wood to contrive that structure or this visual effect. But it takes two to make a structure—the builder as well as the material. And it takes two to make an aesthetic—the observer as well as the observed object.

To me the builder and the observer and the carver and the engraver are as interesting as the common material they all perform upon. What is it that they see in wood, what gratifications do they derive from working on it, why are they sufficiently "hung up" about it to talk and argue about it? For, let us face it, we are not considering the structural, operational, and visual exploitations of a mere natural resource, a raw material like any other. We are considering a material that is loaded with meanings, a material which inspires strong feelings in most of us.

We are here concerned with a material which is not brewed up at the behest of our own immediate will in vats and furnaces, nor laid down by geological process millions of years ago, but a material which commonly grows at a speed comparable to the speed at which we grow, so that a man who plants a seedling tree in middle age can just about expect to see it out-top himself before he dies. A material which, like man, grows upright and at right angles to the surface of the earth—a growth habit unique to man among the primates and unique to wood among his structural materials. No wonder we can identify so closely that we see men as trees walking, or mistake wind-shaken trees for men waving. No wonder they say that where a tree won't grow, a man won't grow.

And little wonder that we crave the presence of wood so deeply and so indiscriminately that we will settle for its painted or printed appearance even when its substance is present. And no wonder that every one has a ready answer to the rhetorical question which is the title of this paper.

Yes, Virginia, there is a substitute for wood-grain plastic—it is wood itself. But let us face the fact that for most employments and deployments, natural wood is a poor physical substitute for the many and sundry processed and perfected reincarnations of wood which now come coolly and unemotionally to hand.

Rationally and reasonably, the future lies with wood products, we must all suspect, rather than wood as it grows, but in our hearts we know that we will always prefer the old unreliable, twisty, shaky, knotty random lengths from the lumber yard—and *because* of those imperfections, not in spite of them.

Design and the Product in the Future Economy

CARL KOCH
Carl Koch and Associates
Boston, Massachusetts

A graduate in architecture from Harvard University, Carl Koch worked with Sven Markelius and with Gropius and Breur. He established his own firm in 1946. The many honors that have come to his firm include American Institute for Architects awards for the Wellesley Free Llibrary, Bennington College Library, Armco Techbuilt House, and the Acorn House. A lecturer and critic at MIT, he has contributed to many professional journals and is co-author of At Home with Tomorrow. *He is a Fellow of AIA and a member of its Committee on Residential Architecture.*

I want to make a plea for a return in the future to a more traditional use of wood, in a very specific sense, as the individual man's material for coping with his environment. The chief characteristic of wood as a material is and always has been its adaptability —using the simplest tools and a modicum of skill—to practically any purpose. When wood was the most abundant and available material, it was used for everything. Now that we are beginning to feel a scarcity, not only of woods but wooded land, we must reassess the uses to which we put this most versatile material. It is axiomatic that for a material which performs so many differing functions, a substitute can be found to perform *any one* of them better and cheaper if technology be aimed in that direction. We are in a position to choose which functions this material can perform best and most usefully and to effectively supplant wood in functions which seem, in the face of dwindling resources, wasteful. Although there are hundreds of new uses of wood appearing every day, it is not clear that it is the part of wisdom to put wood to work everywhere. The protean capability of wood can be replaced on the industrial level by many other products.

There are very few of us who don't have

a very special attachment to wood and this comes out of a deep past, our very beginnings—when wood was our friend and faithful helper in our long and tortuous journey toward an ordered, civilized world. Wood made it possible for us to control and use fire, to move out of damp, dark caves into the sun, and invent the wheel. Wood helped us launch ourselves on the sea and today many of the most imaginative and interesting uses of wood are for vessels which still carry us across the oceans. I hope the time will never come when man will cease to keep himself warm in front of a wood-burning fireplace or find himself far from wood he can touch, feel, and be sheltered by in his home wherever he makes it.

Wood is the only rigid organic material which is familiar to man, readily available to him, is intellectually comprehensible, provides a material which can be utilized in an infinite number of ways, and is naturally self-restoring. No other commonly used material elicits such an immediate response of "warmth," "beauty," "character." These terms are universally applied. No one talks of an "ugly" piece of wood or a "cold" one. Man has always used wood for his most primitive needs and to express his highest aspirations. Part of this appeal must stem from the fact that a tree is more than a raw material. A tree standing has a personal history expressed uniquely in its own form. It participates in a useful way in the ecology, affording man an irreplaceable service while it still stands. The use of wood should evidence respect, as it has in the past, for this unique history, as well as wood's unique qualities.

I noticed in the New York Times that the world's largest tree was to be cut down. It was nearly 400 feet tall. It was not in anybody's way, but it contained a great deal of saleable lumber. It seems somehow that such a magnificent creature ought to be worth a great deal left standing. It is clear anyway that any discussion of wood only brings up again the point that man's position in the physical and spiritual ecology of this planet is long overdue for reassessment.

There are a number of reasons we should be searching for better ways to use wood. The most obvious is its growing scarcity accompanied by a population explosion. Hans Landsberg, in his book Natural Resources for U. S. Growth, puts it this way:

By the year 2000 demand for domestic forest products is projected at over 29 billion cubic feet and net growth at only a little over 12 billion. Can new forests be planted in sufficient quantity to plug this gap of 17 billion cubic feet? The U. S. Forest Service estimates that some 55 cubic feet of realizable growth can be harvested from one acre of commercial forest land. On that basis, some 300 million acres would have to be planted to fill the gap, and they would have to be planted soon. New technology, such as faster breeding, higher rates of fertilization, etc., might reduce this figure, but not substantially. Furthermore, much of the land converted to forest would be in small lots, scattered over the country, with little relationship to points of processing or consumption. Further shrinkage of commercial forest land is generally believed to be ahead. Hence, the projected demand is incompatible with preservation of the nation's forests.*

Later he states that almost certainly, without a great change in present practice, eastern forests will be on the way to extinction by 2000.

* Landsberg, Hans H. Natural Resources for U. S. Growth, A Look Ahead to the Year 2000. Published for Resources for the Future, Inc. The Johns Hopkins Press. 1964.

The indignation about the redwood parks in California points up a very important problem—that of the further depletion of our forests. I get the impression from the reading I have done on the subject that the lumbering industry is like the typical builder in underestimating the human and social *and* economic value of good-sized trees. They will always grow, but this takes a kind of patience we don't see much of anywhere in the modern scene and a kind of space which our cities may soon demand. Many of us as parents and grandparents are disturbed at the changes in our woodland cover which make it more and more difficult to provide the coming generation with the easy natural access that was taken for granted in our childhood.

To satisfy the need for lumber there are for the years ahead large forest resources in the developing countries in Africa, South America, and Asia. We should encourage the importing of both lumber and wood products as a way of helping them develop markets and thus become customers for our own sophisticated products as well as sparing our own forests.

A very important way to use wood more effectively is to develop uses that take advantage of its visual as well as its structural qualities. It is too wasteful, I believe, to continue to use wood in its present structural form. As joists, rafters, studs, and rough sheathing, it is buried usually under far inferior materials which we then see, touch, and smell often with distaste and dissatisfaction. The abundance of wood imitations in our society represents a rather wrong-headed approach toward this problem. Instead of providing the proper wood, with the proper finishes, used in a graceful and satisfying way, most wood is still used as structure and hidden, while plastic and metal substitute on the surface in various ways, often disguised, usually unsatisfactory. Certainly a large market for wood in

the future lies in the production of hardwoods and the propagation of finishes and treatments which can make wood available to the eye and the hand. Real wood will justify considerable premium in this usage, not in rafters.

Fortunately we are beginning to reverse the process of wood-using inside the structure and are putting it outside where it belongs. As long ago as 1946 I worked out, with the help of John Bemis, a house which adopted this approach, putting the wood on the outside where it could be seen and cutting down the thickness of wood from the two-inch equivalent in conventional construction to slightly over one-half inch by gluing two skins of one-quarter inch plywood to a one-and-one-half inch core of corrugated, plastic-impregnated paper. The Acorn house has never been in production but there are many sandwich panels available now which use wood far more effectively than conventional sized two-by-four studs, sixteen inches on center, to which sheathing of various types is applied. As architects we should continue to encourage the use of wood in ways which best employ its unique qualities, both structural and psychological, and discourage its waste.

On the same basis, but much less effectively, we adapted this principle to a series of mobile homes which we developed for the Air Force a few years ago. This type of sectional house is now being manufactured and shipped for great distances in the private market and will, I believe, soon take over the bulk of the trailer market—and perhaps eventually the conventional, single-family home market.

Here, however, wood may well give way to other more suitable materials to meet the structural and weathering needs of a lightweight box-girder type of construction. We worked on a project with Kaiser Industries utilizing single panels up to ten feet by sixty feet, two inches thick, of surface hardened polyurethane foam, providing a U factor of .09 with very thin skins of aluminum on each side finished with a twenty-year, polyvinyl fluoride coating. This panel costs considerably less than any wood combination of anywhere near the same strength, insulation, or maintenance-free qualities. To me this merely frees wood to perform a far more necessary function—to make this functional shelter into a soul-satisfying home.

Our "Techbuilt" houses—a panelized building system utilizing plywood, two-by-four studs, wood posts, and laminated timber beams—make use of wood inside where it counts the most in human terms.

Our "Techbuilt" furniture, one of a number of examples of a building system of storage units, suggested a desirable way to use wood where it counts the most. Though this project had to be abandoned because we could not get enough quality or volume to justify the effort, tooling, and capital costs involved, the climate is perhaps better now for a really successful effort in this area. It offers a chance for people to participate more in the furnishing of their home —and arranging pleasantly and usefully the storage and work spaces to undertake the many activities that must be housed in the less and less space that can be afforded to them.

The last few years, I have been primarily concerned with a reasonable, human, systematic approach to an urban living environment—in the latest terminology, a "building systems" approach. We have got to make our cities fit to live in for the new millions who need and want to live there and at a building cost of about half the present, out-of-hand levels. So far, we have not gotten much beyond the structure and here, obviously, there are more fire, sound, and maintenance-proof materials than wood. Our approach has been to pick a building block large enough to provide a

roomy, variously arrangeable, modular shelter, using large precast elements with an infinite variety of ways to be put together, to provide the shell, circulatory system, and mechanics necessary for a modern, urban life. Using such a building system, we hope that the family, of whatever size, composition, or economic level, can find the necessary space and functional requirements to then arrange it, furnish, and adapt it to suit themselves.

In our latest plans we expect to cover the concrete floors with wood and hope to get to a furniture and storage unit system that will use wood naturally and well. Certain it is that wood is essential where you can touch and see it to flesh out a skeletal framework, an organized organic system, into a desirable living environment.

Our use of wood today, and the uses of wood which have died out recently, provide an unhappy index of many of our maladjustments to this confusing world. To cite one such, take the plastic models which have replaced wooden model kits. Today most of the work is already done by machine, the parts go together with a satisfying click, and the dullest child can fill his room with models, exquisite in detail, in the time it took me to build a single, mediocre model aeroplane out of wood. The image of being swamped with production and overcared for by the machine of course is a cliche, but in speaking of legitimate uses for wood, it is significant to hold in mind that it is the woodworker's skill which determines the beauty of the wooden model, not the perfection of the moulds at the factory far away. The wooden object demands greater personal involvement, providing more satisfaction. Surely the possibility of working wood by nonindustrial processes is an important part of its key value.

This leads me to the main point I would like to make—how can we use wood to help us create a better, more friendly living environment—a buffer between us and the fast-moving and ever more confusing world in which we find ourselves.

None of us who have visited Japan have failed to be bowled over by the Japanese approach to living—exemplified by their handling and feeling for wood. This is true in modern work as well as the traditional work which still exists and is still practiced in Japan. This is a natural outgrowth of Japan's very beginnings in the eighth century under the Shinto religion. The attitude of man toward trees, as to all nature, was a very sympathetic one. The woodcutter never cut down the tree without appealing first to the kami or spirit which he believed resided in it. Today as then the Japanese woodworking is done with the same respect for the spirit of the wood. For instance, Langdon Warner tells us in his book *The Enduring Art of Japan* that thirty years ago a fresh log for the repair of the huge Daibutsuden temple in Nara was laid out on blocks to keep it from the damp earth and a mat shed was built above. He was told it had been felled three years before, three more moons must pass before it was hewn, more moons still before it could be sawn and then the planks wedged apart for air in the pile, still an unspecified number of moons before the planks could be pegged in place on the great building. By that time the spirit, Kino Kami, who writhes in agony and splits the log, would have made her escape. Mr. Warner goes on to say it is neither sentimental nostalgia nor worship of the good old days which makes us recognize the large measure of human good in this society. Their material culture was fostered by a natural system of craftsmen priests compared with the complex structuring of today's industrialized society. It is certain that fewer conveniences were produced, but one necessary thing we lack today was then available. This necessity we

lack is the prime requirement that a man's trade should permit and train him to grow into a complete man. Our growing specialization quite blocks the complete development of potential skills of hand and mind and soul. Without it no one can be called whole or wholesome.

The confidence in one's ability to create wood objects which are beautiful and useful, or, to reformulate that slightly, to create ourselves the objects we desire in a real material, grows in importance as we realize that it is a key on the one hand to the world of art, and on the other, to a personal involvement with the objects of everyday life. It is here that our present educational system shows its flaws most vividly. Woodworking is just another drill where children make someone else's thing without any real desire or understanding. The child is induced to make poorly designed towel racks, napkin holders, and other trivia instead of beginning at the beginning to relate his effort to real needs through the creation of useful, beautiful objects. Here is certainly a chance, which is going to waste, to create both a market and an indigenous art. Public knowledge of wood is limited, and need not be. Skills with tools, confidence, and respect for the material could be taught in schools, but is not. The child is confronted with another tedious adult exercise which does nothing positive, but is seemingly contrived just to waste his time.

I believe that the lumber industry, the tool makers, and producers of quality wood products of all kinds have a great challenge and opportunity before them which I hope they are visionary enough to pick up —to encourage, educate, and reward the craftsman-artist who uses wood well.

Whatever its present flaws, there is a growing ferment in education, a growing awareness that our survival depends on the wit and skill of our citizens from the top to the bottom of society. This calls for more than the specialized and relatively narrow list of qualities and qualifications which place a man high on the acceptance lists.

And yet narrow specialization is pressed upon us by our condition. It is no longer necessary for physical survival to use our hands and bodies with skill—a man need no longer protect himself with sword or cudgel or know how to ride a horse. A woman who sews is unusual—and even baking a cake has become a matter of adding an egg. We are in danger of eliminating not only the drudgery but the joy and feeling of accomplishment in our lives.

There are growing signs that our younger generation at least feels this lack of full experiencing and feels it strongly. The phrase "do your thing" is the demand of our offspring who insist that they understand and experience for themselves in heart, mind, and body enough of the job they are doing to know where they fit, so they, like the Japanese carpenter, can become whole men.

I am probably biased because the one teacher that remains vivid in memory, and that is from before the fifth grade, was my manual arts instructor. None of my five sons in either public or private school has had any comparable school experience. The obsequious machine is so dextrous and can multiply the craftsmanship of a very few to such an extent that we have as a society lost our manual dexterity and even our respect for it. The art of painting today has for the most part become a matter of feeling, color, mood and accident. There is little in our modern artwork to indicate the discipline and training of the hand to obey the eye and mind and heart —so evident in the past. A return to the creative teaching of manual dexterity— preeminently of woodworking skills—would do more to raise the level of all designed product quality and increase the demand for such quality in the future than anything else I can think of.

What I would like to suggest is a search for products and techniques and approaches which will take advantage of wood's character—of the fact that every piece of wood is different from every other piece—and look to a means emphasizing this quality, making wood into products which have the maximum opportunity to provide the response which it evokes.

This is not to say that we should stop making particleboard, masonite, or plywood. These are excellent materials and they all have a place in any creative woodworkers "vocabulary." But we should be increasingly particular and selective in this use of wood. We should be much more respectful of wood's qualities and use it much more effectively in its unique ways. There is a tremendous untapped market in the area of useful, decorative, sculptural household objects. Again, what is needed is a better understanding of the real meaning, the lasting meaning of art.

Part of the real meaning of art is real involvement with life, whether it be the complex statement of a novel, hidden beauty revealed in picture or sculpture, a gracefully formed piece of furniture, or a clever and effective door knob. Behind the carpenter is a potentially more effective art than the painter's, for his art includes the possibility of introducing beauty and personality into useful objects as well as expressing "pure" art. Art is nothing but the process of doing anything well.

Part of the reason we are willing to surround ourselves with junk, listen to junk, look at junk, is because we have lost the ability or opportunity to make anything well. Wood provides us better than almost any other material with a medium for satisfying creativity. My son's easel paintings have long since disappeared—but the salad bowl he turned for us one Christmas long ago still has the place of honor at our table.

Much, I am convinced, of the relatively unsatisfactory pastime of museum and gallery going is another aspect of the organized effort to turn us all into narrow specialists, spectators, and consumers. If we made more things for ourselves, we could better appreciate and evaluate the products with which our machines provide us and insist that they be *well* made before we will buy them.

We have come to equate art with that which is deposited in a museum and artists with those who paint or sculpt objects for the museum—rather than asking artists to use their sense of color, manual skill, and feeling for form to make our useful equipment and living environment all a work of art.

Wood in Aesthetics and Art

PAUL WEISS
Heffer Professor of Philosophy
Catholic University of America
Washington, D. C.

A graduate of City College, New York, Paul Weiss received his doctorate from Harvard University. He has served on the faculties of Harvard University, Radcliffe, and of Yale University, where he held the chair of Sterling Professor of Philosophy, and is now at Catholic University. At Bryn Mawr he was chairman of the Department of Philosophy. Formerly Fellow of Ezra Stiles College, he was also visiting professor of philosophy at Hebrew University, lecturer at Aspen Institute, Rhodes lecturer at Haverford, a Townsend Harris medalist, founding member and president of C. S. Peirce Society and of the Metaphysical Society of America. He is the author of numerous books, among them Modes of Being, Nine Basic Arts, The God We Seek, *and* The Making of Men.

I would like to begin with some indication of the nature of a philosophic approach to our topic. I can then perhaps make clear why aesthetics is a significant enterprise and what it entails.

The philosopher has at least two tasks. One is criticism, the examination of basic enterprises to see exactly what they are claiming and how far they are justified in their claims. Every other enterprise is somewhat practical in the sense that it takes certain things for granted and then begins to operate. This is true even of such austere subjects as mathematics or nuclear physics. Though they have gone to almost the limit of human knowledge, they do make presuppositions regarding method and the nature of things and reality. No one except the philosopher tries to find out what has been presupposed by any and all inquiries. This critical task is primary for most Anglo-Saxon philosophers. They have given up almost every other interest to concentrate on criticism.

Philosophy is also vision. Its task is to

offer an all-comprehensive outlook on the universe. Everyone has some vision incorporated in his inherited language, in his practice, and in the customs and outlook of his day. Most of us are unreflecting, quasi-Aristotelians. We use such a term as "information" in a good Aristotelian way, to mean having the essence of something in us. It is good Aristotle to say, "Realize what you are doing." Matter and form, power or potentiality are Aristotelian terms. The true philosopher is not content with accepting that inherited vision. He must forge a new one in order to do justice to what we have learned in art and science, politics and philosophy.

Neither of these two stresses in their purity is the main business of this symposium. I will not speak of the nature of being, the reality of God, the meaning of ideals, causality, creation, freedom, or nature of the soul. Aesthetics is our present concern. I will try to deal with it philosophically, i.e., critically and sympathetically, without getting into an abstract discourse about ultimate issues.

The aesthetic is the immediate, what is present, the object as not mediated by ideas or concepts, merely as presented, merely phenomenal, open to inspection, or sensing, or experiencing. Everything has an aesthetic dimension. But when we try to think of something as immediate, as unmediated by concepts, we run a great risk—the risk of losing all content. Were it possible to free ourselves from all conceptualization, we could not tell the difference between wood and stone, a horse and a cat, between hardness and softness, light or dark. That we do experience these is true, but if we have no conceptual apparatus, no judgment or thoughts, we would just have to live through them the way perhaps an oyster does. If we do, we will be experiencing, but will not yet have an aesthetic experience.

The aesthetic is not mediated by concepts, but this does not mean that it is completely alien to all use of concepts. To have an aesthetic experience is to submit oneself to the content. Concepts become merged, lost in, are subject to that content. Aesthetic experiencing cannot really be taught except negatively, by pointing out what has been overlooked. But it can be intensified by drugs, by various ascetic practices, by bringing oneself to concentrate on what is before one.

Wood, our present concern, is sensed primarily by sight and touch. The aesthetic of wood has to do with its color and shape and size, its smoothness, hardness, roughness, softness, lightness, and heaviness, perhaps even with its resistance and malleability, or workability as grasped by touch. Of course, there are facets of it where we can bring in smell and taste, but these are not primary.

Others in this symposium refer to the life or vitality or vibrancy of wood which we get, not by mere touch or sight, but by a kind of organic interplay with it, particularly when it is alive. There are some Indian thinkers who have gone so far as to say that even a tree feels, and that they are able to sympathize with it. But I think we do not have to make such a claim, and yet need not deny that an aesthetic appreciation penetrates below the surface and allows for a vital participation in what is alive.

The aesthetic is also that which is non-pragmatic, that which is cut away from the ordinary uses of every day. At present there is a great deal of interest in the aesthetic in this sense. There is in the United States a growing awareness of Eastern thought, with its stress on detachment; there is also an insistence on the need to free oneself from the conventions and the categories of every day. Many young people today want to escape from an involvement in what had been established; they want to experience the world in its richness with all its nuances, free from the limitations that practical concerns and convention have imposed on them. But it is impossible to avoid involving oneself in the practical world, just as much as it is impossible to avoid having a degree of detachment at times.

Religion—not at this very moment, when it has become so activistic, but traditionally—mathematics, theoretical science, speculative philosophy, art, all try to see what things are like when freed from their ordinary use. Artists even want to free themselves from the traditions of art itself. Artists today are as artists have always been, but today they are more than ever acutely aware of the fact that past art is held down by its traditions, that all artists have learned from other artists, and that all are caught in ways in which they ideally should not be caught. The artist is becoming more and more acutely aware of the necessity of dealing with art objects in complete detachment, not only from pragmatic concerns but from the past as well, and not merely from the general past, but from the past even of art. Art, he knows, should tap man's basic creativity; it should always be fresh and original.

So far my talking about the aesthetic has had nothing to do with either craftsmanship or art, but only with an experience open to everyone. Everyone has aesthetic experiences, but they can be more or less acute, more or less variegated, subtle, nuanced.

I suppose most people are interested in wood as an object of craftsmanship and not in wood as an aesthetic object. Craftsmanship is not art. Very often art and craft are thought to be continuous with one another; but this too I think is an error, one held even by such great philosophers as Leibnitz and John Dewey.

Though it is true that artists must master their craft, though they must exhibit a high degree of skill in order to produce a work of art, a work of art has a different kind of objective and a different kind of a character and aesthetic nature from a work of craftsmanship. A work of craftsmanship is made for an objective beyond itself; it is made in order that something else be achieved. It, therefore, has to be tested in terms of its efficiency as well as in terms of its pleasantness. We ask of the craftsman that he make something so that it fulfills its function well. But the artist makes what is good in itself, what is self-sufficient which has no function to serve. It is made to *be*.

If a carpenter were to make a chair, it would be one on which we could sit without falling to the ground; it would allow us to put our feet to the ground and rest our back. If it did not do this, if we sat on it and it fell apart, no matter how attractive it would have been to see, it would be a failure as a chair.

Ask a sculptor to make a chair. Would he make it of wood? Not necessarily. It could be made of paper or strings. How many legs would it have? I don't know; it could have eighty-four; eighteen of them could be standing out one way, six could be pointing to the ceiling. What about the seat? It could be vertical, horizontal, on a slant. It could touch the ceiling; it could occupy the entire room. But a carpenter's chair, a chair of a master craftsman, is one on which we can sit. The objectives of carpenter and sculptor are here evidently distinct. None of the conditions imposed upon the carpenter are imposed upon the sculptor. We could also have a musical composition called "The Chair" which had nothing to do with the chair on which we sit.

There is no condition of a pragmatic sort that you can impose on the artist; but there are pragmatic conditions to be imposed upon the craftsman. This fact comes out most acutely in architecture, which is at once a business, a craft, and an art. Most architects are businessmen, some are craftsmen, and a few are artists; the best of architects are all three, but so far as they are artists they have objectives which have nothing to do with profit or utility. Other arts have no involvement or very little involvement in business or craftsmanship; their artistic status is more evident.

The master carpenter has skill; he has learned how to use his powers and equipment in order to be in control of the structure and potentialities of the material with which he works. He has served an apprenticeship when he became habituated under a master. It was then that he learned the power and the range of the material on which he worked—how far it could be bent, how far it could be turned, what it will reveal in this context or that. To know how to use wood as a craftsman, one must have experience of working with it.

The craftsman can use wood as a background on which he is going to build other things. He can use it together with some other material; he can combine it with metal or stone to make an ax; he can combine the wood with something else so as to produce a single unified object. Most important, perhaps, he has to struggle with it, actually work with it. All use of equipment, all making things to harmonize with other things, involves some kind of a struggle. Because I do not own my own body altogether, I must learn to become one with it —that is one of the reasons I should control my appetite, exercise, and perhaps even train and engage in a sport. The world is even more difficult to possess; to own even a part of it I must do many different things. Craftsmanship is work which involves my having direct contact with material and thereby discovering who I am in relationship to what it is and what I can do with it.

The aesthetic, as we normally think of it in the realm of craftsmanship, has to do with the heightening of the effect so that it is enjoyable. The outcome is the pretty or the graceful, but not the beautiful. The graceful, the pretty, the pleasing, the aesthetically satisfying work of craftsmanship decorates, heightens or enhances; the high polish, the extra sheen, the excellent harmony of the various parts is, however, subservient to the function of the object.

Wood, like fur, is a natural material. Like stone, it has considerable capacity to support and resist to a degree other common substances cannot. Its peculiar capacity is made manifest by the master craftsman. He reveals to us what wood is really like—not as alive, when it might be said to be subservient to life itself—but when it is detached from life and then confronted by a man having his own various needs and objectives.

A craftsman attends to what wood can and cannot do, refusing to make it appear as though it were some other substance. But he does not necessarily keep it in its raw state. One does not necessarily do justice to a material by keeping it in the brute, rough, undeveloped, unpolished guise that it had in its natural setting. Polishing, even if it does nothing more than reveal the grain, the sheen, the tonality of the object itself, makes us see clearly what the object is.

The crafted work is the objective counterpart of what psychedelic experiments are trying to accomplish. They try to heighten the individual sensitivity, where the craftsman heightens the object's availability to our sensibility. A work of craftsmanship is a kind of objective LSD.

In contrast with the craftsman who is concerned with making something which functions well, the artist is concerned with making something excellent. If there is grace to the work of the craftsman, it has value beyond its functioning; that grace rides on the back of the functioning. The artist instead concentrates on the creation of something excellent in and of itself. It is, of course, true that there are artists who write or paint or dance for certain purposes, e.g., the poet laureate who has to write poems on the queen's birthday. There are people who write plays in order to make money. You cannot hope to have a movie made in Hollywood unless you conform to certain kinds of conditions, definitely not artistic in character. A work of art is expected to submit to those conditions somewhat as a sonnet requires one to keep to certain kinds of verse and to a certain number of lines. These are not the conditions which define a work as a work of art, but only the conditions within which the artist tries to make something beautiful, something good in itself.

The art work reveals—what? I would say the very nature of existence, the meaning of space or time or dynamism, the guts of the universe. Art is made by turning away from the world, but the outcome reveals what the world in fact is. This, of course, is most obvious in connection with music, where we've been free for a long time from attempts at representationalism, only to become aware, through its agency, of the real lilt of things. In a similar spirit we can say that comedy and tragedy make us aware, not of the actors on the stage, but of the nature of man.

Wood used in art can function as background material. A painter could use it instead of canvas. He can paint on the wood. Or the wood could be contrasted, as we have in almost every building nowadays, with brick and stone. It can be contrasted with a void, with nonbeing, with emptiness. The sharpness of separation of the wood from all else heightens its meaning. But the most important fact is that wood is material with which one can struggle, not as the carpenter does, but in another way. That struggle, in the case of the artist, can at times be violent; it could even violate the potentialities of the wood itself. The carpenter must work in consonance with those potentialities.

The artist, of course, can stay in consonance with the nature of the wood, but he need not. The primary fact for him is his creative need to make that which is beautiful.

The word "beautiful" has fallen into disuse, perhaps disgrace, today. Philosophers refuse to use it. Artists tell me they never use it. But there is no reason why it should not be used and well defined. If we ask ourselves about the use of it, we find that we are confronted with the same kind of question we face when we ask about the nature of unity or being. None of these can be found empirically. If you ask me, where is the brown, or where is the rectangle, I can point to it. But I cannot point to unity, to beauty, or to ugliness. These cannot be located. If someone said to you, "Will you please drive my car around the corner," you'd say, "What car is it?" Suppose he answered, "It's a beautiful car."? You wouldn't be able to find it. What you want to know is whether it's red, has two doors, has such and such license plates, etc.

Beauty is an overall characterization. It tells us what the object is as a totality. Produced through the help of the emotions, it requires an emotional involvement in order to be grasped. The experience of it is quite different from that direct aesthetic experience which required no work and quite different from the aesthetic experience we get when we appreciate a craftsmanship. It is quite different even from the aesthetic experience acquired while making a work of art or in merely enjoying a work of art. To obtain the beautiful in wood, there is no other way but to have an artist make, not something which expresses wood (that would be the craftsman), but something beautiful with wood.

If the artist makes something beautiful with wood, will it necessarily be different from what he makes with steel? Or stone? In some sense it must be different. But how different? The medium always makes a contribution. But the contribution can be slight, minimal. Normally, the wood makes only a minimal difference in a work of art, a greater difference in a work of craftsmanship, and a maximal difference in the purely confrontational situation where we attend to the wood itself, free from an involvement with ideas and practice.

The craftsman has another objective in view besides the work that he is working on. He is trying to exhibit a personality or to please the purchaser or user. But this is not the function of an artist. It is not his task to please you, or to communicate with you, or to pay attention to all the power or capacity of the material he's using. He's trying to make something beautiful that is revelatory of a reality beyond. No matter how noble you make your craftsman, you still are on one side of a dividing line separating you from art. The silver plate, the silver spoon, the chair, the table, the desk have to serve an end beyond themselves, but a painting need not. Sometimes a man may say, "I have a hole in my wall, or I have a space four feet by eight feet, or I have a green room, and therefore need a painting of such and such a size and color." That man is not thinking of a painting as a work of art. Interior decoration is a kind of a craftsmanship. Many things made by craftsmen are more valuable and agreeable than what is made by many so-called artists. Most artists are bunglers, while craftsmen are well-trained. Consequently I think you will find the craftsmen usually succeeding where artists fail. Too many artists are without sufficient discipline.

The object of the artist is not to do justice to wood—but to make something beautiful. Maybe he will do this best by paying attention to what wood can or cannot do, but that's not his main question. He is trying to make a master work; that is, to produce a work which shows mastery. There is no condition to which an artist must submit, but there are many which bind the craftsman.

Some artists today are much concerned with the fact that art is dominated by certain conventions. They spend their energies in breaking away from the conventions. Jasper Johns, Robert Rauschenberg, John Cage, and Merce Cunningham spend their energies innovating. Perhaps they would agree that they have not produced works of art except in the sense of avoiding the limitations characteristic of earlier periods. Once upon a time we thought that music had to be made with certain kinds of instruments—cellos and violins and harpsichords. But music can be made by using any sound whatsoever—including Cocacola bottles falling on the ground. The sound of a Coca-cola bottle falling on the ground doesn't automatically become part of music, but it is a neglected sound, a sound that could be used in a musical work. We are today discovering materials that were never used before in architecture. But we must go on to make works of art using these new sounds and materials. Most of the great figures in the history of thought and art were not innovators but men who closed a period. Shakespeare made very few innovations; he epitomized a whole series of developments. An innovation is not usually beautiful.

Of course craftsmen are inventive and therefore produce new works of craftsmanship. In that sense, of course, we have something "fresh." Art, on the other hand, is always to some degree caught in a tradition. No innovations are as radical as one would ideally like them to be. Artists look at other civilizations, at primitive times, at primitive tribes, at foreign cultures in the effort to escape the limitations of their own time and ways. But it is important to note that the artist is not concerned with being novel but with being free—free from the past and for the future.

Art is more than a skill. Craftsmanship might be said to be a skill sustained by inventiveness, but art emphasizes the creative moment, even when it ends without having produced anything radically new. The creative is distinct from the inventive or the ingenious. These are subordinate to the role the work is to play, but the creative is concerned with an emotional reconstruction of this material, to achieve a maximum integration of diversity. It yields something with which you can live and which opens up to you a world beyond yourself. Unless you have all that, you haven't got beauty.

Creativity, at its best, is a controlled freedom with the objective of attaining beauty, which is to say, perfection or excellence, without any concern for what had been, for what will be, what use it may have, or how well it communicates.

Art, Science, and the Human Enterprise

LAURENCE SCHMECKEBIER
Dean Emeritus, School of Art
Syracuse University, Syracuse, New York

A graduate of the University of Wisconsin, Laurence Schmeckebier has studied at various European universities, receiving his doctorate from the University of Munich. He is a contributing editor to American Artist *and is a trustee of the Everson Museum of Art at Syracuse. He served on the faculties of the University of Wisconsin, Cleveland Institute of Art, and the University of Minnesota, where he was chairman of the Fine Arts Department. He is the author of a number of books, including* Ivan Mestrovic, Sculptor and Patriot, *and also numerous articles on art and art history. Among the places where his wood sculptures have been exhibited are the Cleveland Institute of Art, Cleveland Museum of Art, Munson-Williams-Proctor Institute at Utica, New York, and the Rochester Memorial Museum. He now resides in Lyme, New Hampshire.*

This symposium is a pioneer venture, both as a reexamination of wood as one of our basic material resources and as a cooperative effort by scientists, industrialists, and artists to clarify its practical and aesthetic function in our changing society. In a university environment the artist and designer have been curious anomalies. In those areas where the creative imagination and personal commitment of the individual artist appear to be most needed, the social and natural sciences, they have been little used. The result is that the artists' activities have been confined to the relatively free, open, and spiritual realm of the humanities. Perhaps this is as it should be, but in a world of fantastic change created largely by scientific research and its industrial application, the sensitivity to human values and the spiritual needs of the society which these changes affect can no longer be ignored.

It is therefore of very real significance that this entire symposium is directed toward the design and aesthetics of wood with its integrated respect for both the practical and philosophical points of view. The basic problem recognized is just this relationship between scientific technology and the needs of society, with its particular emphasis on the ultimate spiritual satisfaction of mankind. Its clarification requires imagination, independence, and the endless creative drive which the artist somehow has to have in order to exist.

This is an old but a revolutionary concept, and in the great political upheavals of modern times many artists have played significant roles, not so much as an expression of change but rather as contributors in the process of clarification and positive development. Thus the names of Courbet and Rodin in France, Gropius and George Grosz in Germany, Orozco, Rivera, and Siqueiros in Mexico, Frank Lloyd Wright, Buckminster Fuller, and Ben Shahn in the United States, represent a variety of individual contributions as painters, sculptors, and architects, as well as major catalysts in the social and political evolution of their respective periods. The dramatic changes taking place today have not found such leadership from the ranks of the artists.

Traditionally museums have served as institutions for the care and preservation of works of art. From the smallest community to the major museums of the great cities and the nation, they have become the conservators of our artistic and cultural heritage. To this has been added the scholarly function in the historical and technical research necessary for the identification and preservation of these works of art. In modern times a third function has developed, particularly in the United States, whereby the museum has become an active educational as well as cultural center so that classrooms, libraries, visual aids, and a teaching faculty are now devoted to the aesthetic education of the public and com-

mand a substantial share of the annual budget.

Today a new function has been added through the museum's recognition that it has a responsibility for the art of the present and must share in the development of the future. The attitude was clearly expressed some time ago by Dr. Evan Turner, the genial director of the Philadelphia Museum of Art, in an address to a group of educators at the annual meeting of the National Association of Schools of Art. "We are educators along with you," he commented, "and have the special responsibility of assembling significant works of art in an appropriate setting so that the public can make its own decision." The aesthetic experience is therefore no longer restricted to the Temple on the Hill—figurative and often very real—but is brought down to the market place, to create a kind of silent forum, where the individual has the opportunity to study, compare, and make his own decision. This in itself is a creative act which cannot be performed by the traditional high priests of education and criticism. As a basic human enterprise, artistic participation is fundamental to the democratic system—in aesthetics as it is in political and social action.

As in politics, spectator participation is often subject to human prejudices and misunderstandings. This participation requires patience, courage, an open mind, and recognition of the fact that contemporary art is basically an experimental enterprise that is as rich, varied, and fantastically exciting as contemporary life itself. Historically this point of view is rooted in the early conflicts —the individual artist against the pressures of technical and spiritual mechanization in the second half of the nineteenth century. In painting it appeared in the attempts of individualists like Courbet and Manet to look at nature and artistic expression with their own eyes rather than through the refracting lens of tradition. In sculpture it meant the fresh and inspired craftsmanship of Rodin which brought about the rejuvenation of the classic form, as in his famous "Age of Bronze" and eventually led to the new ideal of vitality rather than classic beauty in his Balzac figures.

It is this concept of vitality that has become the determining characteristic of contemporary sculpture from Rodin through the Cubists and the art of our time. Perhaps nowhere was personal freedom, independence, and poetic individuality better revealed than in the recent retrospective exhibition of sculptures by Pablo Picasso in New York's Museum of Modern Art. The variety and ingenuity of forms, ideas, and expressions revealed in the sixty-year public career of this remarkable genius constitute a concentrated reflection of contemporary sculpture as a whole.

From the individualism of this older generation, which rejected science and technology, has now developed a new tradition of the 1960s and 1970s in which young artists have accepted science as a means of achieving greater scale and a stronger form in an expanded environment. The result is an enrichment. Once it was the fascination of movement, the magical mysteries of totems or spaces, the weird assemblages of discarded forms and the startling juxtaposition of visual symbols which tended to focus contemplation on the limited world of the individual spectator. Now there has developed a sense of vastness which recognizes in the urban gas tank, the rural grain elevator, and the United Nations building forms of new and greater significance.

In reviewing the following photographs there are several general observations which may be useful to the reader. The objects photographed were selected from one of the most extensive, original, challenging, and rewarding exhibitions we have ever attempted on the campus of Syracuse University. It was not a laboratory but a presentation of ideas that were fully conceived and realized. The selection of the work, as well as the total design and installation of the exhibition, was done by Professor Lee DuSell and a group of design students from the Syracuse University School of Art.

There is a variety of styles revealed in the work of individual artists which is not a matter of historical sequence from realism to abstraction, classic to modern, or older to younger generation, but one of aesthetic competition. The speed of communication through radio, television, the press, and critical publications has scrambled traditional notions of logical sequence so that visual and technical inventions become common knowledge as soon as they appear. Indeed, the disparity of historical period and geographical distance has been absorbed in the vital competition of visual ideas that make them in a sense all live and contemporary.

A common characteristic of the objects illustrated is, of course, the universal respect for the nature of the material. To the contemporary sculptor this attitude stems largely from Brancusi, whose devotion to the medium often determined the content: the craftsman's "thinking hand discovering the thoughts of the material." The endless process and problem of communicating these "discovered thoughts" is what distinguishes the genuine artist from the traditional craftsman.

There is also the incredible versatility of the machine and the technical processes used in the development of wood products. From the primitive carving to the most sophisticated modern architectural design, each product is man-conceived and manufactured. The machine remains as a tool, an extension of the hand, a means for the practical and aesthetic fulfillment of human desires.

Thus a rich and rewarding panorama unfolds before us. The classic forms persist, some of them quiet and restrained, others dynamic and expressive in monumental terms as seen in the figures of Jose de Creeft, Elliot Offner, Khoren der Harootian, and Leonard Baskin. There are the assemblages of diverse bits and pieces from the builders scrap pile or the household trash can which are transformed into the mysterious wood pieces of a Louise Nevelson or Joseph Cornell. The aesthetic shockers—the Pop artists' reaction to traditional public apathy—are seen in the work of Robert Indiana and Andy Warhol, whose wooden box silk-screened with "Motts Apple Juice" was almost discarded on the shipping dock during the assembly of the exhibition.

There is sculpture designed primarily as fun pieces, including a variety of carved animals, houses with little people, and mobiles with little Viking sailboats. Toys, building blocks, playground sculpture, and even the carved decorative screens show a verve, humor, and creative distinction which are a far cry from the traditional mechanical forms inherited from the nineteenth century.

Hidden beauty indeed is to be found in man's ingenious way of using wood as seen in the Old Town trapper's canoe, the laminated woods of propeller blades, sailing ships (note the incredibly beautiful keel section of the yacht, "Intrepid"), and the superb structural detailing of modern Scandinavian furniture. In principle it is only a step from these details to the gigantic structures of Buckminster Fuller's geodesic domes, yet the scale and shape of this concept demonstrates Mr. Fuller's unquestioned position as one of the greatest artistic geniuses of the twentieth century.

Perhaps through the continuous process of review and reappraisal provided by this kind of symposium and the kind of exhibition from which these photographs originate, we can keep alive the unique combination of creative faith, respect for material and environment, and the working skill of the craftsman by which the future well-being of mankind can be assured.

Design and Aesthetics in Wood Exhibit

Assembled by D. Lee DuSell
Chairman of Experimental Studies
School of Art, Syracuse University
Notes by Laurence Schmeckebier
Photographs by Randy McKay

D. Lee DuSell studied at the American Academy of Art, Chicago; Esquela de Belles Artes, San Miguel de Allende, Mexico; and Cranbrook Academy of Art, Bloomfield Hills, Michigan. Prior to joining Syracuse University, he served on the faculties of the School of Art at Salt Lake City and the Society of Arts and Crafts at Detroit. Having served both as an independent designer and sculptor as well as a consultant, his commissions include, among many others, the entrance doors for McGregor Memorial Community Conference Center, Wayne State University; street lighting fixtures for General Electric Company, Hendersonville, North Carolina; the Suspended Cross for Lynwood Reformed Church, Schenectady; and the elevator and door hardware for the World Trade Center, New York City. His work has been exhibited in many places, among them the Detroit Art Institute where he received the W. B. Ford Award for a sofa; and the Brooklyn Museum, where he received the Hillis Baker prize for a dining table. Photographs of his furniture were featured in Look *magazine in 1956.*

Sculpture in Wood

Louise Nevelson is a veteran woman sculptor whose recent exhibitions have assured her position as one of the great artists of our time. She is particularly famous for her skill in the assemblage of wood fragments, frequently found objects, whose simple and elementary shapes she composes into a unique and personal expression. In this case it is a series of boxes enclosing forms and spaces in a relief design painted a simple tone of black to give it unity. Many of these small-sized reliefs she has developed in large scale to create monumental wall decorations.

Gabriel Kohn uses the common tech-

The Exhibition Symbol
This graphic symbol by Jerome Malinowski, based on the tree form, was used throughout the exhibition on all programs, announcements, and catalogs. It appears here as an abstract sculptural form dramatizing the entrance to the main exhibition.

niques of the wood joiner, carpenter, and shipbuilder to develop the unique forms that have revealed him as one of the most original wood sculptors in America today. Note particularly here the clean geometric shapes, their off-balance composition which gives movement and tension to the whole, and the laminated sections which produce patterns of light and texture from the natural wood.

Joseph Cornell's "Still Life" is an assemblage of totally unrelated and unlikely objects into a strangely gentle and poetic mood piece. The contrast of texture and materials—glass, porcelain, and metal as opposed to worn and weathered painted wood—is enhanced by the space and light composition with a distinctly Surrealist character.

The Pop artists caused considerable discussions among critics and the popular press when they first became prominent in the 1960s. Their work is based largely on the use of common and often discredited symbols of contemporary mass culture presented with direct and sometimes brutal frankness. The most striking is perhaps Andy Warhol's "Motts" with its design, shocking in its commercial realism, stenciled directly on the wood box. Robert Indiana's "Star" is a more complicated combination of blocks and wheel forms with stenciled stars and numbers. More refined in both technique and idea is Sidney Simon's "CPA" with its beautiful lamination of walnut and birch slabs combined with a myriad of number shapes associated with the mechanized mind. A deeper sense of doubt and introspection is reflected in Simon's "Who am I," with its contrast of highly polished and range-hewn surfaces.

Technical crudity and the rough surfaces of common woods frequently lend strength and power to the sculptural expressions as seen in Victor Colby's "Centaur" and Wolf-gang Behl's "Oracle." The particular feature of the Schmeckebier "Prophet" is its total design based on the triangular section of the split walnut log.

Leonard Baskin's "Grieving Angel" and Elliot Offner's "Woman of the Exodus" may be considered significant pieces through their use of the more traditional techniques of the wood carver, their monumental scale (even though the Offner figure is only fifty inches high), their sensitive use of the material, and the integration of these qualities into a mood expressive of our times.

Louise Nevelson
Ancient Secrets, 1964,
Black painted wood 34″ x 27″ x 4″
Loaned by The Pace Gallery,
New York

Gabriel Kown
Pitcairn
Laminated 22½″ x 48″
Loaned by Knox-Albright Museum

Bernard Langlais
Eagle
Relief applied woods 4′ x 8′
Loaned by the artist

Robert Indiana
Star
Timber and metal 76″ x 16½″
Loaned by Albright-Knox Art Gallery

Leonard Baskin
Grieving Angel 1958
Black walnut 6' h.
Loaned by Munson-Williams-Proctor Institute

Elliot Offner
Woman of the Exodus
Willow, 50" h.
Loaned by the artist

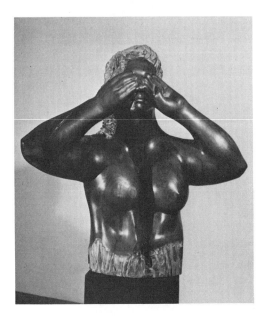

Wolfgang Behl
Oracle 1965
Laminated wood 60" h.
Loaned by the artist

Victor Colby
Centaur 1962
Pine and hemlock 48" x 35"
Loaned by the artist

Sidney Simon
Who Am I 1966
Black walnut 38" h. x 38" w. x 19"
Loaned by the artist

Laurence Schmeckebier
Head of a Prophet 1957
Walnut 29½″ x 15½″
Loaned by the artist

Joseph Cornell
Still Life
Assemblage 9½″ x 15″
Loaned by the artist

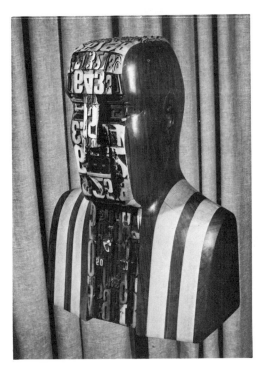

Sidney Simon
C.P.A. 1966
Black walnut, birch laminated
Wooden type, Steel 72″ h. x 22″ x 14″
Loaned by the artist

Thomas Simpson
"Two People . . ." 1966
Pine and acrylic paint 60″ x 38″ x 25″
Loaned by the artist

Andy Warhol
Mott's 1964
Silk screen on wood 18″ x 22″ x 30″
Loaned by Leo Castelli Gallery

William A. Keyser, Jr.
Quad-Looper 1976
Oak 50″ x 24″ x 38″
Loaned by the artist

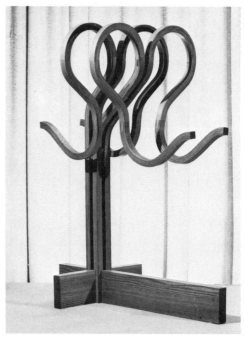

Doris Chase
Brown Catalyst
Laminated oak 15″ h.
Loaned by Ruth White Gallery

H. C. Westermann
A Small Negative Thought 1962
Douglas fir 28″ h.
Loaned by Wadsworth Atheneum

Jules Engel
Porta Organa
Raw umber stained wood 11½″ h. x 10″ w.
Loaned by Ruth White Gallery

Gene Vass
Slate O 1967
Painted wood 44½″ x 44″ x 7½″
Loaned by the artist

American Indian
Northwest Coast
Haida Mask
Loaned by Syracuse University

Norwegian Design
Two Vikings
Oak 7¼″ h.
Loaned by Syracuse University

Arne Tjomsland
Elk Family
Oak 11″ x 9″ x 7″ h.
Loaned by Syracuse University

Sam Maloof
Music Stand
40″ (adjustable)
Loaned by the artist

Wharton Esherick
Spiral Ladder 1967
Cherry 48″ x 17″ x 25″
Loaned by the artist

Wendell Castle
Two-People Chair 1967
Loaned by the artist

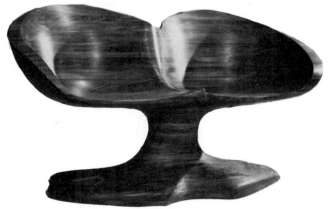

Robert Charles Whitley, II
Library Steps 1967
Walnut 67″ h. x 23″ x 43″
Loaned by the artist

Edsel Martin
Appalachian Dulcimer 1967
Willow, walnut, white pine
45″ l. x 5″ w. x 3″ h.
Loaned by Blue Ridge Crafts, Inc.

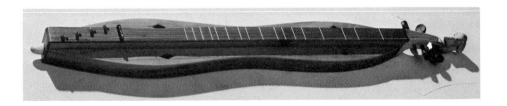

Lee M. Rhode
Salad Bowl
Teak 11″ d.
Serving Plate
Teak 13″ x 14″
Loaned by the artist

Richard R. Breitenbach
Tray 1966
Black walnut 4½″ h. x 13″ x 9″
Loaned by the artist

New Technology in Wood

This group of examples suggests some of the more significant advances in modern wood technology which have had a profound influence on both aesthetic and utilitarian developments in contemporary design in wood.

Improved adhesives and production methods together with advanced knowledge of wood have enabled engineers to produce structural members in wood which have challenged the now traditional domination of steel and concrete and have inspired architects to return to wood as a structural medium.

New possibilities for the designer have been opened through the use of ammonia in the bending of wood and by the various wood-polymers which permit new approaches to wood finishing and improve some of the strength properties of the wood.

An endless variety of fantastically beautiful designs has been made possible by the development of more precise cutting and finishing machines whose products are not the result of imitation, established historical styles but the exploration of new ideas through the understanding of the material and the unique possibilities of the machine itself. The sculptured wood panel is one example of the aesthetic effect that can be accomplished with such equipment by the resourceful manufacturer.

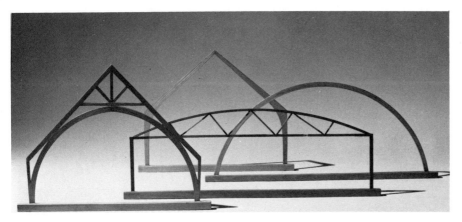

Models of Structural Members
American Institute of Timber Construction
1700 K Street, Washington, D. C.

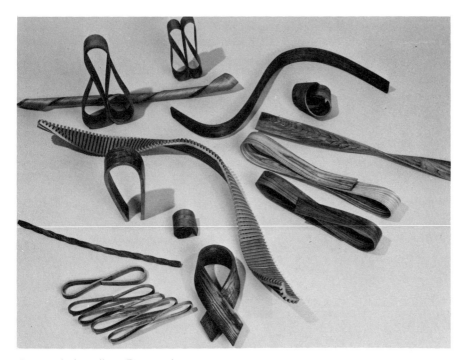

Ammonia bending, Research
Loaned by State University of New York
College of Environmental Science and Forestry

Sculpture Wood Panels
Loaned by Penberthy Lumber Company
5800 S. Boyce Avenue
Los Angeles, California

Wood polymers, Research
Loaned by State University of New York
College of Environmental Science
and Forestry

From the Market Place

Translating the designer's sketches into manufacturable form is just a stage in production. The objects pictured here—chairs, bobbins, shuttles, wine racks, toys—have gone through this process and are all products of industry, both domestic and foreign. Each of them has something special in design and craftsmanship. Surprisingly, a device intended to be used and not seen in some manufacturing process may turn out to be a most attractive object, for example, the shuttle, which moves at dizzying speeds in a weaving loom.

The stress of mass production in highly competitive markets has forced rapid development in every step of manufacture. From selecting the right wood species to drying the green wood, industrial processing has been greatly refined since the day of the individual craftsman. The most precise machining, durable glues, and finest finishes are used to bring out the grain and color of the wood and to achieve in the final result an article both useful and attractive.

How the endless variation in wood can be exploited without reverting to hand labor is always a problem. That it is by no means insoluble can be seen in some of the uniquely designed wood products in the photographs. When not wholly of wood, they show how it can be successfully united with other materials to set off the best features of each.

Especially delightful are the children's toys. The toy rocking horse loaned by the Valenza children will jog many a fond mamory. A wooly lamb, a miniature weaving loom, pull toys, and all sorts of other playthings are, in their light-colored woods, particularly attractive.

While wood can be imitated and copied in minute surface detail, long contact with a table, a chair, or a sculptured object of wood only serves to emphasize its origin in the living world of the forest. A nick, a scratch, or a dent does not send the piece to the junk pile but makes it instead a diary of events that, more felt than seen, serves as a reminder of the little experiences that make up so much of life.

Helicopter blade section and hub
Loaned by Kaman Aircraft
Bloomfield, Conn.

Canoe, Old Town Trapper model
Loaned by Syracuse Yacht Sales, Inc.
6100 E. Genesee Street
Fayetteville, New York

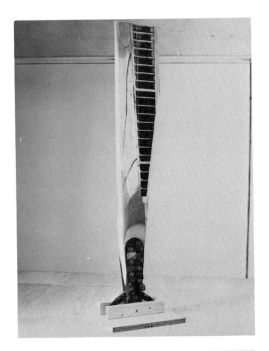

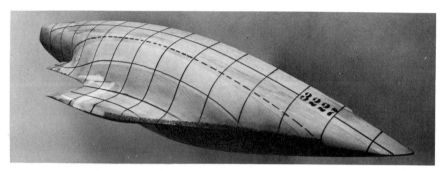

"Intrepid," 12 meter yacht
Experimental model
Loaned by Stevens Institute of Technology,
Davidson Laboratory
Castle Point Station
Hoboken, New Jersey 07030

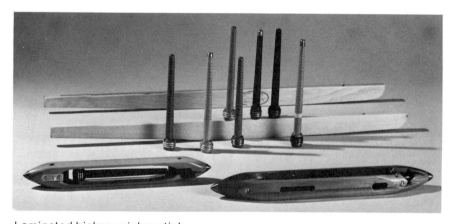

Laminated hickory picker stick,
CW-1-D6, for power loom
Six varied type bobbins, for power loom
H1D hickory picker stick, for power loom
Shuttle No. 1632-13, 16″ long, for
power loom
Shuttle No. 2621-4, 19½″ long,
for power loom
Loaned by Steele Heddle Mfg. Company
P. O. Box 1867
Greenville, South Carolina

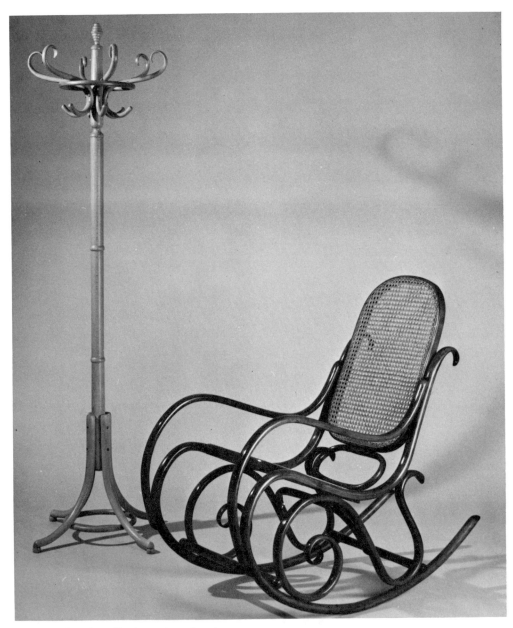

Bentwood rocker, Bentwood coatrack
Loaned by Thonet, One Park Avenue, New York, New York

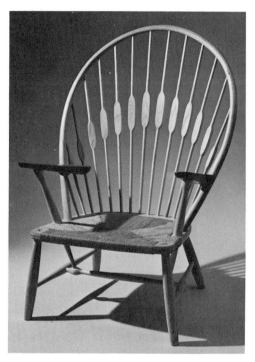

Hans J. Wegner
"Windsor" chair JH 550
Loaned by Georg Jensen Inc.
Furniture and Lighting
27 East 53rd Street
New York, New York

(left) Hans J. Wegner
"Wishbone" chair CH 24
Loaned by Georg Jensen Inc.
27 East 53rd Street
New York, New York
(right) Armchair E-92-3
Loaned by George Tanier, Inc.
305 E. 63rd Street
New York, New York

Scarpa
Lounge chair, Model 925
Dining chair, Model 121
Loaned by Atelier International, Ltd.
6 East 53rd Street
New York, New York

(left) Frattini Stacking tables,
set of four
Loaned by Atelier International, Ltd.
6 East 53rd Street
New York, New York
(right) Armchair, Model 6003
Loaned by Fritz Hansen Inc.
979 Third Avenue
New York, New York

(left) Stacking chair, Model 3107
(center) Stacking chair, Model 3100
Loaned by Fritz Hansen Inc.
979 Third Avenue
New York, New York 10022
(right) Wirkkala Stacking chair,
no. 9019
Loaned by Stendig Inc.
410 East 62nd Street
New York, New York 10021

Adjustable chair 6025
Loaned by DUX Incorporated
5000 City Line Road
Newport News, Virginia

Alvar Aalto Stacking stools, Model 60
Chair, Model 41
Loaned by International Contract
Furnishings
145 E. 57th Street
New York, New York

(right) Armchair, Model 4216
Loaned by Fritz Hansen Inc.
979 Third Avenue
New York, New York
(left) Chair
Loaned by Georg Jensen
27 E. 53rd Street
New York, New York

(right) Knoll Associates
arm chair 13050
Loaned by Nichols Business Equipment Co.
Syracuse, New York
(left) Mathsson chair in
black webbing T105
Loaned by Scandinavian Design, Inc.
15 East 53rd Street
New York, New York 10022

Borge Mogensen Chest of
drawers BM 59
Loaned by Georg Jensen Inc.
27 East 53rd Street
New York, New York

Hans J. Wegner
Sewing table AT 33
Loaned by Georg Jensen Inc.
27 East 53rd Street
New York, New York

Stool, Danish
Rosewood wine rack, Swedish
Loaned by Bonniers, Inc.
605 Madison Avenue
New York, New York
Mathsson table, T614
Loaned by Scandinavian Design, Inc.
15 East 43rd Street
New York, New York 10022

Octagonal table
Hexagonal stools
Loaned by Bell Designs Inc.
37 East 50th Street
New York, New York 10022

Ceiling light fixture,
pine wood, S-9-35
Loaned by George Tanier, Inc.
305 E. 63rd Street
New York, New York

Nordic lyre
Chordal dulcimer
Loaned by Educational Musical Instruments
46 Shilton Road
Agincourt, Ontario, Canada

Large bread board, Verpaco
Butchers block, Verpaco No. 55
Small bread board, Verpaco No. 8C
Oval cutting board, Verpaco No. 2214
Cutting Board, Verpaco
Loaned by Bonniers, Inc.
605 Madison Avenue
New York, New York

Cutting boards, Verpaco
Wooden shoes, Swedish
Loaned by Bonniers, Inc.
605 Madison Avenue
New York, New York
Candlesticks A-47, Boda
Stools H-29, Boda
Chairs G-2, Skrivrit
Weaving loom J-7, Brio
Ladles B-14-16, S. Kalmar
Lans Hemsl. 1.
Twig cock C-4, S. Kalmar
Lans Hemsl. 1.
Loaned by Swedish
Information Service
161 East 42nd Street
New York, New York

Salt and pepper shakers,
4″ high
Salad servers, B33
Salad bowls, B6-30
Lazy Susan, 14″ diameter
Candy dish, B6
Cookie plate, B8
Biscuit plate, B10
Candle holders, B86–90
Loaned by The Leavitts
Alberton
Prince Edward Island
Canada

Toys, West German
Loaned by Consulate General
Federal Republic of Germany
New York, New York

Crane truck, B 894
Sculptured wood animal set, B 583
Ride Em Choo Choo, Q 796 M
Jumbo cargo carrier, B 250
Stacking owl, R 010
Large dominoes, N 146
Loaned by Creative Playthings
12 Station Road
Princeton Junction, New Jersey

(left) Woolly lamb—B 835 M
Loaned by Creative Playthings
12 Station Road
Princeton Junction, New Jersey
(center) Wooden horse with
rope tail, Swedish
Loaned by Bonniers, Inc.
605 Madison Avenue
New York, New York
(right) Animal
Loaned by Consulate General of
the Federal Republic of Germany
460 Park Avenue
New York, New York

Daniel L. Valenza
Toy Rocking Horse:
Alexander 1964
Pine and sugar Maple
24″ h. x 39″ l. x 22″ w.
Loaned by Karen, Susan,
Christine & James Valenza

PART II

Wood as Architectural Material

Four architects, each with extensive practical experience, comprise this section and look to wood's future use in architecture from quite different angles. Charles W. Moore begins more philosophically and historically, reminding one of Banham's paper, for he dwells on the historical distinctions between the northern wood cultures and the Mediterranean stone cultures. By photographic documentation he shows a variety of expressions wood has achieved in past construction in the United States and in Japan and he relates the values in these older examples to those behind recent work his firm has done both in small houses and other small structures and in condominiums.

While Moore emphasizes common-sense reasonableness in his most dramatic uses of wood, Victor Lundy's approach is more poetic. He views the living tree itself, and not merely its fascinating product, as an inspirational form offering a kind of architectural truth. Only the perversity of traditional attitudes keeps man from realizing these truths in unfettered architectural expression. Quite unlike Carl Koch, who condemns modern painting, attributing its negativism to a lack of the "whole man" approach of the craftsman, Lundy feels that architecture should emulate the liberated spirit of modern painting. "Architects are behind other creators. Their work is too static—bound up—frozen." He blames alike the architects, the wood industries, and the building codes. He suggests as a basic cause—and here he is closer to Koch—a "machine ethic" in the United States, an "antiseptic trend" toward the safe comfort of middle-aged mediocrity. He calls for questioning youth to jolt the restrictions of complacency.

A. Quincy Jones, like Lundy, attacks the building codes, but he does it with specific charges and examples of the complacency which Lundy only mentions. He gives interesting documentation of outworn prejudices, the ridiculous inconsistencies of unthinking bureaucracy, and the failure to associate public health with attractive design; the building-code approach to public safety and health is well analyzed. He expresses perhaps his greatest concern for the physical safety of people in terms of their "mental health"; living as they do in progressively inhuman densities of population, their surroundings are "unsafe" as an environmental living experience. Held responsible with the code makers and interpreters are the practitioners, who should press to reform the codes, and the wood-producing industries, who can through technical improvement of wood make possible and stimulate new approaches to our urban problems.

R. A. Eckert, after identifying the nature of our current dynamic building program, which is ever accelerating through rapid technological changes, and then describing the "building systems" methods of meeting these crisis demands, levels his criticism principally at the wood industry for not keeping up with other industry in closing the gap between the industry and the designer. He charges that the industry neither produces the needed product for system development nor has any real design involvement. He asserts that the wood-products industry is just now learning to be "market oriented" rather than "product oriented," when the real need of the current situation is for "design orientation." He points out the obligation of the design profession to respond to any moves that would close this gap, but charges the industry with making the first move in this race to keep up with human needs. Taken somewhat out of its context, one idea of Mr. Eckert's recurs in many forms throughout the symposium papers but perhaps it is best to say it here. "The major difference between something that is needed and something that is desired is design."

Wood Construction in the Planned Community

CHARLES W. MOORE
Chairman, Department of Architecture
Yale University, New Haven, Connecticut

A graduate in architecture from the University of Michigan, Charles W. Moore received his doctorate from Princeton University. He has served on the faculties at the University of Utah, the University of California at Berkeley, and Princeton University. He has been associated with several architectural firms and is now a partner of Moore and Turnbull of New Haven and Berkeley. He has received awards for his buildings from Progressive Architecture Magazine, *the American Institute of Architects,* Architectural Record. *He also received the California Governor's Design Award for Sea Ranch Condominium. He is a member of the Architectural Advisory Group, National Bureau of Standards; the Architectural Board of Consultation, Southern Illinois University; and the Board of the National Council of Arts in Education.*

In England and in this country during the four hundred years that Sir Banister Fletcher thought belonged to the Renaissance there has existed an "over culture" of Mediterranean persuasion which has dreamed of sunlight glistening on marble in the piazza and of ideas as round and full and permanent as the stone muscles on the statues. The dream is an urban dream. Naturally, for this dream to be the topdog dream there has had to persist an underdog (like dark Dravidians on the Indian subcontinent), the "under culture" of the northern forests dark with dreams of shadows flickering over the orgiastic enthusiasts of Nazidom or a Bergmann film. It's no wonder, given the embarrassment of it all, the hairy shame of our two nations' unreliable northern beginnings, that the drums have been so relentlessly beat for urbanity, solidly of masonry and full of bright Mediterranean delights.

But at a point in our history when the underdogs are urgently and dramatically rising, it is perhaps appropriate to face the

House—a box in Sturbridge Village

facts without shame. High-rise construction of hard materials like steel and concrete is still too expensive, really, for any except the very rich and the subsidized. The amenities most people value most do not require housing eternally free from the prospect of decay. Indeed the very immunity from decay is as obscene, in its way, as the shiny imperviousness of an aluminum roof on a weathering barn. Inexpensive wooden suburban housing, already favored by everybody except architecture students and their teachers, may be ready to come into its own, even without such precautions as the Potemkin village configured of piazza and riva which provides a respectable photogenic Mediterranean false front for the wooden houses of Reston.

I am no architect's messiah, to exhort you to a realization of the second coming of wood, or, in the vernacular, to "Wood Power." I only ask that you note how refreshingly easy it is, even in the late twentieth century—especially in the late twentieth century—to saw these slightly dissimilar sticks in quantity and to bang them together with so much ease that enough energy might be spared for the subsequent enjoyment of the product.

The first picture shows a house, a very simple house, which someone has bothered to move to Sturbridge Village, Massachusetts. It is a box made in the fashion of the eighteenth century, based on sizeable sticks cladded over with wooden clapboards, which turned out to be more suitable to the North American climate than the wattle and daub arrangements between the members which had been adequate for the British Isles. The clapboards wouldn't look any different if under them lay the nineteenth-century system of prefabricated pieces which built the North American west. Those nineteenth-century pieces were smaller, less than two by four inches in section, and held together by that most

ingenious and most flexible of modern prefabricated joints, the wire nail. This wooden box of a house in the picture is altogether without any overdog Mediterranean overtones. It is, in fact, without overtones of any sort except that it does suggest a certain separation between the out-of-doors, where the snow is, and the inside, where the possibility of being comfortable exists.

Next we have a house in Nantucket which demonstrates, I think, with considerable charm, the Mediterranean overdog pretensions which come to us all the way from the porches where pre-Greek mayors sat in order to dispense justice to their friends and underlings. The column, which started presumably as a fertility symbol and was then multiplied and capped with a gable roof to become a symbol of kingly power, appears here made out of boards and surrounding, still, the wood box house.

Another New England house, this time in Sheffield, Massachusetts, has the pretensions from the Mediterranean part of our past grown grander yet in the period of the Greek Revival. Although it demonstrates the desire to confuse wood with stone, the victory of the Mediterranean mood must not be regarded as permanent. This is not dissimilar, really, to the first house, the one without pretension. It too is made of boards which cover up the difficulties inherent in the wattle and daub construction of its English forebears. This, like the Nantucket house, serves as a rather grand example of the Mediterranean overlay applied to an entirely wood building, which gives us at once the weather tightness of the wood skin and the memory of our conqueror's heritage. The Greek Revival's colonnade was not quite large enough to cover the need for a kitchen and service area, so the temple sticks out the back of the colonnade a little.

A Nantucket house with pretensions

House in Sheffield with lots of pretensions

Houses in Williamsburg, Virginia

The Jeffersonian notion was that even in our northern forest, the parallel between our new republic and an imagined Graeco-Roman republican ideal was close enough to make an architectural point of. It is even possible to multiply the wooden box, as the example from Williamsburg, Virginia shows, to cause housing to occur rather more densely than in the individual buildings we have seen.

An authentic wooden idiom from the northern forests came the other way around the world from Russia to the west coast of the United States at Ft. Ross, California. This is a recent revisitation of a building which I am sure was much less handsome before some students of Warren Callister rebuilt it. In this very scholarly reconstruction of a Russian structure of redwood, the qualities of the boards themselves are more than evident; we have here not a wood frame but rather a solid wood structure detailed with enormous skill so that the very special quality of wood, its urge to change its dimension, is used to pull together the structure into greater and greater tightness over time, making positive use of that changeability which is so distressing to furniture makers.

Fort Ross, California:
a real wood idiom from the North

The flammability of wood construction creates an argument used in favor of materials presumed to be more fireproof such as steel (which melts) and concrete (which pops). The argument against wood for the high densities which occur increasingly in a highly populated world is pressed less in Japan, where, as in this shopping street in Nara, and as in the wooden community depicted on the screen in a Tokyo museum, many things are pushed close together but left on the ground. Indeed the whole system of planned communities in wood probably comes out more articulately in this highly organized medieval Japanese example, than it does in anything I can find yet from modern America.

Nara, Japan: high density of people, low building

Screen in Tokyo museum

Katsura—to wood that which is wood's

Some boards at the Katsura Villa in Japan render unto wood that which is wood's and manage to put some other material, in this case stucco, in positions where water is more likely to appear or where the more unpleasant forms of decay can occur. Other examples from Japan could have shown much more highly developed joints than this.

A building at Horyuji has lasted since before A.D. 739. Admittedly, the climate has had to be very special in Horyuji. One cannot always expect boards to last twelve hundred years, but the capacity of this simple system to endure and even to give some sense of its continuing endurance is, I think, evident. An alternative arrangement with wood is not to fix it so it will not rot, but rather to take considerable ritual pleasure in its rotting. This shows up at the Ise Shrine in Japan, where the buildings are rebuilt every generation, fitted out with gold and other metal trappings as a link with previous logs that had the same trappings on them, and built in the same way that the previous ones were, so that every generation has the opportunity to renew its ties with the past in a much more affirmative fashion than simply to sign a pledge with the local preservation society. Japan is fascinating for our purposes, I think, because it represents a sort of freedman brother, the respectable liberated kin of our own slave past in the northern forest. The Japanese didn't realize that there was a Mediterranean topdog until very lately, therefore they had the opportunity to use the sticks and boards which they sawed out of the forest in ways which they thought contained adequate overdog tones. Here at Ise again the system memorializes the forest by sticking great round wooden boards directly into the ground, where it is all right if they rot because they will be replaced in twenty-one years anyway. Though this

Horyuji—twelve hundred years of endurance

Shrine at Ise—there are kinds and kinds of eternity (every generation a renewal)

*Ise—Japan as the respectable liberated kin of our own slave past in the
northern forest (the forest freed)*

makes the most of what wood is and what
it grows out of, it is clear that when there
is something that should not rot, items that
should be stored in a storage shed, they
must be kept out of the way of the rotting
agencies of nature's forest, up off the
ground and in the air.

At Nijo, wood is used in close relation with
paint to make what is at once a wood panel
and a sky; it is very special, and altogether different from a piece of Formica.

Nijo Palace—the wood aesthetic developed

The nearness of the wood is in this porch floor at Daitokuji. The quality it conveys of having been rubbed by stocking feet and sat close to makes this material much different from what would happen if it were, say, vinyl asbestos or something more readily reproducible.

Daitokuji-porch—the nearness of wood

The only clear instance I have seen on the North American continent of prefabrication based on the special qualities of wood is made by Tarascan Indians in the hills above Patzcuaro in Michoacan, Mexico. The idea is that when you get married you receive a house that father gives you which he has made out of these reluctant sticks; it is all in a bundle and you take it off to where you and your bride want to go and you set it up. It is a simple system. The mobile-home people and others in our society have the same general idea but they miss some of the qualities the Tarascan father has managed to include. He has attended to pieces which are repeatable in function but are given precise shapes which fit them onto corbels and then under a beam while the whole is made out of boards still decipherable in their forest form, yet put together in a beautifully organized version of what in the houses of the Swedes becomes a log cabin. This Tarascan house does not include certain late-twentieth-century technological achievements such as plumbing, but the desire that puts this prefabricated house together, that lets it then go where its inhabitants need to go, is curiously germane to our own needs and concerns: the house in the picture is now located three hundred miles away from the hills of Michoacan.

Tarascan prefab

At Croton Falls is another aspect of the joy of sticks, by now long enough neglected so that we can examine it anew as a stick aesthetic, casual and full of joy, not really a slave tradition or the outgrowth of a stone architecture, but rather a perfectly good way, as one enjoys the long winter evenings, of hacking at some boards, banging them together, and then painting them (horror of horrors) white, so that the light can fall on them in ways to make particularly clear what they are doing. The idiom seems to be Gothic, sticks are sticks, and such preelectric tools as the lathe were taken full advantage of. The boardness of each of the pieces is played with to make clearer than ever what each one is, and it is altogether evident and altogether appropriate to enjoy sticking some especially nice piece on if no place else can be found for it in the system. This represents a freedom from restraint that is doubtless well worth cherishing.

Croton Falls—a stick aesthetic, casual and full of joy, not really a wood outgrowth of stone

Bonham cabin, Santa Cruz County

Indeed, much American work of the eighteenth, nineteenth, and twentieth centuries has been free of that sense of underdogism to the Mediterranean culture. The Bonham cabin is an effort of my own firm to achieve this freedom from restraint and from the taint of money. It is an extraordinarily cheap cabin in a redwood forest in California; it is made cheap because "Texture 111" plywood has been tacked on to its outside, because tar paper has been tacked on to its roof, and because such appurtenances as a metal chimney, which blows off during heavy winds but can readily be replaced (it is quite light), have promoted the reduction of the cost to a point where the owner was indeed able to build the building, a point which seemed important. The prehistoric and other concerns represented by these shanties can, I think, have considerable power on the human mind.

The Jobson house done by my firm in Monterey, California, is a small, inexpenisve house deep in the woods. One of the ideas on which it is based is a four-poster center (it used to be a hearth in some primitive houses, surrounded by an exterior that was capable of being manipulated to handle the requirements special to the location of the house or the needs of the inhabitants). This firm middle is a place related to the aediculae in which medieval saints used to stand. Its coupling with a surround which has the capacity for complexity makes it an appropriate place to live, at once central to family life and able to cope with life's specific daily requirements. In this particular house rather than a chimney being in the middle, a very active family mostly concerned with running around seemed appropriately monumentalized by a stair which allows children to run up and down in the center of the house.

Jobson house, interior

The house, as a tentmaker from Germany pointed out, is a big redwood tent. The advantage of the tent being redwood made cheaply, quickly and roughly on the spot is of course that it can cope with what is right there and needful of being coped with.

Jobson house, exterior

As the roof goes down a long way it makes it possible, indeed makes it mandatory, to have a lower, wider space. Windows can be introduced to look at something special, in this case a little stream.

As the roof descends not so far, over a dining space, the space is automatically higher, and the opportunity exists to look out of high windows at a high redwood tree, to have an entirely different sense of what lies around. This occurs within a system of considering the problem and within the capacity of small boards (which are more or less alike) to be sawed to any length with minimum extra trouble. A multitude of other examples are available to demonstrate the ease and rapidity of slapping up two-by-fours using diagonal pieces or plywood for stability in wind or earthquake. This is the system which, as Siegfried Giedion has pointed out to us, built the West: all one has to do is take nails and pin those light wood pieces together and cover them up with something. Now, depending upon the part of the country in which you are, the system is still three or four or five dollars a square foot cheaper than anything else available and it can be made to contain in it all the amenities, short of the amenities of midtown Manhattan, which most people seek in their houses. The possibility of changing the method with changing times of course exists.

Jobson living room

Jobson dining space

The structure at New Zion was built by first-year Yale students and represents both the strengths and shortcomings of wood as a material; the students were beginners and so did not know when the man at the lumberyard told them that oak, the local wood, was the cheapest thing they could get for siding, that their first thousand nails would bend on the surface of it, but they now have vigorous understanding of the capacities of oak. This building had to be erected in something under three weeks by thirty students, so methods of using a lot of people at once had to be devised; the methods were sometimes a little hectic, but the idea was that the component pieces could be built bigger than is usual by three-man or four-man carpenter crews and then with the plethora of manpower, could be lifted into place, to stand ready to be joined by others. Our cult object in southeastern Connecticut at this point is a sabre saw, which has the most incredible capacity to make whatever you want to have happen, happen in a sheet of plywood without strain or even preplanning; the capacity exists to go around curves as readily as to go in a straight line.

New Zion—community center built by thirty people at once

The New Haven building inspectors would be more relaxed if they could regard the part of a house at 403 Elm shown in the photograph as a piece of furniture. The capacities of this particular kind of reconstituted plywood provide endless enjoyment to people free of the prejudice against applying color to wood and interested in the wielding of the sabre saw.

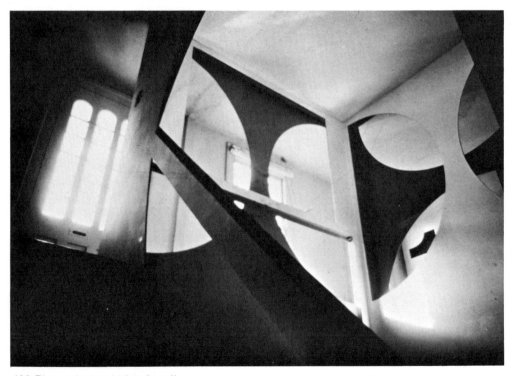

403 Elm—plywood "furniture"

The capacities of the balloon frame were understood beautifully by a number of architects, many of them British, many of them Eastern American, who settled in San Francisco during the first decade of the twentieth century. A group of houses, covered with shingles to make the exterior waterproof, were built on Pacific Street in San Francisco by an architect named Coxhead; these houses show most of the qualities which I think are inherent in this medium, at once very flexible and very simple, multiplied in a planned community.

Coxhead houses, San Francisco

The Villa del Monte model illustrates how our firm attempted to increase the density in an elderly housing community while taking advantage of a system that allowed for small shop-fabricated wooden houses with whole walls which can be put into place at once, very cheaply, with a travelling crane. It owes I suppose a considerable debt to our Mediterranean past; it tries to provide privacy for a one- or two-room house by having a yard behind a wall which is, at the same time, very close to a rather tight pedestrian circulation route. For cheapness and simplicity, wood walls are considered as planes; their balloon-framed stud walls are sheathed in plywood and covered with stucco rather than articulated as separate sticks. They are separated into groups so that only a portion can burn at once and there is a lane left for the firetrucks which have been such a colorful part of the American community since its inception.

Villa del Monte, Seaside, California

The site for the Sea Ranch development lies along ten miles of coast in northern California. It is a magnificent piece of natural landscape which used to be forested; the trees were cut down except along the ridge where Bishop pine and redwood remain. This beautiful, cold, windy coast is therefore innocent of trees, except that cypress hedgerows had been planted some fifty years ago and they constitute now probably the strongest single element in the landscape. The ten miles of coast was bought for a planned community of second homes. These are not vacation homes for most of the people who are there; they are places away from urban requirements for people who don't have that many urban requirements; and the idea of the plan was that houses could be built as close to the hedgerows as circumstances allowed. In some places, however, there were no hedgerows and something else had to be done to maintain the quality of the landscape, to maintain the qualities which make it worthwhile being there in the first place. The clients asked for and we decided to make a scheme for some kind of cluster housing which was, at first, modeled on a Mediterranean village like Mykonos, close-packed on the greensward by the coast and providing everybody with a chance to huddle out of the wind and away from the view. That, the clients decided, was probably not the best way of luring people to a place a hundred miles from San Francisco and fifty-five miles from the nearest town.

Sea Ranch Site

So, we made sugar-cube models to study how close we could put how many together still insuring for each residence a view of the sea, preferably either up or down the coast rather than straight out into the glare of the western ocean. It is probably coincidence that at the scale the model was made the sugar cubes were twenty-four feet on a side, and that was the module that we finally adopted. What was important to us in the planning was that we expected, even without computer aid (although we would have been delighted to have computer aid), to be able to develop a set of dwellings which were part of a system that was readily repeatable but could be thought about one by one by one. We had not just a blind repetition of anonymous housing units on a particularly beautiful site but had, rather, within late-twentieth-century limits of time and money, the opportunity to design especially for individual people's desires and sites. Our idea was to have one sample condominium which would have as many varieties of things happening within the system as we could manage so that the separate units could be looked at by potential clients who would then say, "Dandy, I would like the same, this part of this one and that part of that one, all up on the site which you will show me where the flag is planted to mark my house." The only thing that went wrong with this is that the salesmen became panic-stricken, they had never seen condominium units and they were sure they couldn't sell any, so they insisted that we try to sell the ones that were already built. When the first ten which had been built all sold immediately, then the salesmen said, "Now —we don't have any models anymore, we can't sell from them, we'll have to go and sell lots on which we make more money anyway." So that was that, except there are going to be some more, we hope, to start this process over again. Even though

what is shown on the sugar-cube model has not yet come to pass, I think that the images it generates have certainly been useful in selling individual lots, some of them fairly small and close together, which characterize the part of the property to the north which has so far been developed.

It seemed at the time of its inception an economical system, since big timbers were to be found in this area. As it turned out, it was not quite that economical because floods prevented the delivery of some of the big wood that was to come from the coastal forests to the north and it had to come from the California High Sierra instead. The structure went up as a wood frame with two-inch fir boarding over it, then building paper, and another inch of redwood. A friend delighted us as it took form by describing it as a large wooden rock.

Although there were many drawbacks to this way of doing things, one of the good things about having this wooden frame instead of some more rigid prefabricated arrangement was that we could cope with the irregularities of the site and still have a strong simple form on the landscape.

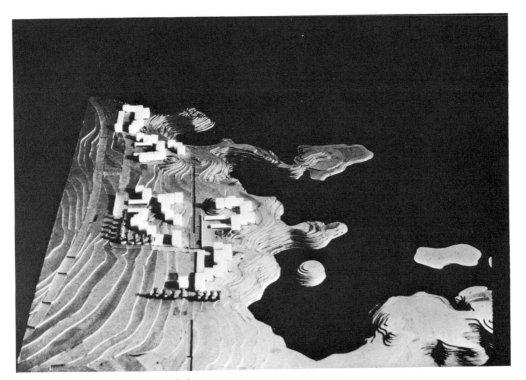

Sea Ranch—sugar cube model

The structure is made of ten-by-ten Douglas fir columns, and then four-by-ten fir girts, the girts applied to the outside of the columns with one girt always resting on another more securely placed one, so that all the way down the hill these pieces had to fall precisely onto one another. Above the top one, then, four-by-four posts held up much more simply the three-inch decking of the roof. Because of earthquakes and the need for diagonal bracing, the problem of making some bolted connection that was capable of taking all kinds of different angles was a very real one and threatened to become very expensive.

Sea Ranch structures

It was solved, thanks to an idea of the contractor, by a device which someone called our "Japanese hardware," a big steel plate that has holes all around it so that spikes can be driven through whichever hole comes over the four-by-four diagonal bracing. Since this structure is not all held together like the two-by-four stud arrangement of most houses, these ten-by-tens are just barely adequate, according to our engineer, to stand up against the wind on this exposed site. As each twenty-four-foot-by-twenty-four-foot module works, there are on opposite sides two columns with the girt between making a fairly stable frame. Each of the alternate sides is a single column with a girt balancing on it and resting at its ends on the other girts. The girts can be extended past the twenty-four-foot square to hold up additional bays. You will notice that unlike the Japanese things we have looked at, this is not wood that you'd love to touch, indeed you would get splinters in your fingers if you tried. It is a big heavy barn which is supposed to maintain considerable distance from you even when you are inside it.

Sea Ranch—Japanese hardware

Meant to be approached much more closely are pieces of wooden "furniture" sometimes three stories high which contain kitchen, stairs, bath, and closets. This is smooth painted wood, much more approachable than the rough framework which stands in contrast to it. Here in my own apartment, blue paint goes on the three-story piece of furniture.

In other apartments the hearth lies under a four-poster aedicula and over it a bed chamber achieves visual but not acoustical privacy when one lets down a great canvas sail with a zipper in it. The framework of the building can be extended, for instance, to make bays with particular views of the ocean. Between the twenty-four-foot modules, seizing whatever opportunities availed themselves, we were able to put rooms, porches, and whatever the space allowed.

One building does not constitute a community, however high may be our hopes for it. The individual houses surrounded with far more than enough land still excite the minds and itch the palms far more than do these condominia, though I do have the (selfish) suspicion that the vision of open land included in the concept of the condominium has raised the hopes of buyers of lots and contributed to the phenomenal financial success of the Sea Ranch. Lot sales in this remote location, fifty-five miles from the nearest town, must total well over two million by now. This may be a good note to end on, with the assertion repeated: wood construction is not dead. It is only our saws that are rusty.

Sea Ranch—interior furniture

Wood in the Big Perspective of Architecture

VICTOR A. LUNDY
Architect, New York City

Educated at Harvard University, Victor Lundy served there as a critic in Advanced Design. He has also been a visiting lecturer at the Universities of California and Florida as well as at Columbia and Yale. A few of his many works include the US Tax Court Building, Washington, D. C.; the US Embassy, Colombo, Ceylon; the IBM Garden State Office, Cranford, New Jersey; and the Ski Center, Lincoln National Forest, Ruidoso, New Mexico. He is a fellow of the American Institute of Architects and has received many honors, a few of which are First Honor Award, Connecticut Chapter, for the First Unitarian Church at Hartford; the First Honor Award, Homes for Better Living, AIA, House and Home, McCall's Magazine; and Silver Medal Award, Architectural League of New Mexico, in the 1965 Gold Medal Exhibition for the Travelling Exhibition Building and Exhibit, United States Atomic Energy Commission, in South America.

There will always be many individual paths to the truths that unite us as creative men. One of the significant things of this Symposium on Design and Aesthetics in Wood is its evidence of the deeds of many people, working by themselves in different places, and how these deeds privately accomplished, often without knowledge of the experiments of others, belong to all of us when a great universal truth is realized or a beautiful building or idea created. This, it seems to me, is the main excitement and the value of such a symposium—the awareness that we are all united as creative people in this search for truth, and the pleasure we all share when a real work or a new idea of visual truth is accomplished —a work or idea that has meaning for all men.

Our people are not building an architecture equal to our time. All the "points" are tritely "connected"—mostly current stylish inspiration is caught and frozen in a way that quickly palls and tires as does any transient fashion. Its spirit is not liberated and free like some of the new painting and sculpture. Architects are behind other creators. Their work is too static—bound up—frozen.

In this sense, wood structures—structures out of and within a live material—offer a great possibility in the hands of creative architects and engineers of becoming new forms of wonder and stimulation that are truly of our time. Wood structures can be of this age and open our vision into the future.

Why should buildings be so static? Is what we see about us the best that man can do for a people that seeks inspiration from nature? Look at the dull boxes about us, with their insipid colors and competitive arrangement, each trying to outdo the other in frozen bad taste, frozen evidence of man's failure to realize his opportunities in providing spaces for shelter and human activity.

Nature is never pedestrian, never insipid or dull. A tree dances, it is alive. Look at the leaves of an aspen tree trembling in the wind. Look up at the amazing intricacy of a roof top of leaves. What vault or roof of man has yet compared with the arching tracery of a tree. Look at the powerful unafraid boldness and yet with it the subtlety of nature. The greens of grass and leaves. The lavender skies. Sunsets are never dull, only man's depictions of them. There is always some new insight to truth revealed in nature.

Why the preoccupation with ponderous, thick walls, brought along with us from ancient or medieval stone cultures, when we have the miraculous discoveries about spanning space—lightly, delicately—discoveries from nature's structures, such as the tree.

Wood's magic is its aliveness—a renewable self-replenishing thing of nature. It is a living, renewable resource—an especially contemporary material for structures. We should draw inspiration from its own visual truth.

Wood is a living, resilient material.

It is totally unlike steel or concrete.

It has air in it. It comes mainly from above the earth, not beneath the earth. It isn't mined. It has resilience, moisture, and air—it is alive. As material it should be a modern medium of construction. It should be given as much consideration as a contemporary construction medium as steel or concrete. New techniques can make it go beyond the limits of tree sizes, tree strengths, and natural fire resistance. These techniques are permissible when they don't violate or torture the true nature of wood.

But traditional attitudes toward wood persist. Its structural use is burdened by a complexity of limits. The only all-wood structures allowed by most building codes the country over are one-story, or sometimes two-story, buildings, churches, schools, gymnasia, auditoria—buildings and rooms essentially on the ground. Our fire codes permit no more. Without some release as a building medium and as a means to architecture, there are just too many shackles on the use of wood to capture and excite the creative architect. One just does not think of wood as a structural means in large multistory buildings and yet there is no technical reason why not and many architectural reasons why one should.

In my architecture I am discouraged by the limits put on the use of wood—by the limits the law imposes on creativity in the use of wood in construction. There are just so many laminated wood churches one can do. By necessity I am working now with other palettes as well. Wood is relegated by custom and law, it would seem, to a small scale, very restricted use—to a kind of virtuosity in laminated wood structures for one- or two-story buildings; as an applique in limited ways as finish panellings; as flooring; in plywoods; on doors; in cabinet work; in furniture; in the individual house and now more and more in larger prefabricated and standardized parts.

We live in a time when we cannot afford to think in a big sense of the old values of hand craftsmanship and tender working of wood by artist woodworkers at the site. And even if we could, it is our obligation to build buildings of our time and make things of our age—not lean on sentimental yearnings for times and ways that are gone. But this need not rule out craftsmanship.

Its place is more and more in the plant, away from the site. Here high standards of craftsmanship can absorb the high cost of labor by efficient utilization under controlled plant conditions and by increased production of the wood industry serving more people.

However, the wood industry really hasn't done what might be expected of it to free its possibilities and stimulate a renewed interest in its product.

Far from keeping up with its present-day potential, it has been very ineffective in pressuring codes toward a point where creative architects could dream of expanded concepts for wood use.

The choices and combinations in the use of wood are, of course, varied and wonderful, and marvelous things will constantly result in the hands of the artist—choosing combinations and finishes—like making paintings out of wonderful colors and textures. The possibilities should be unlimited —the limits done away with. Why can't we build huge buildings out of wood or perhaps in an integral combination with other materials—steel, concrete. Why not some real strength and some brilliant effective action against the codes. Look at some of

the superb and huge wood structures of Japan. Look at Kizhi in Russia. Look at the wood lintels that remained so many centuries on the Mayan ruins of stone at Uxmal, Palenque in the Yucatan, at Tikal in Guatemala—in the damp humidity of tropical jungle.

Wood by its very nature suggests exciting, alive new directions in buildings. For example, by combination with steel cables in tension, interesting and alive buildings have been made. Perhaps there is a hint of such possibilities in the abstract analogy we can make with a tree. Why should not or cannot buildings be more like the tree —why so static and frozen? Air-supported structures react beautifully to wind and even hurricane forces—bending malleably with the wind and recovering their initial form. Buildings can perhaps become more movable, flexible, not tied in so much—like the tree that bends in the wind and recovers its shape.

What a marvelous structure is the tree. Even with all of its snow load, or the weight of water on it in the rain, it stands there equal to its burden—stands on its graceful stem and thrusts up the tracery of its branches. Its leaves wet with water, tons of leaves weighing its elegant members! What contemporary edifices do we know of that are as thrilling? And still we continue to build our simplified blocks. And they get simpler and simpler, and duller, and more alike, because our system, rather than rewarding those who dare to be brave, often penalizes and in fact prohibits by law in some areas any departure from the simple and dull.

Perhaps the restrictions on the use of wood in building have to do with an antiseptic trend in the United States—a machine esthetic—toward over-safety, over-maintenance-free, over-fireproofed, over-clean, over-insured, over-democratized toward an over-equality. We have become so conditioned to equality that there is less and less a reward for excellence, for being best, for being brave, for venturing into the new. That is the mark of middle age. I would like to continue to think of our country as young.

The wood industry should be jolted out of its complacency. It is like the stereotype New Englander, so secure in his traditions that he no longer belongs to his time.

And architects are just as bad—why don't they demand more? With all our know-how, we could make wood so it would not rot and would not burn, and it could be done so that it still is wood, not a tortured, inert, dead, salted-out thing. If the demand were there, surely our chemical industry and our scientists would be equal to such a call.

Perhaps also the question of permanence in buildings should be reexamined. Wood structures certainly last an adequate length of time. On the other hand, so-called permanent buildings of steel, concrete, and stone facing in the United States and elsewhere seem to be torn down after fifty years to make way for something new. At a time when labor costs in the United States make prohibitive the permanent construction that codes are based on, why not a more transient architecture for some purposes?

We cannot really mean this though. That would be exposition building. And we mean something different. Architecture is an art. It should be eternal. To create architecture is difficult, and it is of wood structures as a possibility for a total permanent architecture that I speak. It is a responsible act which guides and leads us to the future. It will last the longest when the lines and the decisions are inevitable and true. The architect's instincts make him custodian of the big, continuing, timeless vision of man's life on earth. His instincts must be equal to the vision of the future. His architecture must seek to be timeless in its truth. Architecture is more than a question of building. It is involved in seeking values that will have meaning for all men always, now and in the future.

History proves the endless variation and profound creative resources of man— man's will to make, to make different, to exceed, to go beyond. It teaches the short-cut, the reality of the instincts and feelings of the true artist, his sense of choice, of commitment—that in some strange way makes him a visionary of the future, as the scientist is.

It will take true artist-architects working in collaboration with creative engineers to make great architecture out of the wood-structure possibility. Great buildings are made out of more than architecturally defined intellectual purpose—intellect must be coupled with instinct, feelings, and these with a sense of the endless reactions and interactions of men.

Man must control and guide his opportunities for shelter and structure purposefully, with resolution and with his art, into poetic, brilliant forms, making spaces of appropriateness and high aspiration.

Safety in Wood Construction in Schools and Public Buildings

A. QUINCY JONES
Jones and Emmons, Los Angeles, California

A graduate in architecture of the University of Washington, A. Quincy Jones is a Fellow of the American Institute of Architects and a member of the architectural firm of Jones and Emmons. His firm has received over sixty awards for a wide variety of structures. His individual awards include an Award for Innovations in Building from American Builder Magazine *and the Alcoa Industrial Design Award. He has been president of the Southern California Chapter of AIA and chairman of their Fellowship Committee. He was a working delegate to the Housing Commission as AIA Member representing the United States at the International Union of Architects and has served on many committees of AIA*

This symposium is important—important because the principles—not the rules, but the principles—that govern the good uses and design of wood are the same principles that should govern the design and planning of our communities.

In 1918 the Englishman Sir W. R. Lethaby said, "Our towns have to be made delightful homes to live in, rather than delightful to get away from." This beautiful quotation may have been true in England at the time of the Lethaby statement, but assuredly it is all too true today in our country. Unless we have the knowledge and wisdom to properly rehabilitate our existing communities, design and execute the presently needed new communities, and plan for the needs of the foreseeable future, it becomes academic whether we can solve the current and future problems of the world or of outer space.

When I first accepted the assignment to discuss "Safety in Wood Construction in Schools and Public Buildings," it occurred to me that I might have to do considerable research in the building codes. Actually, this was true, and I did study the code requirements, but these requirements should be only a part of all of our concern for "safety" in our approach to "design and concern for aesthetics" in the use of wood, or any other building material for that matter. The building codes—and I use the plural because architects all work under many more than one code—always state that they are written and enforced in order to protect and insure the "public health and safety." However, health and safety have positive aspects that are not recognized in the codes.

From this point, I want to discuss the following general subjects which seem to be related to the topic of public health and safety in its broadest sense:

Prejudices—the building prejudices of the lay public and within the architectural and design professions.
Building Materials—steel, concrete, aluminum, and wood: their honest uses, distinctive characteristics and safety.
Building Codes—types of construction and how wood may be used in these various building types.
Building Codes—their inconsistencies and how these inconsistencies adversely affect design.
Technology—technology within the lumber industry as related to the work of architects and how cooperation should lead toward a common goal.

At this point, I want to make the protective statement that I do not pretend to be an expert on codes, safety, public or school buildings, or even on wood, although I must admit that I have used a great deal of wood in housing, schools, and public buildings. I do have a great love for wood and a great horror for its misuse.

On the point of prejudices, I am happy to report that the lay public is prejudiced in *favor* of wood for uses in their homes, offices, places of worship, places to play, work, and learn. Most people associate wood in "structure" and applied finishes with the words "warmth," "livability," "tradition," "home," "hearth," "abode," etc.

In the many projects that I have designed through the years, this association of good things with wood has prevailed. When the client discussions get around to exposed finishes, there is hardly ever a disagreement when the material I have selected happens to be wood. The kinds and finishes of wood may come up for considerable discussion, but the material itself seems to be universally accepted. True, the matter of maintenance and safety and the question of fire hazard become client concerns in some instances, but more on these later.

It has occurred to me that the quick acceptance of wood may relate to nostalgia, because most of us have been exposed to extensive experiences of wood in the home throughout our lives. If we were to think about this, could we not establish the following postulate?

What if two thousand years ago people knew as much about steel, aluminum, concrete, glass, and plastics as we do today —and what if they had not used wood, nor ever thought of its use in conjunction with their buildings? What would happen then, if suddenly today, a new industry invented the gang saw, lathes, and plywood presses? Would we accept wood immediately as a building material, or would our attitude differ from the prevailing acceptance we know today? I have no rational indications on which to base any kind of answer, but my glands tell me that acceptance certainly would be different. I bring up this question as a means of strengthening my point that we all have the responsibility of using wood products well and not using wood as a substitute for another material that will do the job better. There are so many honest and good uses for wood that the industry does not have to suggest wood as a substitute for other materials.

Ironically I have made this point many times before—said as a reverse kind of statement—when talking about steel and aluminum building products. I think that the steel and aluminum industries have not done themselves, or architects, or the public, a favor by producing metal siding that deliberately "looks like" wood, or metal roofing that "looks like" wood shingles or shakes. There is something wrong if the best possible design of a shingle or piece of siding looks the same regardless of whether it is made of metal or wood. These two kinds of materials are not at all the same in their properties or their characteristics. For them to function properly in relation to their use, they should be designed to take advantage of their own best qualities. And as part of this function I cannot believe that metal shingles should be designed to look like wood shingles. Likewise the wood industry has the responsibility to itself, as well as the public, to encourage honest and good uses of wood without exploring fields of fakery. I must hasten to add that the industry, with few exceptions, has acted with integrity on this matter.

As for more negative prejudices harbored through misinformation, recently our office was master planning a new state college campus that would have an enrollment of some twenty thousand students within the next twenty to twenty-five years. Although it was not possible to start construction on the initial facilities until December, the college wanted these facilities ready by the next September for its first six hundred students.

Rather than follow the usual procedure of starting the campus in "temporary buildings," our office decided that we could design the buildings to house the first five hundred students, who were to be in a "college within a college," at the beginning

and use it during the formulative years as the initial buildings to house the early campus enrollment and convert the space when needed to serve the permanent use as indicated in the curriculum plan.

After the administration accepted our concept, we made several basic decisions as we developed our design. The first was to provide a structural system that was easy to adapt for the changing functions as required during the first five years for the initial buildings and, finally, convert to the permanent use for the college within the college. In any event, we elected to use a structural scheme that is similar to the old "mill-type" construction, with a crawl-space, wood-floor joist system that provided us with a continuous duct space under all areas. This crawl-space makes it quite easy to remodel, or rework, the various utility functions of the building, items such as telephone, heating, air conditioning, electrical, computer, and audio-visual utility requirements. The structural system, encompassing the crawl-space, was based on a laminated post-and-beam frame with laminated roof decking, three inches thick, and concrete-block nonbearing filler walls.

Now, back to the subject of prejudices. The college administration and trustees had the kind of first reaction that we anticipated. They posed the following questions and, I think, believed that the answers would lead our office to abandon the system:

Is wood construction permanent? "We want these buildings to last at least one hundred years," one of them said.
What about fire?
What about maintenance?
What about cost of this system versus temporary wood frame or prefabricated steel buildings?

The last question arose because the state wanted to compare costs of the so-called temporary buildings they usually built with the "permanent" buildings we wanted to build.

It was easy enough to point out many examples of mill construction that are more than one hundred years old and in good state of repair despite minimum maintenance. One example that is warm to the hearts of people in California are the old Spanish missions. A difference is that the filler walls—and in some cases the load-bearing walls—are of adobe (hardly an aid to permanence) instead of concrete block. Another difference is that the beams are of solid stock without the additional attributes of long life and structural stability that are inherent with the laminated posts and beams that we are using.

As to fire safety, the building code supported our decision. Our selected system of construction is rated by the state fire marshal as a Type-Three building, the second highest in fire rating, falling just under Types One and Two that include reinforced concrete or fire-proofed steel consturction, normally used in high-rise construction with a four-hour fire rating. By comparison, temporary buildings of the kind usually built for the initial needs of a campus are the Type-Five construction and at best have a one-hour fire rating.

It was also easy enough for us to prove that the wood elements of our scheme required no more maintenance than painted surfaces of plaster or concrete structures that are painted.

As to cost, we had a direct comparison. The state had built many temporary buildings (which we all know are more permanent than "permanent" buildings when they think of tearing down the "temporary" structures) and their costs averaged about $18 a square foot when finally made ready for occupancy. Our buildings when out for bid, were estimated at $18.50 a square foot.

The point of all this is that we could not have met the prejudice problem we faced and solved it satisfactorily if we had not been able to prove that our solution was feasible. More important, through the use of an exposed-wood structural system, we now have a facility that is aesthetically pleasing and functionally flexible, with the highest fire rating we could get without going to an expensive Type-One or Type-Two building. Most important, we have a solution that is compatible with the kind of environment one associates with the learning experience. Prejudice through misinformation could have prevented this.

In a structural system we used in a food market in 1952 and in a church designed in 1959, we have examples of the same advantages from the standpoint of safety and, at the same time, a wood structural system that provides an environment that did not have to be compromised because of the justified concern we all have for the safety of the occupants.

Enough now about prejudices and on to building materials where comparisons can be made regarding safety, use, and characteristics while, at the same time, remembering that one of the most important functions of any building is the quality of experience provided.

As an aside in connection with the comparison, it can be pointed out that in more cases than not, as we all know, building a reinforced concrete structure required the contractor to build what amounts to a disposable wood building. Admittedly, the increasing reuse of forms, whether they be steel, aluminum, or plastic-lined forms, as well as slip-forms, is increasingly cutting into this shadow business of the lumber industry, but the fact remains that the lumber industry continues to supply a considerable amount of these forms for concrete structures.

Concerning safety, I find it difficult not to worry about the hazards of fire when one uses a structural system that involves pre-stressed or post-tensioned concrete. We have heard of failures that occurred in Japan, for instance, when the building walls, with the thin protection that is usually characteristic of prestressed or post-tensioned systems, have been exposed to excessive heat. If adequate concrete is provided to insulate the reinforcing steel to the proper degree, these systems lose some of the advantage gained otherwise in the "economy of materials."

There have been many predictions regarding the future of plastics as structural materials, particularly on the advantages of lighter weight within a structure and inexpensive fibre materials for use in reinforcing. I cannot help but recognize these advantages, but the fire problem and the simple heat problems have not been solved yet within this industry. If these problems can be solved, there will be great and honest avenues of use open in the plastics industry. It is possible that the space-development research will uncover ways to meet the problems of high heat.

When we are concerned with safety, it is readily possible to rule out structural failure in any of the materials. If properly engineered, none of them should fail structurally unless influenced by other factors such as heat or water.

Fire is really the major point of concern. We can assume proper structural engineering. As a matter of fact, the building codes, including the uniform code, define their five types of structures based only on fire ratings. Types of occupancies are to be within certain building types because of the pre-calculated fire risks for the users of the buildings.

It is truly unfortunate that, after all these years, architects and engineers have not been successful in getting one building code that serves the entire country, with only the minor variations for regional char-acteristics such as earthquakes, temperature, weather, soil, and similar local conditions. Instead, we have many codes and even in contiguous communities these codes are often contradictory. Within a radius of one hundred miles of Los Angeles, for instance, we work under more than twenty different building codes that are in effect to provide for the public health and safety of their respective communities. It might seem that somehow the individuals in these communities vary from each other and have different built-in safety and health tolerances, but people living across the street from each other, separated only by jurisdictional boundaries, look very much alike and do not have different requirements for health and safety.

One of my personal concerns with the code is the part that is supposed to protect the public health. To me, it seems that the mental health of the people can be affected by the plaster box that is written into the code by indirection; plaster boxes with ugly ceilings that divide into the unsightly rows of strip fluorescent lights in a forest of ceiling diffusers, registers, ventilators, and sprinkler heads. These chaotic ceiling surfaces in most structures usually clash with other surfaces in the rooms.

Actually, within the codes as they are now written, there are many safe and permitted uses of wood. Type-One and Type-Two buildings that are usually classified as four-hour, fire-rated structures permit the use of wood for nonbearing permanent partitions as well as ceilings if the wood has an approved fire-retardant treatment. In other words, the architect has considerable latitude in a high-rise building that is a rigid-frame concrete or fireproofed steel structure. The wood industry, however, has a real responsibility to come up with a type of fire-retardant treatment that permits the architect to make multiple choices in the final finish of the wood, choices that are acceptable in terms of aesthetics as well as safety.

Type-Three construction permits combustible materials in all structural and finish elements of a building, except for the exterior walls, but wood must be heavy timber. Usually, this means that no beams are under six inches by twelve inches and no columns are under eight inches by eight inches. The roof decking is at least three inches thick. These requirements leave the door wide open for the safe use of wood products.

Type-Four is rated for incombustible materials, but it permits the use of fire-retardant treated lumber for the nonbearing permanent partitions and roof framing. The possible uses of wood products in a Type-Four building are as extensive as they are in Type-One and Type-Two buildings.

A Type-Five building that has the requirement of one-hour fire rating can use heavy timber the same as Type-Four, of course, and a Type-Five without the fire requirement is open for all kinds of wonderful wood-product uses.

I point out these specific opportunities because sometimes we fail to realize the opportunities of using wood imaginatively. Often, we assume there are safety hazards when, in fact, wood may be safer than another choice of material, particularly exposed steel.

Too often, the codes as written—even without the technology of the possible fire-retardant finishes of wood—are not explored sufficiently for the many possible imaginative uses of wood. I think this is an important point, because the continued lack of sensitivity in the design of habitable spaces produces results that are not safe from the standpoint of public mental health. Safety, in other words, must consider the long-time exposure of building occupants to their surroundings. In the same way, safety must also consider the damaging ef-

fects of atmospheric and water pollution upon individuals over a long term.

There is a further responsibility of the architects and the industry that I want to discuss. The building codes have many requirements that do not concern the principle of public health and safety, and many times these codes are inconsistent, as mentioned earlier. In some instances the codes seem to be irrational. In any case, we must constantly exert every possible effort to change and bring these codes up to date. If the practitioners involved in design do not do it, there is no reason to believe that it will ever be done.

Here are a few examples of code inconsistencies that illustrate my point.

The first has to do with a church. We wanted to build a garden wall some fifteen feet away from the glass walls of a square nave and altar space. The concept envisioned that the visual boundary of the nave space would extend to the garden wall and provide a garden place of worship within the privacy of this garden wall.

The nave was framed with laminated beams in a pyramidal form and the roof was sheathed with two-inch tongue and groove. The point of the pyramid was at fifty-five feet, the maximum height permitted for this occupancy in heavy-timber construction. The glass wall was to be eight feet high to the soffit of the eave that projected from ninety-foot-long sides of the square plan.

In this case the code considered the glass to be a wall, not a window. The code stated that 25 percent of the wall must have a one-hour fire rating. I could not find any explanation for this requirement of solid wall in relation to glass, so I went to the building department and asked, "What part of the wall should be one-hour?" The answer was, "We do not care."

It turned out that the building department would accept a continuous sill-bulkhead, two-feet high; or a continuous head over the glass, two-feet high; or a solution that split the difference with one foot of one-hour wall at the head and one foot at the sill. In addition, we were told that we could thicken the mullions to eight inches by eight inches and count the areas of the mullion surface as part of the wall requirement. It appeared obvious to me that regardless of the original intention of this requirement, its watered-down and arbitrary interpretation had nothing to do with safety. I am still hoping that we can change this particular code requirement since safety is not a factor, but we will not be successful, unfortunately, until more people are affected and interested in the change. Obviously, the quality of design suffers under such arbitrary rules.

The point I am trying to make here is that we should support every effort possible to get a performance-type code rather than one that merely states rules upon rules. Good building codes help all of us, we need the freedom for quality design and we need the protection of good code requirements. We do not need unnecessary and ambiguous requirements that keep us from doing our design job well.

Another example also has to do with a church. This church was designed for a shingle roof. It was situated in the middle of a four-acre piece of property with roads and open space on all but one short side. Across the street there were rows and rows of two-story apartments, spaced with the minimum side yards, which means they were within ten feet of each other. These apartments were already built and had shingle roofs. Incidentally, our church seated two hundred persons and was open to gardens with doors on three exterior sides.

The building code, newly adopted since the 1961 Bel Air-Brentwood fire in Los Angeles, did not permit shingle roofs on churches or other buildings for assembly type of occupancy. We talked to the building department about a shingle roof for this particular church. We pointed out that the new apartments across the street housed more people than the church could seat and that people sleep in the apartments and can be caught in a night fire. On the other hand, the church, presumably, is used only by people who are awake (the minister complimented me on this observation, incidentally).

We were turned down not only on our request for a shingle roof, but even on the use of fire-retardant treated shingles. Our only choice was to change to shingle tile, metal roof, or asbestos-composition shingles. Two of these added to the cost, and none of them fulfilled our design objectives in this particular instance.

Here again, we need a performance-type code to provide a sound basis for interpretation of what *is* and what is *not* "safe." Is it naive to wonder why it is safe to sleep under a shingle roof in an apartment building on one side of the street, but across the street it is unsafe to sit in a church, especially when its exits are easily accessible at all times?

A third example has to do with the code requirements for a marquee that extends over a public sidewalk. In commercial areas outside of the fire hazard zones in Los Angeles, we are able to build Type-Five combustible buildings to the sidewalk line and project a canopy or marquee over the sidewalk. The code's inconsistency is that the marquee must be of incombustible material, despite the fact it is supported structurally by a combustible wall. In the context of today's so-called "sick" humor, one can happily project the thought that in case of a fire the entire marquee can fall in one piece on the lucky firemen.

These three examples are only a few of the many code inconsistencies, but I hope they illustrate the need for our continued effort and participation by the building industry to bring codes up to date and make it possible to use all building materials in the best possible manner. More important, however, these inconsistencies make it increasingly difficult to design buildings that will upgrade the environment where all of us live.

Now, may I call attention to some concerns that I have which involve the lumber industry as well as other segments of our society, particularly the planners and architects.

We hear talk about technology and the effect of new developments upon our lives. I am hanging my hat on two points. First, safety and the various other considerations in any building type should apply to schools in particular; and second, that all buildings are public buildings. Regarding technology, there is no doubt that new developments and future products will change buildings. It is vital that we make these buildings inviting and comfortable for people to use.

School buildings and public buildings will change, but people who use these buildings are more or less a constant factor. Certain needs of people will change, but essentially the individuals using these new buildings will have much the same inner requirements for shelter, pleasant surroundings, and a good environment as the users of today's buildings.

Like many of you, I have traveled around this country and in several foreign lands. I am becoming alarmed for the physical safety of people and their future mental health unless a way can be found for technology to provide the kind of environment that is conducive to an atmosphere of emotional stability.

Some years ago, as a representative of this country at the International Union of Architects' Congress in Prague, I saw re-

cent examples of schools, public buildings, and housing that were designed from precast concrete components out of the "catalog." We saw row after row of five, eight, and twelve-story apartment buildings. The schools were one to five-story buildings. The same applied to most of the new public buildings. The same "catalog" precast floor units, wall units, beams, and roof slabs were used in each building type. The buildings have few amenities and they are not human in scale. Regardless, these buildings represent a tremendous step forward for postwar Czechoslovakia where a critical shortage exists in housing and schools in particular. But even under these critical conditions, one wishes the new housing were better than it is. One of my concerns is that these same higher and higher densities of living patterns are starting to influence us in this country in a way that can be equally as "unsafe" as similar experiences are for people in other countries.

I do not know how much of these negative aspects of the housing we saw can be credited to the prevailing socialist form of government, nor do I know how much of the negative aspects of the housing in our country can be blamed upon the free enterprise system in this, our democracy. I do know, however, that when we start to think in terms of housing people in units of five to ten thousand and more, we confront problems that are "inhuman" in scale. It is important that we face this problem, whether we live on that side of the world or in this country. These are the things that are happening in all parts of the world. I believe this subject of how we are housing people is pertinent to safety, and to safety in all kinds of buildings.

We are building more and more high-rise housing and large communities all at one time in our own country. It is our responsibility to make the new living patterns livable. One important way is to provide the component parts that represent warmth, livability, tradition, home, hearth, abode,and scale. We must recognize that any totally new community, regardless of whether it is for a few thousand or many thousands of inhabitants, presents a serious social challenge and responsibility. Most existing communities throughout history grew slowly and the residents had relatively few problems in adjusting to their environment. It is much different when we build new towns and large-scale developments in existing towns.

The lumber industry can become an important contributor through research and applied technology. One way is to improve the methods of fireproofing lumber products. If chemical means of fireproofing are feasible, and we change the statement from fire-retardant to fireproof, we can make one big step in the right direction.

What about other innovations? Will the lumber industry be successful in molding wood chips and other waste materials into shapes such as one-piece bathroom units, for example, or other elements that will enable us in this country to get on with our business of solving economically some of our critical housing problems?

We should not set our sights too low. We cannot set them too high. It is good to talk about these things. Perhaps someone today has the idea that will stimulate the rest of us to take another look at our own backyard and our own urban areas.

The Gap Between Industry and the Designer

ROBERT A. ECKERT
Manager of Architectural Services
Marketing Program Planning Department
Weyerhaeuser Company,
Tacoma, Washington

A graduate of the University of Washington, Robert A. Eckert did advanced work in architecture at Massachusetts Institute of Technology. At the Weyerhaeuser Company he is responsible for program planning for their Architectural Marketing Program, planning and supervision of professional design and technical support for all marketing programs, and design planning for new products and systems. He is active in the Southwest Washington Chapter of the American Institute of Architects.

There are ten critical, dynamic, explosive, challenging years ahead! How does this relate to the gap between industry and the designer? It identifies problem areas; and problems in industry are resolved through planning. The goal on long-range planning is the traditional ten-year period.

A few years ago, if there was a gap between an industry and those in design, it could be closed with known, and fairly reliable, remedies. A market survey, perhaps . . . a revised Sweet's Catalog . . . and some new ads or brochures. It wasn't an industry matter, but rather a company problem, generally one of mechanics.

I suggest that there is a new kind of gap, and it's different in at least two key ways from anything we have known before.

The first difference is the speed of technological change that is involved. There has always been change in this business, but nothing like we see today—and if the predictions for future technological change are even close, what is happening now is nothing to what will happen in the next decade. That, then, is the first *major* difference.

The second is that attitudes are changing much more slowly than technology. The present need for buildings, and the way they are being built, are profoundly modifying the roles that manufacturers and designers have played in construction. Yet, a good many industries and a good many designers continue to assume traditional roles.

For the moment, let's consider the first difference—technology. At just about every recent AIA, CSI, or Producers' Council Conference, the following forecast has been made: *There will be as much building completed in the next ten years as there has been in the last one hundred years.*

The accelerated pace of building isn't merely industry gossip—it's a matter of high national concern. When President Johnson signed the bill that created the Department of Housing and Urban Development (itself a significant change), he stated it this way: "By the year 2000 we must literally build a new America. We must create, in thirty-five short years, as many homes, schools, churches, hospitals, parks, roads, offices, warehouses, and public buildings as we have since the pilgrims arrived on these shores."

This new America cannot be built—or designed—like the old one. There just isn't time. Nor are the old skills available. The carpenters tell us that we are losing more journeymen than we are gaining apprentices, and that the attrition rate is getting worse. Most of the building crafts report similar problems. So we will have to build differently.

The most significant trend to different methods is the development of predesigned packages of materials—more often called "building systems." Walk into the typical office building today. The ceiling is made up of elements representing acoustic materials with prefinished surfaces, a support system, and often integrated environmental control and lighting units. About a third of the walls in a typical new office are completely predesigned, preengineered, movable partitions. If it is a sophisticated space for data processing, the building probably has a predesigned and preengineered floor

system. The exterior walls can be a predesigned and preengineered cladding system —and it is possible now to support all of these elements on a completely preengineered structural system.

The pace of building is increasingly fast. Cypress Junior College in Orange County, California is an example. It has about 3,000 students on a campus that was put together in approximately three months. Junior colleges are a big part of this new America—they are being started at the rate of one per week.

The technology is exciting—so much so that it may obscure the most significant aspect of its existence—*that is the fact that the responsibility for design and development work on these building systems is in the hands of the building-materials industries.* Like it or not, that is what has happened, and we are bound to see even more of it. We may not be able to—or want to— change the trend. I believe, however, that we in the industry can make this design trend a beneficial one.

There is a constant interest and pressure to upgrade these new building systems, to better integrate building processes into them and thus to include larger portions of the structures being built today.

Consider the school-construction-systems development program in California. It is complete now—and it has been reported that five of the seven new building systems developed for the program were put on the market. At least one of them has become an eight-million-dollar-a-year business. This program, in turn, has stimulated other states and school districts to start development of their own systems programs. This systems development program was followed with the university-residential-building-systems program in California.

All of this activity has one overriding objective: to force industry to design and develop integrated building elements to help solve tomorrow's building needs.

Every system being developed for these programs has to be designed and developed in conjunction with the other related systems in the structure. If you study this goal and the experience so far in this kind of systems approach, you come to a startling (but logical) conclusion: we are in a race for time, and the goal is to be able to design and build almost simultaneously.

I think it is clear that systems will continue to be an ever larger part of our building business. The pressures supporting this trend include the positive fact of demand for more rapid development of buildings—and the negative fact of our inability to produce buildings fast enough in the conventional manner. Labor costs are rising—on-site labor costs at a much higher rate than off-site labor costs.

Where is the wood industry in all of this?

There is a tremendous challenge ahead—that is getting ourselves in a position to be able to participate in programs such as the school-construction-systems-development program and the university-residential-building-systems program. In the university-residential-building-systems program, it was impossible for the wood industry to submit a proposal for structural systems. A subsequent addendum to the program allowed a Type-Three, one-hour construction for the low-rise; however, low-rise could not be bid separately from high-rise. I'm sure this was not done intentionally to rule out wood—rather, I believe it was a reflection on the assumed capabilities of the wood industry in terms of past performance.

In any event, the present position of the wood industry indicates the first of two factors that widen the gap between the designer and the industry; that is simply, *the lack of product and/or systems development* to support the designer in meeting tomorrow's building needs.

To see the second contributing factor better, let us assume for the moment that we are either proceeding or planning to proceed in the direction of closing this aspect of the gap, and that we are making some headway. After we begin to develop and present packages of materials, we find new complications related to obtaining and presenting information about performance requirements, specifications, technical data, etc., as it relates to these new products and/or systems.

The second factor in the gap, then, is in the area of *communications*. We must find a better way to get the designer involved with these new products and systems.

Here's the situation: there is a clear trend toward systems development. We must begin to produce the systems and products that are the trend of the future and, at the same time, we must keep one step ahead of ourselves and prepare to communicate information about our new systems in a new way.

There *is* a way to close the gap between industry and the design profession. It is involvement in *competent professional design*.

It is a little like the three strangers sitting together on a plane. When the first man was asked what his occupation was, he said he was a dentist, but that he liked to paint on weekends. The second man said that he was a neurologist—and that he, also, painted on weekends. "And what do you do?" the dentist then asked the third man. "Well," he answered, "I'm a painter." The dentist then asked our painter if that was all he did to occupy his time.

The painter answered, "No, on weekends I'm a brain surgeon."

The point is that we, as an industry, have to stop being weekend brain surgeons. We have to get the professional designers involved in our activities, both from outside our companies and from within. To close the communication and product-development gap between industry and the designer, industry has to take the initiative. The designer cannot because he has neither the time nor the money to research systems on his own. For most of the wood industry, taking design initiative is a new concept.

As a part of our communications gap, let's talk about advertising and promotion for a moment. If we are to close the gap with the designer in the realm of advertising and promotion, *what we do* is very important. I think most of us in industry know *what* we have to do; however, *how we do it* is more significant. A very discerning landlady I remember when I was in college had a favorite phrase to describe the situation. She would very often comment, "We see our own thinking."

What are we saying then? If we are to reach the designer where he is thinking, we have to reach him in the area of design. At this point, I would like to differentiate between the typical type of advertising design and substitute in its place design that is accepted and understood by the professional in the building industry. I am not going to try to identify the difference at this time, but I am going to assure you that there is one! The only way I know to accomplish this is, again, to *get the designer involved*. It's not the easy way, but I can guarantee that it does get results.

In the area of technical information and good professional specifications, the design profession has already made contributions. We would do well to consider carefully the spec-data program developed by the CSI and the CSI Format. These are all tools to help close the gap.

Look at it this way: industry suddenly finds itself with the responsibility for systems development and, therefore, with a new role in design and construction. At the same time, the designers' interests and roles are changing. In the last ten years, there has been relatively little discussion at national AIA conventions about building design as such. The whole profession has taken a step from the highway of building design to the new freeway of planning, urban development, comprehensive service, etc. From the standpoint of the wood-products industry, the new role in design is imposed at a time when we are going through a major change—we are just learning to be market-oriented rather than product-oriented.

And now we have to learn to be *design-oriented!*

Fortunately there are already some noteworthy examples in other industries. Westinghouse, for instance, recently set up a complete design center for their corporation. The assignment covers not only building-materials design, but all of the firm's industrial design, their corporate image programs, and their own building programs. A good many others have moved in this direction—including IBM and Container Corporation of America. They have recognized the value of design in all aspects of their operations.

I've said the responsibility that industry faces is that of becoming design-oriented, but it's more than that, really—industry must become completely absorbed in design.

We have been manufacturing materials that were needed. We are now on the threshold of developing end-use products and systems that are desired. The major difference between something that is needed and something that is desired is *design*.

The decision to become design-oriented has to happen at top-management level, and the needle to keep things moving in this area must always point down. When that needle gets turned around, it is referred to in our department as "situation up needle," and as William Oncken, Jr., a professional management consultant, says,

"This is not the most efficient way to accomplish anything in any business organization."

As with any problem involving communications, however, it's a two-way street. If it is up to industry to initiate action, then it is up to the design profession to be involved —to participate. I cannot emphasize enough the importance of the need for the professional designer's being both within the industry and on the outside as a consultant, thoroughly versed in industry's needs. For example, I do not know of a professional design organization in the country that has a balance representing, and completely understanding, market needs, manufacturing processes, and building design. This is what is required for the design and development of good end-use products and/or building systems. As a result, a good share of the knowledge and skill necessary to devise a well-designed building system has to come from within industry itself.

I'll mention just a few things the profession could, and is, doing to help.

A short time ago, Robert Durham, president of the American Institute of Architects, mentioned to me that over a third of our graduating architectural students were now going into industry. The question the Institute and industry is concerned with is, "Are these students properly trained for this activity?"

There is a change in the profession relating to the designer who is working in industry. The traditional attitude has been one of polite scorn—the architect in industry was likely to be considered at best a seeker of security or at worst the kind of designer who failed to respond to the challenge of private practice. If that was ever the case, neither the profession nor industry can afford to let it be the case now.

In systems design, industry is where the action is—and the highest capabilities of both industrial management and the design profession are essential to favorable results. As we have mentioned before, industry is now dealing not only in basic materials, but also in design and construction. The amateur designer is about as pertinent to this context as our old friend, the amateur brain surgeon!

On its part, industry must assume the responsibility for systems design that is being thrust upon it. But it must, in the process, acquire a new understanding and rapport with the profession, developing its new systems with the highest quality of professional design and presenting information about them in a comprehensive, technically accurate, well-organized, and aesthetically pleasing manner. Designers, on the other hand, must react to this "open-door" policy of industry, if this amalgamation of productive capacity and creative design is to occur.

Industry in these next ten critical years has to somehow attract professionals, both as industry members and as industrial consultants, to do the job. The profession has to find a way to supply the talent.

PART III
Design in a
Dynamic Technology

While many of the contributors in the earlier art and architecture sections extend their interest in wood into a broader concern for the total condition of man—his psychological well-being, his social well-being, his environmental well-being—the two papers in this section are almost entirely centered on this broader aspect. They are panoramic in their consideration of the environmental quality of human existence. For them wood is merely a deeply significant and potentially rich element that can contribute substantially to this quality.

As a landscape architect, Karl Linn does speak of wood in quite a different way—as a living organism or living sculpture in which its growth, development, and aging process must be anticipated to be well "integrated with environment." But his concern is in the integration—the "ecological aesthetic" he calls it—in which wood and other materials "show the impact of the forces that surround them." Their design should create, in his words, "an ecologically integrated architecture," a "microenvironment, which is deeply responsive to the natural surroundings." But Linn's greater interest lies not in "physical" but in "human ecology." Architecture should not only reflect the impact of those who use it, but ideally they, the users, should have a hand in its construction. The genuine human contact with basic natural materials —natural materials like sand, wood, and water that delight man—is what for Linn gives quality to life. And these natural materials, as so many of the other papers have urged, must be honestly presented, not veneered or falsely finished or imitated. Finally, in proposing some theoretical reasons for man's universal attraction to wood, he urges us to trust that which we like strongly, suggesting that intuition or "knowledge unthought of" can lead us to truth.

Buckminster Fuller moves out on a still

wider canvas—incredibly wide. He turns the earth into a spaceship and the ecological unit he considers is the universe. His range is not only vast in spaciousness but at the same time detailed and specific. He moves easily from history into the future, forward and backward, just as he moves back and forth from physical to human interests and concerns. He views the ecological balance chemically. He graphically accounts for structural tension and compression of the tree and its marvelous structural system, but at the same time he optimistically sees man as "essential to the complementary functioning of the universe," and he sees man as moving toward the "great challenge of our day" . . . "that the design-science revolution could make possible all of humanity's enjoying all of our spherical space-vehicle earth without anyone interfering with another and without anyone being advantaged at the expense of another." His view is breathtaking and its very size relegates wood to a smaller role than it has in the other papers. Readers narrowly searching out the subject of wood may be disappointed, but those interested in design and in wood as a marvelous structure of natural design—as well as a material for design—will find in this paper a structure of relationships and idea-giving concepts—a kind of creative release for design thinking—that is unique in design literature.

Toward an Ecological Aesthetic and the Use of Wood in Design

KARL LINN
Landscape Architect, New York City

*Trained in psychology at the New School
for Social Research, Karl Linn also holds
degrees from Psychotechnical Institute, Zu-
rich, Switzerland, and Kadoorie Agricultural
School, Israel. He founded the Neighborhood Commons organization in Philadelphia, Washington, and Baltimore and is a
member of the Executive Committees of
the Architects Renewal Committee for Har-
lem and the New York City Council of
Parks and Playgrounds. He is a neighbor-
hood-resource planner and consultant on
establishment of urban-extension projects
and Model-Cities neighborhood programs.*

I have an axe to grind. A few years ago
when my little boy was three, we went to a
Howard Johnson's restaurant. He reached
out to a little philodendron leaf and
touched it. Recoiling from it, he cringed
and grimaced and exclaimed his disap-
pointment because it was an artificial
flower. In a similar way I have a very definite bias against imitation wood, because I
like wood, I like to use wood, in its organic
form where its strength and its very nature
can become part of the environment. I do
not mind stylizations, of flowers for instance; I like the Mexican paper flowers
that are large and colorful, but I do not like
imitations of flowers or wood.

As a landscape architect, I have often
pondered on what makes this field unique
and different from that of other design disciplines. What distinguished landscape architecture to me years ago was the fact
that one designed with living organisms,
with living plants. At one point in my practice, I used plants more sculpturally, as
"living sculptures"—not only as mass—
and was involved with the intricate structure of cut-leaf maple specimens and
gnarly bonzai trees. Landscape architecture must be involved with the anticipation
of growth. One has to anticipate and incor-

porate growth into one's composition. The landscape architect is only successful, then, if that which he anticipates comes true. I remember when I came back five years later to a place where I had planted a rockspray (*Cotoneaster praecox*) amidst some rock outcropping. It had become so intricate—I could not have done it alone. I might have sensed that which a rockspray wanted to be; that the gnarliness of its branches echoed the angular lines of the rock, and that the two were somehow isomorphically related. Both were the result of similar climatic conditions. I only had to find the proper ecological niche through which the true potential of the plant could unfold. So I merely sensed a possibility. But the form was inherent in the plant, and all the forces in its surroundings contributed to its unfolding. Maybe as a landscape architect, I was only a good midwife.

Even lumber used as a structural organic material seems to grow with age if well used. We all know what the forces of weather can do to change wood, and how we want cypress and cedar to bleach as years go by, and how important it is for structures to age with grace. We all know what patina means. This seems to be an even more profound challenge. It was difficult enough to anticipate the growth of living things, but how does one anticipate the growth of inorganic or inanimate objects, how does one incorporate the change that an inanimate object has to go through to be integrated with the surroundings? This "to be" produces yet a higher level of aesthetics. I'd like to call it an ecological aesthetic and it represents a profound challenge today to architecture, which inadvertently deals with inanimate, very rigid objects. Today architecture still primarily creates structures that are segregated, isolated from their environment, artificially lit, with hermetically sealed air-conditioning. This architectural ambition

is still on the order of mechanistic aspiration to prove an independence of nature, a testimony to man's arrogance. But there is a beginning of a growing ecological awareness that aspires to structures that are integrated with environment, that are part of their environment, that show the impact of the forces that surround them. Instead of making buildings look virginally new, untouched, by sandblasting, at least the Seagram Building used acid to hasten the weathering of the bronze exterior.

In addition to weathering, advances have been made toward the development of ecologically integrated manmade environments. The stainless steel Saarinen Arch in St. Louis, reflecting the rising and the setting sun and constantly changing, is one such achievement. Another is Louis Kahn's girls' dormitory in Bryn Mawr, which, faced with grey slate, has vertical apertures at the funneled entrances to the building that allow the changing light of the sun to cast a shifting shadow on the slate, transforming the building into a sundial. Louis Kahn was also commissioned to design an altar in New York to commemorate six million Jews, victims of Nazi terror, but he didn't want to restrict its significance only to Jews that died in gas chambers. He chose to build it all out of glass, and every butterfly or leaf that intercepts the rays of the sun outside the building will cast a shadow upon its surface. Thus the building attains an infinite resonance in tune with every stirring that takes place in its environment.

When the Japanese built a building, they sometimes put the wooden columns on curved rocks. I thought they were put there to prevent the wood from rotting. I learned that the buildings were deliberately so designed to make them resilient to the earthquakes, so there would be a little give. This to me is a responsive environment, a responsive manmade environment, a more lasting environment because it can yield. It is not a rigid, finite structure. It incorporates the possibilities of change and flexibility. I like to call this kind of building "Judo Architecture."

I remember another building by Louis Kahn—the embassy in Angola. He topped the building with another ceiling to prevent the sun from heating it. The building was also surrounded by a set of separate sections opposite the windows to prevent the sun from directly penetrating into it. He created, unintentionally, an air vector, which made air-conditioning almost unnecessary.

When we spent three months in Puerto Rico, I met a young architect who studied wind currents for five years in England. He experimented with wind tunnels and came to the conclusion that in Puerto Rico one of the most significant resources is the northeasterly wind prevailing at all times; that if you turn the buildings in the direction of the wind you can create comfort zones without air-conditioning. You only need a little fan for three hours during the midday for three months of the year; but the louvers had to be vertical instead of the horizontal ones that produce currents that bypass the body zone.

This to me is a true, new challenge to the design profession. It's an ecological challenge. It's no longer adequate to take pride that we can isolate man from his environment and put him in an artificially illuminated, hermetically sealed, air-conditioned room. We must create a man-made environment, a microenvironment, which is deeply responsive to the natural surroundings, to the specific prevailing forces. The great technological challenge is to create an ecologically integrated architecture, and we are capable of doing so. Only then will cities not look alike any more. When you go to Syracuse you know you are in Syracuse and not in New York; if you go to the

West Coast, you know you are on the West Coast. Airports would not all look alike and buildings would not all look alike. It's really a renaissance of the primitive, because in early centuries people had to build in response to their environment and draw on local materials in order to survive. Consequently, that architecture was infinitely more intricate, full of nuances. There is the beginning of a reaction in America against homogeneity that a low-level mechanistic technology brought about. But many are still taking tremendous pride in that they can isolate men and put them in artificial environments, and thus they are even building schools underground, going from the sublime to the ridiculous. These underground schools are supposed to be air-raid shelters, bunker-schools.

I would like to consider another aspect of an environmental aesthetic. Lancelot Whyte was asked by Edgar Kauffman, Jr. to make some comments on architecture. He complained that because of assembly-line construction, the physical environment manifested too low a level of complexity. It is very repetitive in its rhythm. He feels that as men penetrate more deeply into the incredible complexity of organic structure, men's art has to follow suit. The only way Lancelot Whyte sees that a greater complexity can be injected into the development of the physical environment, though he didn't know how to translate it into specific design applications, is through synchronization, through orchestration of different, independently existing, working systems.

This principle of orchestration is also really the essence of a democracy. You work through bargaining and compromise. One does not dictatorially predetermine. So the specific answers are never known, because whatever evolves will be the result of many people with different interests having to get together. We have the Senate and the House of Representatives and they have to work things out with the executive branch. It is a difficult process.

The musical composers of today compose in such a way that the score has an open structure, so that it's played differently each time, with the minutia and the detail new in each performance. This means open-structured design, planned indeterminacy. It is not accidental that composers, poets, and philosophers are pacesetters, since their metier is fluid. It is much more difficult for sculptors and especially for architects to follow suit. It is easier to manipulate sounds, words, and paint than steel and concrete.

I somehow feel that environment, if it is to attain an environmental aesthetic of quality with a high level of complexity, has to be the result of a three-fold partnership, a triumvirate of builders: first, the resident; second, the professional; and third, the climate. We have referred to two so far—the professional and the forces of climate and weather. We have referred to physical ecology and man-made physical environment which should be in resonance with the forces of natural surroundings. To it I'd like to add the consideration of human ecology, the third partner, and transpose the dynamics of physical ecology to the consideration of a human ecology.

Our challenge as builders of space is to create habitats for living, not to create finite structures. Unfortunately, so many people in our field still take it upon themselves to pursue the challenge that the sculptors of yesterday—not even of today —went after, to create finite buildings imbued with a message, "Do not touch." Walls made out of marble or travertine are not only prohibitively expensive but also prohibit human touch. Any little expression is called desecration of the physical environment. Even rich people moving into fancy buildings are prevented from driving so much as a nail into the wall. And hired decorators take all possibility for expression away from those who inhabit their structures by predesigning every hi-fi component and its case.

But we know today from mental health science that unless people are given an opportunity to contribute to the unfolding and molding of their immediate environment they become deeply alienated from it, which undermines their mental health and makes them strangers to their own living quarters.

So how can we create the kind of physical environment that invites expression, that makes it easier for people to make a home out of a house? Only if those who reside within the physical structure can gradually develop a sense of home, do they develop a sense of belonging, a sense of pride. Only then do they, as growing children, develop a greater sense of assertiveness, of self-confidence, because they are given the opportunity to gradually test their strength as they reach out farther and farther to participate in the molding of their own environment. You have to start with the small—unless a child can be given a chance to create his environment, he will never develop the kind of confidence that we so badly need today, since we are all called upon to contribute to the molding of our destiny.

There are as yet only a few examples of an architecture that allows its residents to assert their impact on its structure. Neil Mitchell, who taught engineering at Harvard Graduate School of Design, developed a lightweight concrete specifically designed to enable poor people in South America to build their own houses, independent of large equipment. His flexible structural system also makes possible erector-set-like modifications to accommodate changing needs of growing and shrinking families. Jan Wompler won the first "Progressive Architecture" award for his open concrete platforms which he designed to allow the displaced squatters of La Perla in San Juan to bring their buildings along or build new ones on the various concrete levels which incorporated all utilities. This plan encourages the self-expression and mastery over environment that is squelched whenever people are displaced and squeezed into rigid public housing.

In a more poetic way, Charles Eames, a close friend of Sister Corita, in his program statement for the New College of the Immaculate Heart, expresses this goal:

We guard outselves against wants that could be hazardous—such as expressions of form or structure or monumentality or even an overemphasis on beauty—
We want a college that will shelter those within it on the sad days as well as the gay days—
A system of buildings that will not be embarrassed by complete changes of program—
A structure that can be scotch-taped, nailed into, thumb-tacked, and still not lose its dignity—
Spaces that will welcome and enhance teaching machines as well as celebrations and pageants—
Materials that will not tend to become shoddy and will still show a response to care—
One would hope that the experience of the buildings would seem so natural that the question of their having been designed could never come up.
We want these buildings to demand something of those who enter them and to enrich and shelter those who remain within.

We know now why gurus choose caves.

Arthur Koestler made public in *The New York Times* a story in which he said that none of us really realize how deeply we are affected in our unconscious by the new technology that the Atomic Era brought with it. He asked that we imagine that we receive a wire from an intergalaxial insurance company congratulating us because we have come of age with the invention of atomic energy. They deplore very much, however, that they have to cancel our insurance policy, because the risk is too high; they have seen many planets blow themselves up. But since we have come of age, they extend their blessings to us, saying that it's all up to us now. And as masters of our destiny, we cannot afford to be prophets of doom any longer. We have to become prophets of hope.

I consider the importance of the use of wood in the environment in this context. In these days of great uncertainties and the invasion of our lives by synthetic materials, we are all involved in the search for elemental things. We need less fancy, contrived play equipment and more big sand mounds, big bodies of water, fire, and wood—to climb on and to build with, and more human contact.

Our cities should also be designed in such a way that the framework of the larger landscape is accessible to its citizens, so that they are in touch with the sky and the horizon; the rivers that frame or dissect many cities also reinforce a sense of belonging. This need is especially felt in Manhattan, where one is usually overwhelmed by the canyons of buildings. I suggested once that Manhattan, especially from 59th to 110th Streets, really should have been built like a dromedary. One high point should have been over Broadway and the other over Lexington Avenue. Like Habitat '67, the buildings would taper down to the Hudson on one side and down to Central Park on the other; they would rise and then taper down again towards the East River, so that more citizens, more people, could have a chance to see the rising and setting sun. This is the physical-ecological context to our cities. We really shouldn't just put the biggest buildings up for a few people next to the water, river fronts, and parks, which relegates everybody else to their shadows.

There are many aspects of wood to talk about. One often, as the saying goes, doesn't see the forest for the trees. I would like to talk about woods too for a minute, not just wood. A physician who is also a bio-physicist at the University of Pennsylvania once explained that forests and trees produce negative ions in the process of transpiration. This negative ionization of the atmosphere has a beneficial effect on one's organism, it soothes the thorax. Fountains as they refract water particles have the same effect. Then perhaps I understood why the only place I can sing decently is in the shower and perhaps why so many of us feel like taking a deep breath when we come into the midst of a forest. The landscape architect fortunately doesn't have to rely any longer on his romanticism to explain why he likes woods, but can justify his psychological experience by the knowledge of the underlying physiological event. So if we really like wood so much— good, solid wood, maybe someday someone will find a scientific reason for it. In the meantime, let's just enjoy it and speculate about it.

As wood is being polished, its grain emerges more and more vividly. There is something honest about its inwardness, its organicness. I think we are getting away from the concept of beauty that is just a masked beauty. I once wrote a little synopsis to the students that said, "Love is really not blinding, but it ignites a spark which illuminates a face." There is something that is being expressed that emerges and radiates outward. Before, we thought about the effect of forces in the environment upon structure; now, I am reversing it and thinking of the expression of an inwardness. I think that is why we feel attracted to wood grain, just like my little boy felt cheated when he touched something that pretended to be what it was not. I think that's why it is so difficult for us to deal with veneers, things that are really not what they seem. To discover that only the few strawberries on top of the little basket are very pretty, while the ones below are small or rotten, really hurts. I do not think it is accidental that more and more butcher blocks appear in restaurants, nor am I surprised that butcher blocks as table tops have become such a growing industry. They are strong, real, and honest. It has something to do with the tension of the age. There is so much that shifts these days that we have to hold on to something rooted. In this age of increasing change, we are really in search of universals. A tree is such an incredibly complex element, which joins the realm of the living and the world of structure, that it also helps us to bridge the many different worlds in which we orbit.

Since we have talked about the ionization of our environment, it will behoove the future environmentalist to investigate our surroundings in terms of energy. We know, for instance, that fluorescent light and incandescent light charge the atmosphere with very different wave lengths. I noticed this at the Four Seasons Restaurant where we worked on the effect of different lighting on plant growth. But fluorescent light also affects human beings physiologically. It dulls one's whole state of being, as well as making one look like "death warmed over."

Trusting deeply his intuitive grasp of an audience, Buckminster Fuller often speaks about psychic-energy communication. I heard him not long ago give a talk to the International Congress of Art, Architecture,

and Religion, where he referred to his
being in contact with knowledge that he
has not thought of. So I want to enourage
you to trust that which you like strongly.
We apparently all share a common liking
for wood, and maybe this natural selection
makes us closer to each other than we realize.

Design in a Dynamic Technology

R. BUCKMINSTER FULLER
Professor
Southern Illinois University
Carbondale, Illinois

R. Buckminster Fuller is a prolific writer, dynamic speaker, innovative thinker, philosopher, teacher, designer, inventor, and business executive. He prepared for his career by taking work at Milton Academy, Harvard and the U. S. Naval Academy. He founded Dymaxion Corporation and is president of Geodesics, Inc. He has been Charles Elliott Norton Professor of Poetry at Harvard, is a member of Southern Illinois—NASA, Advanced Structures Research, and was vice-president of the World Society of Ekistics. He is the inventor of the Geodesic Dome, the Plydome, and the Paperboard Dome. He was the architect of the U. S. Pavilion at Montreal's 1967 World Fair. His awards include, among many others, Gran Premio, Triennale de Milan, 1954 and 1957; Plomado de Oro, Society of Mexican Architects, 1963; and the Industrial Designers Society of America First Award of Excellence, 1966.

My first task must be to put myself and my work into correct perspective. I know myself so well that I would be uncomfortable masquerading as somebody that would seem somehow special. Every man is unique. We are all special, but I am quite confident that I don't have anything other human beings don't have. Because I know myself very well and have operated a great deal on my own initiative and with limited funds, I have often been forced to use myself as my own guinea pig. It is quite difficult, but I have learned how to keep records of myself and from time to time it has been necessary to discipline myself quite vigorously.

But I'm quite confident that there is nothing I have been able to do that any human being could not have done who, once born, had not too much misfortune in having damage done that suppressed those innate faculties inherent to all men. Man's innate cerebral and metaphysical capabilities often are frustrated by negative factors of the environment. Not least of the frustrating factors of environment are the people in it who surround every individual. Every child is born a genius but is quickly degeniused either by unwitting humans or by physically unfavorable factors of the environment. The bright ones are those who are less damaged than the others. There are those who have special inbred aptitudes and those more cross-bred who are more comprehensively coordinated. Life as born is inherently comprehensive in its apprehending, comprehending, and coordinating capabilities. Every child is interested in the universe. His questions are universal. Development of specialization has been either a forced training affair or is a product of inbred talent, as in the case of two musician parents who tend to produce children of musical aptitude.

I am quite confident that whatever I've done really represents a good exploration of what other individuals could be able to do and I don't think it's much more than what an average healthy human being should do. The words "genius" and "creativity" have sometimes been used in explanation of my being "well-known." In my way of thinking the only reason that I am known at all is because I set about deliberately in 1927 to be a comprehensivist in an era of almost exclusive trending and formal disciplining toward specialization. Inasmuch as everyone else was becoming a specialist, I didn't have any competition whatsoever. I was such an antithetical standout that whatever I did became prominently obvious, ergo, well-known. I learned that you could train for comprehensivity at the United States Naval Academy. I attended the United States Naval Academy at Annapolis, Maryland, as a special student at the time of World War I.

Before that I had been a student at Har-

vard University where Alfred North Whitehead came early in this twentieth century from the great universities of England. He said that one of the things that was very noticeable at Harvard was that this great private school was initiating a new kind of pattern. It was beginning to build and staff the great graduate schools. The graduate schools dealt in specialization. In England a special preoccupation could be taken up within the general university. There were no special schools. Whitehead said that the American populace applauded the high specialization and Whitehead saw that this pattern was being followed by the other leading private schools, colleges, and universities. Of course the public schools and public universities immediately followed suit, taking on the graduate schools' patterns, because the political representatives of the public saw that their constituents would want the state school to incorporate these educational advances of the rich man's private schools. So specialization in graduate schools also became the "thing."

Whitehead said this meant that we deliberately sorted out the students, sieved them, picked out the bright ones, and persuaded the brights to stay in the university and to go on to the graduate school. This meant that we began to make specialists out of our bright ones. The bright ones within their own special category of their special school went on to develop further special nuances within their special areas. This all worked toward expertise and hybridism in the educational pursuits. It meant that the bright ones would learn much about their special subject. The public thought this to be desirable because people liked the idea of an "all-star team." They thought that if we took groups of all-stars and put them together, our commonwealth would surely prosper.

Whitehead said, "So far so good, and everybody is applauding." But he then said that the educational hybridism would mean that these men who were of high intellectual capabilities would have very high intellectual integrity. As men of high intellectual integrity they would quickly discover that they were making great progress in highly specialized areas of inquiry and thus also they would know how little any other man outside their own field could possibly understand of what was going on inside their own and inside any one field other than their respective specializations. Therefore, no specialist of integrity would think of going into some other expert's field and making quick assumptions as to the significance of that unfamiliar work. This would be considered preposterous. There would thus develop an increasing tendency to break down generalized communications and comprehensive prospecting between these experts. Certainly, they would not tend to join together and say, "I see I am developing this and you are developing that, if we associated them thus and so, such and such would be the economic consequences; therefore let us do so by employing our credit as scientists with the banks in order to fund our undertakings." These men, Whitehead said, would do just the opposite and would become more and more subjective, growing into purer and purer scientists to whom no banker would think of lending money on the basis of intellectual integrity alone. The scientists went in just the opposite direction of applied science. The more expert they were, the less they would think of searching into the concept of how society might enjoy the fruits of their discoveries.

Whitehead pointed out that this system tended to break down the communication between men of high intellectual capability in all special fields. Inasmuch as society wanted to exploit the game of their "all-star" teams, it meant that someone other than the prime intellects had to integrate and exploit their capabilities and their findings.

Then Whitehead said—which came as quite a surprise—"Inasmuch as we have deliberately sorted out the bright ones from the dull ones, we have inadvertently created a class of dull ones." Just as in mining we have a big pile of tailings, and no one thinks much about tailings because they are interested only in the high-grade, quick-cash ore and the net metal that is taken out of the latter. He said that inasmuch as the "bright ones" are not going to be able to realize, integrate, and exploit their own potentials, we will have to leave it to the not-so-brights to put things together. This is what I have termed "Whitehead's dilemma."

I have developed "Whitehead's dilemma" a little further than he could go at that time. I find that there is a second grade of men who get passing marks, but are not selected to be specialists. These men, though not "gleaming bright," have a dull polish and are good healthy fellows, who play good football and are liked by everybody. These second-grade "clean ones" become the first choice for executives in business, which does integrate potentials of demand and supply. Then, as corporation executives, these not-quite-so-brights take on the pure scientist experts and cultivate them like special hybrid egg-laying hens in special houses. The corporations take on the task of putting appropriate specializations together to exploit the synergetic advantage thus accruing. The businessman becomes the integrator of the bright ones' capabilities. The business executive himself, however, tends to be a specialist of a less fine order. Pretty soon he will say, for instance, "I am in the automobile business and don't know anything about stockings, so I am just going to just stick to my automobiles." He might also say, "I find that an automobile won't run across an open field. Therefore it is only half of the invention—automotive transportation. The highway itself is a large part of the invention—high-speed highway transportation." Automobiling is schematically like a monkey wrench—the ratchet half is the "highway" and the thumbscrew-adjustable traveling jaw is the "automobile." The automobile is literally geared by its tire-treads to the road. So the business executive might say, "An automobile company could not possibly afford to build the highways—it is a very difficult political matter. You have to have costly condemnation proceedings and so forth to get a highway through. It is all so expensive that our company would never make a profit if we took the responsibility of providing highways. All we can provide is the automobile. To get the show going, however, we will have a little auto race track over here and we will have automobile shows in many big cities and at county and state fairs. We will get people very excited about the way our automobile can go and how fascinating it looks." Thus it went, and the people began to envision personal use and enjoyment of the automobile "if only they had highways." What the auto executive did was to excite the people into demanding highways for the cars.

We next come down to a duller class of not-so-brights—much duller—who didn't even go to college. This much-duller-class is that of the politicians. The politicians saw that the people in general wanted automobiles and wanted to "joy ride," so they immediately voted for highways to get the people's votes for themselves.

Thus a much bigger, geographical pattern of the automobile emerged than the domain of the factory and the auto executive's specialized territory. The bigger pattern was the total highway system—state, interstate, and federal. We also find that generally speaking the larger (geographi-

cally) the physical task to be done, the duller the conceptual brain that is brought to bear upon the integration of the scientific discovery and its technically realized applications. Finally, we get to international affairs, and you know what is happening today. The most highly polished of the dullest class, scientifically and intellectually speaking, may wear their striped pants very beautifully and be charming fellows, but they have not produced any mutually acceptable, constructive, world-peace-generating ideas. They traffic successfully only in people's troubles and emergency compromises. One of the great mistakes that society has been demonstrating in our last century has been that of leaving the most important problems to the men who are bankrupt in creative thinking ability.

World War I marked the end of the old great masters of the water-ocean-earth commerce. These men were the world "bankers," who were the not-too-dull businessmen who had the high courage and coordination necessary to develop successful world-pattern cartels and trusts quite transcendentally to any one nation's antitrust laws or to any one nation's popular knowledge. They took advantage of the preoccupation men the world around had with their own respective domestic affairs. These old masters kept the world peoples in complete ignorance of their world planning and let it be thought that this planning resulted from the deliberations of the local politicians the people appointed.

At Harvard, just before World War I, the dilemma Whitehead was talking about was developing in a very interesting way. What Whitehead didn't ask was how Harvard could afford those graduate schools. The fact is that neither Harvard nor any other university has ever operated at a profit. Certainly schools, colleges, and universities don't have surplus earnings accruing which they can reinvest. Establishing graduate schools wasn't something private colleges could do on their own. The explanation is that the graduate schools were given to Harvard and the other leading private universities.

The next interesting question is who gave them the graduate specialty schools. Well, the people who gave Harvard the schools were primarily the partners of J. P. Morgan and Company, or they were men who were founders or presidents of companies whose boards were run by J. P. Morgan. J. P. Morgan or his partners were at that time on the boards of nearly every important, powerful company in America. Morgan or his associates were also partners in the great unseen syndicate of world-commerce mastery up to World War I.

If you were an invisible world master of the water-ocean-earth, you had to maintain the capability to create and run the top world navies—you had to have physical control of the biggest patterns. No matter what else we may say of these men today, they were magnificently imaginative, big-scale operators. They had taken all that science, had learned about energy and put it into their navies' faster, further, more accurately hitting power in order to keep in supreme command of the physical affairs of mankind. Now if you were world master, you would not be at all worried about being displaced by a dull one. You would only be apprehensive of, and on guard against, the bright ones. There is the old strategy of "divide-and-conquer." Anticipatory "divide-and-conquer" is more powerful than tardy "divide-and-conquer." The old masters, then, in order to prevent others from displacing them from their great ocean mastery, deliberately went to work taking the young, bright ones as they came along and divided them up anticipatorily into non-self-integratable specializations which made them completely innocuous as chal-

lengers to comprehensive grand-strategy thinking and practical-affairs integration. The bright ones thus became subject to integration of their high potential only at the masters' command. That was the key to the world pattern mastery up to World War I, when general literacy of the rising world democracies posed threats to the old masters' all but impregnable sinecure.

World War I marked the end of the old masters. The old masters had local rulers of their choosing set up all around the world. They invented the political nations. They invented the geographical names—Greece, Italy—their nations were welded out of many tribes and battles. The masters said to their head-men stooges, "You command and hold the fort here. You are the strong man locally, and I will make you head-man. You can stay head-man, because I have the line of supply of maximum hitting power and maximum energy duration. If anybody challenges you, you get the supplies and he doesn't, for I control the oceans which carry those supplies. Therefore you are going to be able to win." This was the old and great pattern of world mastery. The local politician was a man (a king or whatever) put into a position of strength by the great masters who themselves remained scrupulously invisible. They preferred to remain invisible. The more invisible they were, the longer they could stay master. No challenges would arrive, because there was nothing visible to challenge. Secrecy was one of the greatest tools of the old masters. The visible head-man on the beach—the local head-man—was strong, however, simply by virtue of the old invisible master.

During World War I the incumbent world masters had been challenged by the organized "outs," who were the competitor commerce group of potential masters who were beginning to put the new potentials of science together faster than the old masters had seen fit to do. The "outs" invented going under the sea with submarines to break down the line of supply and going above the earth and sea with the airplane.

The old masters were being so vigorously challenged by the expansion of war patterns into new dimensions that they were about to be displaced, when suddenly a powerful scientific suggestion was made in England to the high command. A scientist said that there were ways in which the guns that reached the front could be made to last twice as long. He said, "Wouldn't this be as good as getting twice as many guns to the front? That is, even if the line of supplies was being critically slowed down by sinkings, the guns which did reach the front would last twice as long." The old high command said, "This is nonsense, but what do you have in mind?" Then the scientist said, "Well, we have had it here in the drawer since 1854; chrome-nickel-steel alloy." The old masters had never trusted anything they could not see, touch, or smell. They coordinated by virtue of their extraordinary sensorial ability—they were very physical human beings. They could count masts of ships swiftly, they could knock another guy down, they could play beautiful polo, and they could sail a very fast yacht. They did these things in a sensorial way. But they were suspicious of anything invisible; internal structural functions of alloys were invisible, ergo, they were unaccredited by the old masters.

At the turn of the century we were coming to the point where there were the X-rays, alloys, and all kinds of invisible events that the scientific specialization had discovered, but the old masters didn't want any of that invisible phenomena let loose. They were suspicious of its portent. They said, "The kind of steel we are making is good—it is all right and will do." In America they already owned US Steel and so

forth and were turning out what was called "mild steel." That is not a specification steel at all. It was the steel of the great rust dumps of pre-World War I. Finally, because the submarines were sinking their ships, in order to survive the old masters had to unleash the manufacture of the alloys which made the tools last longer.

Thus in World War I industry suddenly went from a visible to an invisible base, from the track to the trackless, from the wire to the wireless, from visible structuring to invisible structuring in alloys. The big thing about World War I is that man went off the sensorial spectrum as the prime criterion of accrediting initiations forever.

All major advances since World War I have been in the infra and ultra sensorial frequencies of the electromagnetic spectrum. All the important technical affairs of men today are invisible. Thus we see then that the old masters, who were sensorialists, had unleashed a Pandora's box of physical phenomena which were not sensorially controllable and which they had avoided accrediting up to that time. At that great critical moment when they unleashed these phenomena, they suddenly lost their true mastery, because from then on they didn't personally understand what was going on. If you don't understand, you cannot be the master.

Since World War I, the old masters have been extinct. Because they always operated in secret, they of course didn't announce their own demise. As they died secretly, they inadvertently left many accepted patterns such as, for instance, the "head-men" on the world thrones and the university patterns which Whitehead described. As new problems brought about by the old masters' demise arose, everybody began to turn to the local political head-men and new head-men, who arose easily by pushing over the old who no longer had the support of the now-defunct invisible masters.

In respect to "Whitehead's dilemma," everybody tends to believe that the best way to earn a living is by establishing one's own special monopoly at some strategic point in the specialization network. As a consequence of comprehensively undertaken specialization, we have today a general lack of comprehensive thinking. The specialist is therefore, in effect, a slave to the economic system in which he happens to function. The concept of inevitable specialization by the brightest has become approximately absolute in today's social economic reflexing. The fixation is false and is soon to be altered.

I went to the US Naval Academy at that moment in World War I when the grand masters and the British Navy who represented them were for the first time obliged to acknowledge the American Navy as an equal and give it great support or else the old masters were probably going to lose their world mastery. As a consequence, the British Navy began to disclose to the US Navy some of the inner secrets of its grand strategy. In addition to information given to top-rank admirals, much that was of basic strategic significance was disclosed to the young men who were being trained at the US Naval Academy at that moment. To us at Annapolis there were disclosed some of the grand theories as well as special strategies used by the old masters. One of the prime theories I learned as one of those naval-academy students was that in the naval academies of Britain, the United States, and other European countries, in contradistinction to all private and public universities and the military academies, they picked the bright ones to train deliberately as comprehensivists rather than as specialists. In the armies the officers became specialists for life as cavalrymen, artillery men, etc., but the admirals were trained to function ultimately and exclusively as the comprehensive assistants to the great invisible masters who were running the earth.

This comprehensivity of admirals came about in the following manner. The old masters had commanded that the highest economic priority go toward using everything man had learned in physics and chemistry to produce the highest hitting-power navy as the greatest tool with which to master the earth. This was due to the simple fact that you could carry bigger guns on ships than you could pull overland with horses. The navy represented the focused objective for application of all that man knew about science, mathematics, chemistry, and physics. All science was reduced to versatile, mobile practice in the navy. Armies and fortresses were static and good for local war. Navies were the dynamic and most important world tools up to and throughout World War I.

In sending the navy off to the high seas with all the nation's most important hardware, the nation had to develop admirals and captains whom the old masters could not only count on to be their most competent right-hand men but who could also be trusted to command competently and to maintain this most powerful tool, even when out of the old masters' sight. They had to have men who understood the world economic patterns as did the old masters themselves. They needed admirals and officers in general who could take a great navy halfway around the world from home bases and build a new naval base, say in South America or in any other remote place, who understood technology in every way, who could handle thousands of men, millions of dollars, thousands of technical, psychological, and economic problems—

very comprehensive men, the antithesis of specialists. The training scheme in the navy was to pick the brightest and send them first over to the Bureau of Ships where they could learn the theory and history of ships themselves and their great comprehensive patterning. Then the Navy Department deliberately rotated their officers' services, sending these men to sea on different types of ships—every type and kind: submarines, battleships, destroyers, supply ships and airships. Between ship assignments, the navy rotated its line officers into naval stations around the world. They rotated them back and forth, out of the ships into jurisprudence, into managing great naval shipyards which had the most powerful industrial tools of those days, and then to foreign embassies to get world-statesmanship experience, and finally into the study of the comprehensive world-strategy at the Naval War College. The navy's top-rank officers were always selecting which junior officers would be promoted. There was no automatic promotion by numbers in the advance ranks of the navy, as there was in the army. Admirals simply selected the two-and-one-half stripers who were most comprehensively capable and moved them up rapidly. The grand masters were able to pick the officers they most trusted amongst those who had the most comprehensive ability.

Suddenly new industrial technology available through invention changed all this. Lincoln was really the first "wired" president—the first head of a state able to talk directly by telegraph to his generals at the front. This was the first time generals no longer needed sovereign autonomy, because now the head of state became practically available for the highest policy decisions right at the front. World War I brought in the radio, and in World War II, for the first time, the admirals at sea were hooked up directly to Washington. They

didn't need the autonomy they had formerly needed when they took the fleet away for a year with no link to the president other than a messenger sailing ship. Therefore the radio made physical centralization of political authority inevitable, and with political centralization and the demise of the old masters came the end of the autonomous admiral, ergo, the end of the need for comprehensive training. With this came oblivion for the concept of comprehensive capability and "finis" for the comprehensivist educational systems. Today the navy, too, is specialized with "submarine officers" and "naval aviators" and so forth. But, by good fortune, I experienced the naval academy's last era of comprehensive training.

Today, however, all of our universities have been progressively organized for ever-finer specialization. Society assumes that specialization is natural, inevitable, and desirable. Yet, in observing a little child, we find it is interested in everything and spontaneously apprehends, comprehends, and coordinates an ever-expanding inventory of experiences. Children are the enthusiastic planetarium audiences. Nothing seems to be more prominent about human life than its wanting to understand all and put everything together. One of humanity's prime drives is to understand and be understood. All other living creatures are designed for highly specialized tasks. Man seems unique as the comprehensive comprehender and coordinator of local universe affairs.

Of all the species aboard earth, man, as designed, is the least specialized, although for limited moments he seems to employ some of his capabilities to much larger extent than he uses the others. What is unique in the universe with respect to man is the comprehensivity of his adaptability to changing environment through his externalized inventions and the magnitude to which he has detached, deployed, amplified, and made more incisive all of his many organic functionings. Man is unique among all the living phenomena as the most adaptable, omnienvironment, penetrating, exploring, and operating organism, being initially equipped to invent intellectually, and self-disciplined dexterously, to make the tools with which thus to extend himself. The bird, the fish, the tree are all specialized and their special-capability-functioning tools are integral to their bodies, making them incapable of penetrating hostile environments; man, however, externalizes, separates out, and increases each of his specialized-function capabilities by inventing tools as soon as he discovers the need through oft repeated experiences with unfriendly environmental challenges. Thus man only temporarily employs his integral equipment as a specialist and soon shifts that function to detached tools.

At the American Association for the Advancement of Sciences' annual 1961–62 meeting at Philadelphia, among the thousands of papers presented, there were two of special interest to us and our discussion here. One of these papers dealt with all the biological species that have become extinct and the other paper, quite independently, dealt with all the human tribes that have become extinct. These papers searched for characteristics that might account for the extinction. In both cases, it became clear that all the biological species that have become extinct and all the human tribes that have become extinct, became extinct for one reason—overspecialization. Evolution involves constant change. When living species become so specialized that they cannot adapt to an unexpectedly large jump in evolutionary events, they are "out."

Now men in our industrial and educational system have become more and more specialized. Everyone wanting economic security has seemed to think that as a specialist he could command the tollgate of an expressway to unique and essential information. He thought " a great many people will have to go through my specialization tollgate, and I'll have a special-education-guaranteed economic security."

But when we combine the trend toward increasing specialization with our knowledge that overspecialization leads to extinction, we realize that our unwitting human trend toward extinction was about to be realized as we developed the ability, through hyperspecialization in mathematical physics, to take the atom apart and thereafter to develop fission and fusion. Even the scientists, as specializations' victims, knew nothing of how to control the military, commercial, or political evolution of their discoveries.

But just as we are about to blow ourselves up, we discover that nature has invented man with a built-in safety factor: an automated self-destruction-arrester. The safety factor is the built-in propensity not only to invent and develop tools of destruction, but also inadvertently to invent constructive tools that render the destructive inventions obsolete. In this case the constructive tool was the computer which was immediately adapted by the military specialists to control the performance of rocket weapons.

Now here comes the surprise—suddenly, all unrecognized as such by society, the evolutionary antibody to the extinction of humanity through specialization appeared in the form of the computer and its comprehensively commanded automation, which makes man obsolete as a physical-production-and-control specialist. And this happened just in time. Now the computer, as superspecialist, can persevere day and night, day after day, in picking out the pink from the blue at superhumanly sustainable speeds. The computer can also operate in degrees of cold or heat at which man would perish. Man is going to be displaced altogether as a specialist by the computer. Man himself is being forced to reestablish, employ, and enjoy his innate "comprehensivity." Since it was overspecialization that was leading us toward self-extinction, man has, inadvertently, invented his own anti-self-extinction device.

Here I would like to just note another evolutionary trend that countered all of the educational systems and the deliberately increased professional specialization of scientists. This counter current occurred at the beginning of World War II, when extraordinary new scientific instruments were developed and the biologists and chemists and physicists were meeting in Washington on special war missions. But as early as my leaving Harvard, I suspected that nature didn't have separate departments of physics, chemistry, biology, and mathematics, which required meetings of department heads in order to decide how to make bubbles and roses. I had a suspicion that nature had just one department. The exploration capabilities of the scientists of my youth were meager compared to today. What the biologist was able to see with his very low-powered microscope looked very different from what chemists seemed to be dealing with, and the chemist couldn't see what he was dealing with at all. Today's scientists begin to realize that whereas a biologist used to think he was dealing only in cells, and that a chemist was dealing only in molecules, and that a physicist was dealing only in atoms, today they find their new powerful instrumentation and contiguous operations overlapping. Each specialist realizes that he is concerned alike with atoms, molecules, and cells. They are finding that there are no real dividing lines between their professional interests. Scientists didn't mean to do this, but their professional fields are being integrated inadvertently on the scientists' part, but ap-

parently purposefully, by inexorable evolution. So, as of World War II, the scientists began to invent new professional designations, ergo, the biochemist, the biophysicist, and so forth. They were forced to. Despite their deliberate attempts only to specialize, they were being merged into ever more inclusive fields of consideration.

Thus was deliberately specializing man led back unwittingly to employ once more his innately comprehensive capabilities. As I said earlier, man will also be forced to do this by the computer. Many people erroneously fear the computer and the increased industrial automation that it will bring. So I would like to point out that we are already fully automated as human beings. There are over a quadrillion times a quadrillion atoms dynamically intercoordinating in each of our brains, of whose successful local intercoursings, within microcosmic dimensions at seven-hundred million miles an hour, we have no conscious awareness. Nor may we claim any conscious design responsibility for their fantastically successful electromagnetic performances which, all together, result in our consciously cerebrating those sensations and thoughts that integrate as our seemingly simple awareness of just being alive here and now, and in our evolving and considering those self-emergent "thoughts." It is not surprising that we can tune into so exquisitely designed an apparatus carelessly and imperfectly, with superficially misleading results.

And as an example of the inadequacy of our macrocosmic apprehending, I think of students who say to me, "I wonder what it would be like to be on a spaceship?" I always answer the students by saying, "What does it feel like? That's all you have ever been experiencing. You are all astronauts, for you live aboard a very little spaceship called earth. Every once in a while, man launches a little spaceship at a velocity of 15,000 miles an hour from our bigger 67,000-miles-per-hour-speeding spherical spaceship earth, which is only 8,000 miles in diameter. We launch our little ships from our bigger spaceship earth at about one-quarter the speed of our own sun-orbiting travel. Our 8,000-mile diameter may seem big to the only-one-thousandth-of-a-mile-high you or me, but our spaceship's size is negligible in respect to the macro distances of the sky. The nearest space gas station or energy station, from which we get our energy to regenerate life aboard our spherical spaceship, is the sun, which is flying in formation with us at 92,000,000 miles distance. As our spaceship earth flies formation in annual circles around the sun, it rotates 365 times per orbit and thereby exposes all of its surface to the sun's radiation, thus permitting optimum impoundment of this prime life-supporting energy. Our next nearest energy-supply-sky-ship "star" maintains space flight position with us at one-hundred-thousand times greater distance than the sun, as we altogether fly formation through the vast reaches of the ever-transforming galactic nebula."

I am a constant traveler around our spaceship's spherical deck. Together with several million others, I have now, in my lifetime, walked, run, ridden, floated, or flown over three-million miles around the spherical surface of earth. My travel is one-hundred-fold the average distance around the surface of our spaceship earth heretofore accomplished in an average lifetime by any one of the generations before our time.

Lots of people say to me, "You know, I don't like travel, I don't like motion. I couldn't stand your kind of life." And I reply, "You apparently don't know what you are doing. My lifetime's traveling around our spaceship earth's surface is but a negligible mileage addition to the nine-million miles annual spinning around our polar

axis we mutually accomplish, plus our six-and-one-half billion miles annual orbiting around the sun, and our multiquadrillions of annual miles of Milky Way traveling and internebulae deploying. Therefore, my total lifetime's coming and going around our spaceship earth's surface of only three-million miles is only one-millionth of one percent of the macrocosmic traveling of one-hundred-and-forty quadrillion miles that you and I simultaneously accomplish, which enormous total is, however, only one-third the distance simultaneously accomplished in the microcosmos by each of the six-trillion atoms that comprise each of our individual human organic systems."

Spaceship earth is so extraordinarily well invented and designed, that to our knowledge humans have been aboard it for two-million years not even knowing that they are on board a spaceship. And our spaceship is so superbly designed that it can keep life regenerating on board despite the phenomenon entropy, by which all local physical systems lose energy. So we have to obtain our biological life-regenerating energy from another spaceship—the sun.

Our sun is flying in company with us within the vast reaches of the galactic system at just the right distance to give us enough radiation to keep us alive, yet not close enough to burn us up. And the whole scheme of spaceship earth and its live passengers is so superbly designed that the Van Allen belts, which we didn't even know we had until yesterday, filter the sun and other star radiation which, as it impinges upon our spherical ramparts, are so concentrated that if we went naked outside the Van Allen belts, it would kill us.

Our spaceship earth's designed infusion of the stars' radiant energy is processed in such a way that you and I can carry on safely. You and I can go out and take a sun bath but are unable to take in enough energy through our skins to keep us alive. So part of the way the spaceship earth sustains biological life is through the vegetation on the land and the algae in the sea employing photosynthesis to impound the life regenerating energy in an adequate amount.

But we can't eat all that vegetation. As a matter of fact, we can eat very little of it. We can't eat the bark or wood of the trees, nor the grasses. But insects can eat these and there are many other animals and creatures that can. We get the energy relayed to us by taking the milk and meat from the animals. The animals can eat the vegetation and there are a few of the fruits and tender vegetation petals and seeds that we can eat. We have learned to cultivate more of those botanical edibles by genetic inbreeding.

That we are endowed with such intuitive and intellectual capabilities as that of discovering the genes and the RNA and DNA, nuclear energy and the chemical structuring and other fundamental principles governing the fundamental design controls of life systems is part of the extraordinary design of spaceship earth, its equipment, passengers, and internal support systems. It is therefore paradoxical but strategically explicable, as we shall see, that up to now we have been misusing, abusing, and polluting this extraordinary chemical-energy-interchanging system for successfully regenerating all life aboard our planetary spaceship.

One of the interesting things to me about our spaceship is that it is a mechanical vehicle just like an automobile. If you own an automobile, you realize that you must put oil and gas into it and you must put water in the radiator and take care of the entire machine. You know that you are either going to keep the machine in good order, or it's going to be in trouble and fail to function. We have not been seeing our spaceship earth as an integrally designed machine which, to be persistently successful, must be comprehended and serviced in total.

Now there is one outstandingly important fact regarding spaceship earth and that is that no instruction book came with it. I think it very significant that there is no instruction book for successfully operating our ship. In view of the infinite attention to all other details displayed by our ship, it must be taken as deliberate and purposeful that an instruction book was omitted. Lack of instruction has forced us to find that there are two kinds of berries—red berries that will kill us and red berries that will nourish us. And we had to find out ways of telling which was which red berry before we ate it or otherwise we would die. So we were forced, because we lacked an instruction book, to use our intellect, which is our supreme faculty to devise scientific, experimental procedures and to effectively interpret the significance of those experimental findings. Thus, because the instruction manual was missing, we are learning how we can safely anticipate the consequences of an increasing number of alternative ways of extending our satisfactory survival and growth, both physical and metaphysical.

I would say that designed into this spaceship's total wealth was a big safety factor which allowed man to be very ignorant for a long time until he had amassed enough experiences from which to extract progressively the system of generalized principles governing the increases of energy-managing advantages over environment.

The designed omission of the instruction book on how to operate and maintain spaceship earth and its complex life-supporting-and-regenerating systems has forced man to discover retrospectively just what his most important forward capabilities are. His intellect had to discover itself.

Intellect, in turn, had to compound the facts of his experience. Comprehensive reviews of the compounded facts of experiences by intellect brought forth awareness of the generalized principles underlying all special and only superficially sensed experiences. Objective employment of those generalized principles in rearranging the physical resources of environment seems to be leading eventually to humanity's total success and readiness to cope with far vaster problems of the universe.

Now I would like to think with you about developing a grand strategy for swiftly multiplying humanity's effectiveness in mastering his spaceship earth's life-regenerating principles.

How may we use our intellectual capability to higher advantage? Our muscle is very meager as compared to the muscles of many animals. Our integral muscles are as nothing compared to the power of a tornado or to the atom bomb, which society contrived in fear out of the intellect's fearless discoveries of generalized principles governing the fundamental energy behaviors of the physical universe. In organizing our grand strategy, we must first discover where we are now, i.e., what is our present navigational position in the universal scheme of evolution?

To begin our position-fixing aboard our spaceship earth, we must first acknowledge that the abundance of immediately consumable, obviously desirable, or utterly essential resources have been sufficient until now to allow us to carry on despite our ignorance. Being eventually exhaustible and spoilable, they have been adequate only up to this critical moment. This cushion for error in humanity's survival and growth up to now was apparently provided just as the bird inside of the egg is provided with liquid nutriment to develop it to a certain point. But then, by design, the nutriment is exhausted at just the time when the chick is large enough to be able to locomote on its own legs. And so as the chick pecks at the shell seeking more nutriment, it inadvertently breaks open the shell. Stepping forth from its initial sanctuary, the young bird must now forage on its own legs and wings to discover the next phase of its regenerative sustenance.

My own picture of humanity today finds us just about to step out from the pieces of the eggshell we broke just one second ago. Our innocent trial-and-error sustaining nutriment is exhausted. We are faced with an entirely new relationship to the universe. We are going to have to spread our wings of intellect and fly, or we shall perish. That is, we must dare immediately to fly by the generalized principles governing the universe and not by the ground rules of yesterday's superstitious and erroneously conditioned reflexes. As we attempt competent thinking, we immediately begin to reemploy our innate drive for comprehensive understanding. As I have indicated earlier, central to all of humanity's world-around dilemmas is that it lacks comprehension and formal recognition of the comprehensive scope of its fundamental problems; in addition it lacks awareness of how these problems may be solved. For example, society does not have any idea what wealth really is. Since everything economic undertaken by business and government is done so either on a basis of formally acknowledged or "book" wealth, capital expenditure, or on a budgeted matching of outgo by predictable income, ignorance of what present realizable wealth capabilities are, and what practical realizable greater wealth capabilities thus may come to be, must obviously curtail and frustrate humanity's effectively farsighted and adequately detailed dealing with the unrealized, inexorable trend of evolution.

Wealth is not created by man. Wealth is generated by man's discovery and employment of the life-sustaining-and-regenerating principles existing a priori in the universe, many of which, we can infer from past history, are as yet undiscovered by man. Wealth is as limitless as the universe. But aboard spaceship earth, wealth is specifically the product of the regenerative-design-science applications of ever-amplifying metaphysical know-how to the ever more efficiently reassociated physical energies in their complementary condition of matter and radiation. In doing the foregoing, we're taking nothing from the energy capital of the universe. The physicists make it very clear that energy can neither be created nor destroyed. You can't exhaust that kind of wealth. It is not physically exhaustible.

And the metaphysical, or know-how, component of wealth can only increase. For every time we make an experiment with physical-energy wealth, we learn more. Even when we only learn that something we thought might work won't work—that is, in effect, learning more. Every time we make an experiment, we learn more; we cannot learn less. Because universal energy is inexhaustible and our intellectual advantage only gains, our wealth is continually gaining. We're continually upping the relative metabolic advantage of man in the universe.

Our present real wealth is exclusively the tool-organized capability to take energies of the universe which are transforming their patternings in various ways as yet uncontrolled by man and shunt them through channels onto the ends of levers which man invents so that the energy turns wheels and shafts to do his work. When man discovered the lever, he could move objects weighing hundreds of times his own weight and unmoveable by his muscles without the lever. This was the beginning of what is known as mechanical advantage. When man arranged a number of bucket-ended levers around a wheel and put that wheel, mounted in bearings, under a waterfall and connected a pulley on that shaft to pulleys on other shafts by belts, man had shunted the natural energy income patternings of the universe external to his own organic system to work for him and by converting the environmental events of energy to automate his future days during his metabolic regeneration. That event enormously increased his wealth. From then on, his real work became metaphysical development, increasing know-how through discovery, research, invention, and techno-scientific development. And no solutions to problems that now face us today have any value unless they are predicated on this recognition of wealth.

Now I would like to tell you about something else I feel essential to the solution of today's world problems. Consider that up to the time of Thomas Malthus, at the beginning of the nineteenth century, we had had many great world empires. But all the great pre-sixteenth-century world empires, such as those of Genghis Khan, Alexander the Great, the Ottomans, and Rome, were all what I call "flat empires." That is, they were all part of man's same pre-sixteenth-century cosmology which conceived of the earth as flat. The earth was apparently a great island surrounded horizontally to infinity by the sea. All the great empires were flat, postage-stamp empires inside of this great infinity. And the people in the times of Alexander the Great, or the Caesars, or of Saladin, all thought in that flat way. That is why "simple, elementary, plane" geometry is used by and taught to beginners, and "solid" is considered more difficult, and "spherical trig" even more advanced and more difficult.

When you think about the real consequences of that psychologically, philosophically, and mathematically, it is devastating. It means that "inside" the empire we have something we call civilization, while "outside" the empire begins the unknown wilderness with pretty rough people, and outside of that live dragons, and beyond the dragons, flat infinity. What we have in flat land is an only local finiteness and all outwardly around us extends flat infinity. This meant, then, that the Greeks, in attempting to communicate their mathematical conceptioning, defined the circle as "an area bound by a closed line of equal radius from one point" or a triangle as "an area bound by a closed line of three angles, three edges and three vertexes." The Greeks talked only about the area that was "bound" as having validity, finiteness, and identity, while outside, on the other side of the bounding line, there existed only treacherous terrain leading outward to infinity and, therefore, boundless.

This has a tremendous feedback effect and explains the ingrained biases in our present thinking. We tend to think that only one side of a line is definable, organized, and valid. "Our side" is natural, right, and God's country, and vice versa. All humanity has been conditioned to accredit only its own local area of experience as being natural and the logical prototype of all that is good and acceptable, with all else being remote, hostile, treacherous, and infinite. Infinite systems may contain an infinity of variables. The ancient world was imaginatively controlled by an infinity of gods.

The British Empire, on the other hand, was the first empire of man to occur after man knew that the earth was a sphere. A sphere is a mathematically finite, or closed, system. It is an omnisymmetrical, closed system. A sphere is finite unity. In 1810, Thomas Malthus, professor of political economics to the East India Company, was the first economist ever to receive all the vital statistics and economic data from a closed-system world. Once the world is conceived of as a sphere and finite, there are no longer an infinite number of varying possibilities identifiable uniquely as whims of gods.

Because the earth had been discovered by its high-seas masters to be a closed and finite system, the great pirates who controlled the seas took their scientists around the world to discover and disclose to them its exploitable resources. Only because the earth constituted a closed system could the scientists inspect, in effect, all the species and only thus was Darwin able to develop the closed-system theory of evolution of species. Such a theory could not have existed before that. It would have had to include dragons and sea serpents. All the people in all the previous open-edged empires lived in a system within whose bordering infinity anything could happen. Paganism wasn't illogical. Geometrically speaking, the pagans could have any number of gods, because any kind might occur in infinity. There were an infinite number of chances of upsetting the local pattern, which was a most satisfying idea if it happened that the individual didn't like the prevailing local pattern.

It seems strange that we are not taught about the historical, philosophical, and economic significance of the foregoing transition from an open to a closed world system. However, the omission can be explained by realizing that a closed system excludes any variables supposedly operating outside the system. Once a closed system is recognized as exclusively valid, the list of variables and the degrees of freedom are closed and, I might add in parentheses, they are limited to six positive and six negative alternatives of action for each local transformation event in the universe.

In view of Thomas Malthus's discovery that the world's people multiplied themselves much more rapidly than they were able to produce goods to support themselves, what could be done with these hard facts? For approximately a century the world-mastering venturers "classified" Malthus's books as secret information, belonging exclusively to the East India Company. Once "classified," that kind of information leaked out only among the pirates and the scholars. Karl Marx, as a great scholar studying in England, encountered the Malthusian data. It was equally clear to Marx that there was not enough to go around. Marx, therefore, said, "Since there is not enough to go around for all, and not even enough to go around for many, certainly those few who are arbitrarily favored by the prevailing system and thereby enabled to survive their alloted life span of twenty-seven years, ought to be the ones who are most 'worthy' "—and those who do the work were obviously, to Karl Marx, the most "worthy."

Those who opposed him said that daring enterprise, which alone conceived of the great value to be realized by society, could also increase abundance and support more people and that one should concede that the entrepreneurs should be the exclusive few who could and should survive. Others said it should be the bright ones who, by their superior intellectual fitness alone, could increase the numbers of men who could be supported. The choice of who should survive has always underlain all class warfare. Should it be the brightest, the toughest, the bravest, or who should it be?

Certainly the corollary to Darwin's theory of evolution, which expounded survival only of the fittest, seemed to fit neatly with Malthus, who observed that only a few were surviving their full span of years. It was assumed to be obvious by those in power that a scientific law supported and vindicated their position. Despite the great pirates' satisfaction, the question persisted among the "outs" as to who were the fittest. Would it prove, in the end, to be the workers, or would it be some military class, or would it be some intellectual class?

Just before I went to Harvard University in 1913, before the start of World War I, an "uncle" gave me some counsel. He was a very rich "uncle" and a friend of my father who had died when I was quite young. My "uncle" said, "Young man, I think I must tell you some things that won't make you very happy. I know that you are impressed with your grandmother's golden rule, 'Do unto others as you would they should do unto you.' " But my uncle went on to tell me about the discoveries of Thomas Malthus. He spoke about the pre-Malthusian times when there could reasonably have been any number of possibilities. He made it clear that in the early empires the concept of the golden rule was highly plausible. There seemingly were an infinity of chances that it could work. "But," my uncle said, "a few of us now know from the closed-system experts that the golden rule doesn't work. Those few of us who are rich and who really have the figures, know that it is worse than one chance in one-hundred that you can survive your allotted days in any comfort. It is not you or the other fellow, it is you or one-hundred others. And if you are going to survive and have a family of five and wish to prosper, then you're going to have to do it at the expense of five-hundred others. So, do it as neatly and cleanly and politely as you know how and as your conscience will allow. At any rate, that's what you're up against." He went on to say, "I'm not going to try to educate your grandmother, because she's quite happy in thinking her own golden-rule way and, of course unknown to her, I have taken care of her one-hundred alternates." My uncle then said, "There are few even today who know this is so. There are those all around the world who have their gods. They keep dying off short of their potential years, but they keep themselves happy by having their hopes of infinite possibilities. So we just won't bother to tell them about it."

At the present moment in history, we find

ourselves in a fundamentally different economic position. When more than a decade ago Eisenhower went to meet with Khrushchev in Geneva, both had been informed by their military and scientific aides regarding the magnitude of the atomic bomb's destructive capability. And Eisenhower said as he went to that conference, "There is no alternative to peace." I am sure Khrushchev, with the same realization, must have felt the powerful responsibility of that moment. Both being political realists and hard-fact men, they knew that they would not be able to make any important peace agreements solely by themselves. Their proposals and agreements, if any, would have to be backed by their respective political parties and their parties were always in mortal contest at home with their chief opposition who waited upon altruistic moves of the "ins" as opportunities to impeach them for treachery to their respective sovereign powers' ideological premises. Any softhearted step on the leader's part would throw the party out. While Eisenhower and Khrushchev couldn't yield an inch politically, ideologically, and militarily, both of them brought along their atomic scientists and allowed them to talk to each other in a limited manner regarding any possible peaceful uses of the atom.

Only a little over a decade ago, at this meeting in Geneva and at its companion meeting of the United Nations agricultural organization, it came clearly into scientific view (as reported unequivocably by Gerard Piel, publisher of the *Scientific American*) that for the first time in the history of man, it was evident that there could be enough fundamental metabolic and mechanical energy sustenance for everybody to survive at high standards of living and furthermore that there could be enough of everything to take care of an increasing population while also always improving the comprehensive standards of living. Granted the proper integration of world-around potentials by po-

litical unblocking, there could be enough to provide for all man to enjoy all the earth at a higher standard of living than all the yesterday's kings experienced. And this high standard of living could be enjoyed without personal interference and with no one being given advantages at the expense of another.

But clearly both political leaders and their respective states are frustrated by all the political checks and balances each side has set up, in view of yesterday's dictum that there was only enough to support one in a hundred, to protect and help only their own and their allies' side. So all the ages-long fears, all the bad habits, all the short-sighted expedients that have developed in custom and law frustrate whatever might be done to realize the new potential. But the fact to remember is that it was only a little more than a decade ago that man had this completely surprise news that Malthus was indeed wrong and there could be enough to go around handsomely.

The confusions of the world societies regarding what we are reviewing here are great. The fact is, however, that the foregoing economic facts are mankind's most important considerations now. We are faced with the necessity of developing effective ways to educate all humanity as rapidly as possible regarding this new and vital economic situation. The fact is that now, for the first time in the history of man, all the political theories and all the concepts of political functions are completely obsolete. The primacy of political ideologies are obsolete, because they were all developed on the basis that only your party or my party could survive, because there simply would not be enough for both.

The whole realization that mankind now can and may be comprehensively and mutually successful is so startling that we must have it as both the whole and the essence of our forward undertaking. But to have enough to go around for all requires a design revolution. For as now designed, the world's metals are invested in machinery and structures which are so inefficient that they can only take care of 44 percent of humanity. Engineers and scientists agree that the technical knowledge to correct this now exists. So it is also part of the great message to humanity that the world's problems cannot be solved by politics but can only be solved by a physical-invention and design revolution, or what I call a comprehensive anticipatory design revolution.

Although science has discovered that man can be a success, still all our great governments are organized and, as yet, operate on the basis that only you or me can survive, not both of us. Instead of having everybody carrying their own bludgeons, spears, swords, or later, guns, the major nations have professional soldiery and develop enormous mass-killing guns against the day of reckoning when it is decided by war which side is going to survive. Until the day before yesterday, the theory of sovereign autonomy of national ideologies held and, as yet, holds, that only the side whose military can deliver the greatest hitting power the greatest distance in the shortest time with the greatest accuracy and least effort will survive and prosper.

Inherently shortsighted but articulate business and politics, looking only to this year's crop or profit, or next year's elections, has left it to the military in charge of national defense to look ahead and watch widely for the total war enjoinments that are hopefully far off in the future. To attain and maintain their superior power over all comers, the military employ their scientists as masters of energy—energy harnessed into almost totally invisible operative behavior. Progressive reports of the opposing spy systems escalate the scientific undertakings and breakthroughs. Thus science has been employed almost exclusively for both direct and supporting military purposes.

Out of their escalated scientific effort has come a technology which would propose to spend many-fold what their respectively competing societies thought they could afford. When it came to the critical verge of war, however, the opposed people and their political leaders were told by their military they must either buy or die. So unwitting how they might pay, they bought the new hardware. Out of that technological evolution has come this epochal change and already we have gone from the historical ratio of less than 1 percent of humanity to 40 percent of humanity enjoying a higher standard of living than any king ever dreamed of before the turn of the century. This has occurred despite the fact that the full spectrum of elemental resources per man has continually decreased. So the forty-fold increase in the vital supportive capability has come almost exclusively out of the constant doing-of-more-with-less technology that society has acquired, though only under the duress of military crisis.

How did it happen that the historical preoccupation of men with weaponry continually improved the performance per unit of invested resources? It was because the ability to carry the hitting power of weaponry the greatest distance in the shortest time involved ships, and ships have limited displacement due to nature's pattern of floatability. Therefore, the design challenge was always to produce the most powerful ship with the least weight invested in the ship, thus enabling it to carry the greatest load of weaponry, ammunition, and fuel, and to get it there faster. As we went from the ships of the sea to the ships of the air, the performance per pound of equipment and fuel became even more important than on the sea. Finally, with man's breakthrough into rocketry, we see a transition of startling magnitude in speed, distance, and energy load carried per weight of vehicle or ship, and its fuel.

Architects know that neither they nor

their patrons have ever been concerned with the weights of their buildings or with any ratings of performance per units of weight invested. Neither the architects nor society know what buildings weigh. Society knows well what the *Queen Mary* and the Douglas DC 8 weigh. The public knows what the sea and air ships' performance capabilities are. The public thinks of performance per pound ratings, but the world of housing and living has always been a world of opinionated dealing with the leftovers, after the high-priority technologies have been applied exclusively to weaponry and its supporting industries.

It is a fundamental characteristic of industrial evolution that each successful invention is followed by a period of expanding use of the invented tools. In this period more performance by that type of tool is accomplished only by using more of those tools with an increasing capacity until the elephantine level is attained. As for example, in the development of ocean ships— the *Queen Mary*. Thereafter there developed a period of converting the doing-more-with-more phase of that tool into a doing-more-with-less phase which uses new alloys and techniques to accomplish as much as the elephantine tool did with one of lesser size. In the example cited, the tool of lesser size would be the *SS United States,* which carried the same number of passengers and cargo at the same speed, but with 30 percent less dead weight and size than the obsolete *Queen Mary*.

Then follows a third period in which an entirely new type of tool does the same task with only a small fraction of the weight of the previously invested resources, but with a fabulously large investment of completely weightless scientific activity. For instance, one jet airplane can in one year outperform the annual trans-Atlantic passenger-ferrying capability of the *Queen Mary* or the *United States* by, of course, accomplishing many more round trips even

though it has a smaller passenger capacity. Complex radio tubes now replaced by transistors are typical of how the newly invented tool for an old task progressively diminishes in size and weight.

When Sputnik went into the sky, the now suddenly "elephantine" airplane weaponry system yielded its premiership to a weapon-transportation system with enormously increased hitting power which is not only far swifter but which also employs a minuscule fraction of the physical resource tonnage in its supporting tools as well as in the weapons themselves. This new vastly more efficient system requires, however, a fabulous abstract, or no-weight, investment of the essential scientific resource, i.e., man's disciplined mind activity. With the obsolescence of the aircraft industry as a prime weaponry resource, 90 percent of that industry's now obsolete, massive high-performance technology production capacity is potentially released for application to life in general.

But neither the philosophy nor the fundamental desire to transcend immediate economic survival considerations exists in the aircraft munitions industry. If they did, they could inaugurate unprecedented, world-around, air-deliverable high-standard living systems designed at an entirely new level of design-invention competence, such as that now feasible within aircraft technology and production. This latter now could generate an augmentation of technical performance in support of general living systems adequate to supply and maintain a highly developed service for 100 percent of humanity with less than 100 percent of the world's resources. This is feasible through design ingenuity and only through design ingenuity applied directly to living systems.

We discover in the picture that I have given you the fact that raising the performance per pound of the world's resources for improving standards of living has never been a direct objective of the politicians or the military servants of the politicians. Now that we know all humanity can be supported at standards of living higher than any yet have experienced, we do not have to have war. We do not have to brink ourselves into acquiring such capability. We need no longer back into our future doing the right things for the wrong reasons. If the great science-won economic strategies and advances in physical capabilities which we heretofore have been employing only for military purposes were directly employed to make man an economic success, all of humanity could become an economic success within a generation. But all political systems, as yet, operate blindly in respect to the universal economic system of energy, which can provide physical sustenance and general satisfaction for all humanity.

By far, the most important change that has taken place recently is in the maturity and will of our young people. I was brought up in the preautomobile era, when all that we knew by experience was about our little local town. The people in the next town were supposed to be quite ignorant and dangerously unreliable people. As a consequence, we became biased about everything and had to choose sides. We were brought up to look for logic and reliability within the confines of our limited experience, in this case exclusively within the boundaries of our little town. Outsiders were questionable characters. But our young world today has been inadvertently emancipated from this postnatally imposed bias of the common senses by the capability of the new technologies to communicate around the world with the speed of light.

The students at the University of California's Berkeley campus, who in 1965 first gained front-page prominence for the world students' revolution, were members of the first generation of humanity to be brought up with television in the midst of their home life. They averaged one-thousand hours a year listening to television, which was much more time than they had listened to their natural parents. They were the first generation of humanity to be told about the world on the hour, every hour, by their third parent, TV. They are the first generation of humanity not to have a bias. They are imbued with the same idealistic compassion for life that young life has always manifested, but that compassion now includes all of humanity. They will settle for nothing less.

The young are intuitively convinced that the inventive and scientific capabilities and physical resources now squandered making war could be diverted to make all of humanity a success. They do not, as yet, have sufficient experience to know how this might be accomplished. But they will soon evolve that know-how. They will learn that success for all requires that invention revolution for which scientific, technological, and economic comprehension and competence are essential.

Let us remember that man consumes daily, if it is available to him, about two pounds of dry food and six pounds of water, and he breathes in fifty-four pounds of air, out of which he extracts seven pounds of oxygen. The substance he uses most is oxygen. It is interesting that the substance he uses the least, he can go the longest without, for he can go a month without dry food. He cannot go more than a week without liquid. But the air which man uses the most he cannot go without for more than about two minutes. Food has often been scarce, but since there are thirty days in which to find it, man does not get panicky. He can become determined enough to fight for food and has ample strength and time reserve with which to do so. Water has been more plentiful but at times becomes critically scarce. Then man has little time before physical weakness overcomes him. Therefore, intuition leads him into swift battle, if there is a shortage and visible water is being monopolized by others.

But air has always been so plentiful as to be unrecognized by man as a commodity. What we learn here is that when there is abundance to a point of unselfconscious intake of a resource, man does not fight or feel competitive. Though humanity throughout all recorded history has sold both food and water, man has not put meters on air below ten-thousand feet altitude above sea level. Above that altitude air becomes scarce and is metered out of compressed air tanks at a high price. Below sea level, it is even scarcer and more costly, as witnessed by the deep divers' oxygen tanks.

Men have thus fought endlessly throughout history for their food, frequently for their water supply, but only once in a rare while do they stampede one another to death when suffocating for lack of air in a fire disaster. Men have always competed and often fought over a woman because to them she was the only woman. In such cases, the essential regeneration of humanity on earth and the built-in drives of biological balance selectivity are involved. Despite the reflex conditioning which governed past fighting, the usual absence of fighting in respect to abundance discloses that fighting is not an essential human characteristic despite the fact that aggressiveness is an essential of innate curiosity.

There are official wars and unofficial wars. There has never been anything approaching peace. The unofficial wars occur as billions of lives deteriorate prematurely and finally die for lack of vital necessities. These people are deprived by economic warfare which is shrewdly and cruelly waged during the times preposterously called "peacetimes" as well as in anticipatory competition for access to inadequate supplies or in hoarding against feared scarcity.

There are no medals given during unofficial warfare. The brotherly excitation occurring amongst each of the opposed peoples during official warfare are almost entirely lacking in unofficial warfare. Though much discomfort exists, the lowest death rate anywhere on earth is now manifest in the direct combat deaths amongst the official forces fighting each other in Viet Nam. On the other hand, within the economic struggles and their resultant indulgences of those unofficially warfaring people on the North American continent, more lives have been lost in automobiles within the last half century than in the official warfaring of 100 percent of all past humanity. And this death toll is from among only 7 percent of humanity.

Today's youth will soon learn that success for all is the only way of overcoming the need to kill, either in the swift death of official war or in the slow slum death of unofficial war. Because lack of knowledge of how to provide for all produces lethal competition as vast numbers are shunted into poverty and a death far more protractedly painful and humiliating than death in war, today's youth will learn in due course that their idealistic compassion and hope to eliminate war cannot be gratified by political actions, for inherently the last resort of politics is always to physical force, whether actively performed with guns or passively provoked by sitdown blockades. The young will soon discover, hopefully before humanity has bungled its way into extinction, that their ideals can be realized only by a design revolution—that is to say, by undertaking to reform the environment so that man's circumstances of technical advantage will permit his omnisuccess and eliminate the causes of war. This is better than undertaking to reform man by laws and propaganda, hoping unrealistically that he will forsake warring despite an environment which is, as yet, so ill-organized as to be able to keep only a minority alive.

And I don't want you to think that keeping all humanity alive with a high standard of living is in any way linked to those preconceptions of societies which we label "charity." One of the myths of the moment suggests that wealth comes from individual bankers and capitalists. This concept is manifest in the myriad charities that have to beg alms for the poor, disabled, and helpless, young and old in general. These charities are a holdover from the old pirate days when it was thought that there would never be enough to go around. Counseled by our bankers, our politicians say we can't afford the warring and the Great Society too. And because of the mythical concept that the wealth which is dispersed is coming from some magical and secret private source, no free and healthy individual wants that "handout" from the other man, whoever he may be, nor does the individual wish to be on the degrading public "dole."

After World War II, several millions of our well-trained, healthiest young people suddenly came out of military service. Because we had automated during the war to a very considerable degree to meet the "war challenges," there were but few jobs to offer them. In that emergency, we legislated the GI Bill and sent them all to schools, colleges, and universities. This act was interpreted as a dignified fellowship reward and not as a "handout." This produced billions of dollars of new wealth through the increased know-how and intelligence thus released; it also augmented the spontaneous initiative of that younger generation. This "reckless spending" of wealth we didn't know we had produced a condition that brought about the greatest prosperity humanity has ever known, thus exceeding even its most hopeful dreams.

Through all pre-twentieth-century history,

wars were devastating to both winners and losers. The preindustrial wars took men from the fields, and the fields, where germinated the only form of wealth of the time, that of agriculture, were devastated. Therefore, it came as a complete surprise that World War I, which was the first full-fledged war of the industrial era, ended with the United States in particular, but also with Germany, England, France, Belgium, Italy, Japan, and Russia in lesser degree, all coming out of the war with much greater industrial production capabilities than those with which they had entered. That wealth was soon misguidedly invested in World War II, from which all the industrial countries emerged with even greater wealth-producing capabilities despite the superficial knockdown of already obsolete buildings. It was irrefutably proven that the destruction of these buildings by bombing, shellfire, and flames left the machinery almost unharmed. The productive tooling capabilities multiplied unchecked, as did their value.

This unexpected increase in wealth through industrial world wars was caused by several factors, but most prominently by the fact that the result of the process of tooling-up of tools that makes a complex of industrial tools, the number of tools that could only make the end products of war, armaments and ammunition, were negligible in number as compared to the majority whose uses could be redirected. Second, the wars destroyed obsolete structures whose actual availability despite obsolescence, persuaded their owners to overextend their usefulness and exploitability. This had blocked the acquisition of up-to-date tools. Third, there was the surprise of alternate or substitute technologies, which were developed to by-pass destroyed facilities. The latter often proved to be more efficient than the technologies that were destroyed. Fourth, the metals themselves not only were not destroyed but more and more were reinvested in new, vastly higher-performance tools. It was then that the World War losers, such as Germany and Japan, became the postwar industrial mass-production winners.

As we study mass production, we see also that mass production cannot exist unless there is mass consumption. This evolved through the great social struggles of labor to increase wages and spread benefits and to prevent the reduction of the numbers of workers employed. The labor movement made possible mass-purchasing, ergo, mass production, ergo, low prices on vastly improved products and services which have all together established entirely new and higher standards of living for humanity.

But today our labor world and all salaried workers, including school teachers and college professors, are now at least subconsciously if not consciously afraid that automation will take away their jobs. They are afraid they won't be able to do what is called "earning a living," which is short for earning the right to live. This term implies that normally we are supposed to die prematurely and that it is abnormal to be able to earn a living. It is paradoxical that only the abnormal or exceptional are entitled to prosper. It even implies that yesterday success was so very abnormal that only divinely ordained kings and nobles were "entitled" to eat fairly regularly.

It is easy to demonstrate to those who will take the time and the trouble to unbias their thoughts that automation can swiftly multiply the physical-energy part of wealth much more rapidly and profusely than production controlled manually by man's muscle and brain reflexes. On the other hand, humans alone can foresee, integrate, and anticipate the new tasks to be done by the progressively automated wealth-producing machinery. To take advantage of the fabulous magnitudes of real wealth waiting to be employed intelligently by humans and to unblock automation's implementation which organized labor has postponed, we must give each human who is or becomes unemployed a lifetime fellowship in research and development.

This fellowship will permit these people to comprehensively expand and accelerate scientific exploration and experimental-prototype development. For every 100,000 people with research-and-development fellowships, only one will probably make a breakthrough, but that will more than pay for the other 99,999 fellowships. Thus, production will no longer be impeded by humans trying to do what the machines can do better. On the contrary, omniautomated and inanimately powered production will cultivate humanity's unique capability, i.e., its metaphysical capability. Historically speaking, that will probably happen within the next decade. But not without many social crises and consequent educational experience regarding our unlimited wealth.

Through the universal research-and-development fellowships, we're going to start emancipating humanity from being muscle-and-reflex machines. We're going to give everybody a chance to develop their most powerful mental and intuitive faculties. And when I say "everybody," I would also like to give you my thoughts on what has been wrongly named the "population explosion" and so answer the fears this term has often provoked. In looking at the really big picture, the fact that comes first to our attention is that the rate of conversion from an agricultural craft to an industrial economy is directly related to both birth rates and life-span increases in the converted economy. For example, the original European colonists in North America had an average family of thirteen children. Many died soon after birth. Average life expectancy was twenty-seven years. As industrial tools such as community waterworks, electric lighting systems, telegraph, and telephone came into use, birth rate went down and the expectancy of life span increased. Today, the birth rate in the United States is less than two children per family and the average life expectancy is over seventy years. Though there are larger numbers of humans now alive in the USA, the total number of babies born each year is decreasing. The population increase in all industrialized countries in the world, including Russia, is now holding consistently to this same birth-rate decline and life-expectancy increase. Japan has attained approximate population equilibrium.

Because the additional human beings arriving annually are decreasing in all industrial countries, their population increase is due exclusively to people living longer. Because the higher death rate used to occur predominantly in the first four years of life, the decline of death rate in these years means that momentarily a big bulge in population is in the under-twenty-year-old part of the population. That bulge will grow progressively older so that by 1985 the average age of people in industrial countries will be thirty years and the birth rate will be so lowered as to begin to show a total population decrease. The population expansion through birth is today uniquely found in the nonindustrialized India, Africa, Central and South American countries. China, well on its way to industrialization, has already instituted rigorous birth control.

We can say quite clearly that the craftsman's hold on life was poor and that his number multiplied slowly, if at all. We can say that industrial man's chances of living out his "four score and ten" years are high. We can say that the so-called "population explosion" is a misleading name, because the increase in numbers alive is due primarily to death occurring at an ever-advancing age. If man is to live only to ninety, then the population increase will cease when the average age of people alive is forty-five years. If man learns how to keep human life going on indefinitely at a good health, vigor, and agility level, then man may also stop producing new babies. For it is a rule of nature that when chances of survival are low, she makes many, many starts or, in this example, many, many babies.

But the increased chances for survival brought about by industrialization will quickly reduce the birth rate because population characteristics are tied up with industrialization and the accelerating industrial rates of the latest countries to adopt industrialization. So we can foresee a world population maximum in 1990 and a twenty-first century in which world population will begin to decline. As world industrialization advances, the number of babies born will decrease to rates matching those of accidental deaths. Stabilization of world population will probably occur at around 5,000,000,000 people, when there will be five acres of dry land and seventeen acres of water averaging one-half mile deep per each human being on earth. With this condition, life will still be sparse around the surface of our little spaceship and the natural resources for supporting human life will as yet be abundant, provided the greedy race for sea foods does not exterminate fish species.

Now how fast is industrialization? It took England 200 years to industrialize. The United States did the same in 100 years and came to parity with England. During the great economic depression that began in 1929, when the giant United States corporations were almost completely shut down, Russia found much gold in Siberia, purchased and imported prototypes of the USSR's great industrial tool-up primarily from the big US corporations. The biggest

US corporation of almost every industrial product category, glad to have any business, took contracts and put up factories for the Russians and the Russians insisted they be furnished with the very latest machinery of which these corporations could conceive. Thus, Russia started her industrialization at the tool-design phase where the United States had left off. As a consequence, in about fifty years the USSR attained an equivalent industrial technical capability as the United States in respect to the production of scientifically conceived weaponry.

China started where Russia left off and even though the Russians pulled out from helping them with their prototyping, China had adequate scientific capability to reestablish the Russian line of industrial tooling strategy. Thus, China started her industrialization at the automation level. She started with computers, fission, jet, and transistor plus a three-to-five-millenium-old philosophic sophistication, which had originated industrialization. She will probably accomplish her automated industrialization within twenty-five years.

Now may I say something about wood's lessons to us as they relate to the design-science revolution which, through invention, can increase capabilities and efficiencies to a point that will guarantee success to all men. If we really will try to do more with less, then nature has some extraordinary things to teach us when we study the structure of the tree.

First, let me say that there is nothing in nature but structure. Still, I find in engineering and architectural schools, with all of their specialization, that they continue to emphasize courses in materials. In these courses, it is taught that buildings are built out of materials, but I find from my experience that this is not the case. What we, in fact, do is to build visible module structures out of invisible module structures. We have nothing but structures. We have microstructure and macrostructure, but there is nothing but structure. If we look carefully and see what nature is actually doing, what is her patterning, what is her structuring, then we can begin to develop very high capabilities.

I find that man has thought structurally in what I would call compressional logic, in which he piles stone upon stone to make a building. In that kind of building, you find that tension is only a secondary helper and compression is the primary logic employed. This is to say that I find many thinking spontaneously in compressional—might-makes-tight—logic. I found that nature was not using that logic. In our solar system, the earth is not touching and ball-bearing around the moon's surface, and in the atoms, the energy components are equally remote from one another. In the atom, the electron is as remote from the proton in this microstructure as the earth is from the moon in our planetary macrostructure. In terms of relative diameters, we still have the same kind of celestial attraction that we have in the microcosm. There are no "solids" just as there are no "materials," but there are sufficient relative proximities of these masses to cohere. The earth's mass is enough to have it held to the sun even though they are 92,000,000 miles distant. I find that nature here is using continuous tension and discontinuous islanded compression. These are clearly differentiated tension-compression structures, which I call tensional integrities or tensegrity structures. This, as we shall see, is exactly the structure of the tree.

Tension and compression are complementary functions of structure. Therefore, as functions they only coexist. When pulling a tensional rope, its girth contracts in compression. When we load a column in compression, its girth tends to expand in tension. When we investigate tension and compression, we find that compression members have very limited lengths in relation to their cross sections. If they get too long and too slender, they will readily break. Tension members, on the other hand, when pulled, tend to pull approximately, but never entirely, straight instead of trying to curve more and more as do two thin compressionally loaded columns. The contraction of these tension members in their girth when tensionally loaded brings their atoms closer together, which tends to make them even stronger. There is no limit ratio of cross section to length in tensional members of structural systems. There is a fundamental limit ratio in compression. Therefore, when nature has very large tasks to do, such as cohering the solar system or the universe, she arranges her structural systems both in the microcosm and macrocosm using tensegrity.

The tree has an excellent structural lesson to teach us in the efficiency of its tensegrity structure's clearly differentiated tension and compression patternings. To better appreciate this, consider the history of man's structural capabilities. Man's earliest recorded structures clearly express his compressional logic and his lack of an instruction manual for the planet earth. When he built a pyramid, he didn't need tensional efficiency as far as he knew. All that was needed was to make the base wide enough and have the walls clearly leaning over towards the center of gravity of the mass. He used stones that were flat-sided so that they would not roll, and because the ultimate compressive strength of stone is 50,000 pounds per square inch, this permitted the construction of outstanding pyramids.

But the ultimate tensile capability of stone is only fifty pounds per square inch, or only one-thousandth of its ultimate compressive strength; therefore, if a building with great span was needed, it couldn't be realized in stone. A very good vertical wall could be built as long as gravity operated within the mass of the wall. However, when man tried to turn this wall over on its side to get a roof beam, he found that the operating gravity made it bend. Bending makes the top of a beam come together through compression and the bottom come apart under tension. Because stone has so little tensile capability, there cannot be a stone beam. The Greeks employed a system with a very short lintel, which used a stone so deep that there was enough to span a very short distance. An example of this is the gate at Mycenae, where thick stone walls lean towards one another and are spanned for six feet by a stone high enough not to break like a beam. This stone's more than twenty-foot depth at the top of those walls makes it look more like a cornerstone.

Ancient man, wanting a spanning procedure, used wood. Wood has 100 times stone's ultimate tensile strength or about 5,000 pounds per square inch. But the wood beams eventually rotted out or burned, which is why, today, we find only the vertical stone compressive elements of antique man's great building ventures. During all this period, compressive strength never went beyond stone's 50,000 pounds per square inch.

Then for the first time in history, in 1851, production steel brought man's tension capability up to parity with compressive capability. Man had had high-tensile-strength metals before that for swords and armour, but the industrialization from the Civil War produced enough steel with an ultimate strength tensile of 50,000 pounds per square inch to use in buildings. After that, came Roebling's pioneering with steel cable which permitted the 1400-foot span of the Brooklyn Bridge. Man's further research and invention produced alloys with tensile capabilities permitting the suspension spans of 3400 feet for the George

Washington Bridge and 4200 feet for the Golden Gate. Today alloys are so improved that a suspension bridge with a central span of several miles could be realized without increasing the cable girth over that used for the Golden Gate Bridge. Simple piano wire has an ultimate tensile strength of 70,000 pounds per square inch, which clearly shows how man's control of tension efficiencies has surpassed his compression possibilities.

Tension is way, way out ahead. World War I produced aircraft steels with ultimate tensile strengths of 120,000 pounds per square inch from chrome, molybdenum, iron alloys. World War II brought chrome, nickel, steel castings with strength up to 350,000 pounds per square inch. Since World War I, research laboratories developed tensile capabilities of 1,000,000 pounds per square inch from beryllium, aluminum sapphire, glass and other silicates, or iron crystals. Finally, NASA's advanced research has developed borons with up to 2,000,000 pounds per square inch. During all this time, ultimate compressive strengths have never depassed that of stone or 50,000-pounds-per-square-inch ultimate strength. Clearly we see that compressive capability has to be augmented to match our high tensile ability.

It is the tree that can teach us this, for nature has a very great trick in relation to all of these structural strategies. In 1885 the scientist van't Hoff demonstrated to organic chemists that all organic chemistry is tetrahedronally configured. Consider molecules as tetrahedra and those tetrahedra joined vertex to vertex. A constellation of tetrahedra linked together entirely by such one vertex or universal jointing, which is called single bonded, uses lots of space and is very characteristic of the gases. Engineers speak of a single bond as "pin ended." Tetrahedra joined by two vertexes line up to what engineers call a "hinge." A constellation of tetrahedra interlinked only with double or hinge bonding is as yet flexible, but summed totally as an aggregation and space-filling complex is noncompressible as are liquids. When tetrahedra are attached to one another by three vertexes, they are triple bonded. Engineers call tripled bonds "fixed ends." They are rigid, or they are stable like three-point landings of airplanes or like three-legged stools on uneven ground. When tetrahedra are quadrivalent, four bonded, as when soft lightweight carbon contracts to form dense diamonds, all four vertexes are congruent.

How does the tree do its extraordinary work? The tree has to impound all that sun's energy with all of those leaves. It has to expose an enormous amount of leaf structure in order to be able to do so and still not dry up. To do this, nature has the tree water-cooled, sending its roots deep into the ground to find the water to pump through its cooling system. These deep roots also give the tree its great stability, which resists the forces of its great branches and leaves waving around in the wind. If you take a fifty-pound load, such as a bucket of water, you are able to hold it vertically at the end of your arm, but if you try to elevate the bucket towards the horizontal, it becomes more and more difficult. You can't really hold it out there. Because your arm is a pretty good size, this makes you appreciate what the tree is doing with what is called the branch root, the point where the branch joins the trunk. Although relatively small, this area sometimes sustains a branch weight of more than two tons, compared to the fifty pounds with which you were struggling. And the tree is able to do this in winds of hurricane velocity; it can wave those tons around and still not have the branch break off. In the airplane we call that joint where the wing comes into the fuselage the "wing root." The greatest stresses experienced by a flying plane are at the wing root. Some of the great tree branches are cantilevered out from their branch roots as much as forty feet. How can you possibly make such a structure as that?

The tree uses extraordinary structural strategies both in the tension and compression of its tensegrity patterning. The tension is entirely in continuous sheathing of compression-resisting liquids and shock-absorbing gasses. The tension strength in the sheathing fibres comes from getting those masses of atoms closer and closer to each other and thus exerting greater and greater attraction to each other. As they get closer the fibre gets stronger. If examined under a microscope those overlapping fibres are exactly analogous to the Milky Way. One Milky Way approaches another Milky Way and the attraction between their masses becomes enormous. The series of fibres actually overlaps so closely as to act as one great fibre.

The compression strategy is in the use of noncompressible, but very flexible, liquids with their hinging molecules of two-vertex-bonded tetrahedra. We had great hydraulic elevators in New York City in the early days of elevators. I remember going into a building down near the Battery that was twenty stories high with a hydraulic shaft which was just a tube, a beautiful, hollow steel tube, eighteen inches in diameter, that had water pumped inside it. There was a hole for that more-than-twenty-stories-long tube deep down in the ground where it was filled with water. It was closed at the top to prevent the liquid from escaping. It was a beautiful structural column with a slenderness ratio that was three-fold in efficiency over any other man-made structural column yet accomplished. Its extraordinary strength economy came from the metal being entirely in tension and the liquid doing all the work in compression. In compression, liquids are completely noncom-

pressible, and because they are also completely flexible, they distribute load evenly all over the system.

This is just what the tree does. She does all of her compression in hydraulics, and in between the hydraulic, or liquid, molecules, are little gas molecules. They are single-bonded tetrahedra and, therefore, highly compressible. The gas molecules give springiness and absorb shock. They are smaller than the liquid elements and fill the tiny spaces between them. An effective analogy would be oranges in a pile in closest packing. Think, then, of the hydraulic molecules as the oranges with the gas molecules filing in the tiny corners between them. So the shock loads on the tree are taken in the gases and the hydraulics give the tree its firmness and strength. I would say that we're probably going to see an age of high hydraulic compressive capabilities coming in to balance the advantages man already has of high tensive capabilities.

I'll just point out that our tree is the greatest structure I know. That's why if man continues to use wood in a dried state, we shall continue to lose its greatest strength. Incidentally, in order to have more trees regenerated, there cannot be a tree underneath another tree, because the new tree wouldn't get enough sun to sustain it. So nature has the tree produce seeds and the tree imprints a pattern in the seed which is shipped off by wind and water to get implanted where the new life's regenerative needs will be available. Trees are regenerative. Man can actually profitably cut them down and replant them, spread so that each one will thrive to advantage. This structure is built and rebuilt. Nature is continually giving man new structure, which seems to me to be very, very important.

These new structures are part of planet earth's income, and I think we are going to have to learn to live on income. There are two prime sources of energy to be harnessed and expended to do work. One is the capital, energy-saving-and-storage account; the other is the energy-income account. The fossil fuels are certainly a part of capital energy-saving, which took multimillions of years of complex reduction and conservation that progressed from vegetational impoundment of sun radiation by photosynthesis to deep-well storage of this energy below the earth's surface. There is a vast overabundance of income energy at more places around the world at more times, which produces billions-fold the energy now employed by man if he only knew how to store it when it is available for use when it is not available. There are gargantuan energy-income sources available which do not stay nature's own processes of conservation "against a rainy day" of energy within the earth crust. These sources are in water, tides, wind, and desert-impinging sun radiation. An example is the amount of energy unleashed in one minute by one hurricane, which equals all the energy of all the atomic stockpiles of Russia and the United States.

The exploiters of the fossil fuels, coal and oil, say it costs less to produce and burn earth's savings account. This is analagous to saying that it takes less effort to rob a bank than to do the work which the money deposited in the bank represents. The question is cost to whom? To our great-great-grandchildren who will have no fossil fuels to turn the machines? I find that the ignorant acceptance by presently deputized world leaders of the momentarily expedient and their lack of constructive long-distance thinking—let alone comprehensive thinking—would render dubious the case for humanity's earthean future, could we not recognize the plausible over-riding trends.

Clearly, something very important must happen to man on this planet. Fred Hoyle, the great astronomer dealing with the regularities found by astrophysicists in the heavens, has been able to say in all seriousness that he now assumes from these observed regularities that there are at least hundreds of millions of stars with planets that could maintain human life. He finds it logical to assume that human life is present in this universe on at least one hundred million planets. The particular big figure he uses is obviously intended to infer astronomical numbers of humans present in universe.

Dr. Hoyle, who is the Plumiam Professor of Astronomy and Experimental Philosophy at Cambridge University, finds the case of humans on this particular planet to be precarious. He says humans have found atomic energy just in time to overlap the exhaustion of the fossil fuel supplies. Humanity will have to make vitally important moves in a hurry.

I remember asking myself whether there is anything in our experience that could tell us whether man might have an essential function to perform in the universe. Was he needed in the universe or was he—as he seemed to feel, himself—just a chance observer, a theater goer watching a great play called life? I said the only way we can judge whether he has a function or not is to go to our experimental data and the way it comes out is as follows:

The astronomers have given us their observation of the "red shift" which indicates that vast and remote star groups are probably receding from us in all directions because the light coming from them is redder than that from nearer groups, which in turn indicates an expanding universe. The expanding universe is also called for by the law of entropy, or increase of the random elements which must ever fill more space. We have also learned, experimentally, that unique behaviors are usually countered by somewhat opposite behaviors; therefore, an expanding universe must infer a concurrently contracting universe. So I asked myself "What experience do we have that may demonstrate such a contracting universe even though none has been observed or mentioned by the astronomers?"

I saw that around our own planet we have high and low atmospheric pressures which might better be called expanding and contracting atmospheric patterns. I discovered clues to the operation of a contracting universe to be operative on our own planet. Our planet earth is not radiant. It is not sending off energy in any important degree. As compared with a star, it is "dead." Earth is receiving energy from the sun, but is not losing it at the same rate. For instance, we have learned from the geophysical year that we are receiving about 100,000 tons of star dust daily. Our physical imports from the universe are, as yet, much greater than our exports. Therefore, we are a collecting or concentrating center, possibly one amongst myriads in the universe. All planets in the universe may be collecting points as focuses of the contracting phase of the universe.

At the surface of the earth in the topsoil, the ecological balance becomes operative. The vegetation's chlorophyll inhibits the sun's radiation instead of allowing it to be rebroadcast through reflection to the universe. The sun-inhibited energy impounded in the vegetation is further inhibited by insects, worms, and mammals, and both botanicals and zoologicals are gradually pressured into the growing earth crust and finally are concentrated into coal and oil, rather than being broadcast off to the universe in all directions. By dissipating these energy concentrations, man may well be upsetting the expansion-contraction balance of universe.

The ecological balance is fascinating when viewed chemically. We find all biological systems continually sorting and rearranging atoms in methodical molecular structures. To insure performance, each species is genetically and environmentally programmed. Each sorts and reassociates atoms as its genes cope with and alter environment which, in turn, alters the species' behaviors.

Thus, we see that all the stardust, cosmic rays, and other radiation randomly dispersed into the universe by all stars are being methodically converted by the biological activity around the earth's whole surface—in the sea and on the land—into progressively more orderly "organic" chemical structures. Thus biological life on earth is antientropic. Earth is acting as an antientropic center as may all planets in the universe.

Of all the antientropic sorters and rearrangers on earth, none compares with brain-driven man. We find man continually differentiating and sorting out his experiences in his thoughts. As a consequence, we find him continually rearranging his environment so that he may eat, be clean, move about, and communicate in more orderly and swifter ways.

Doctor Wilder G. Penfield is the head of the Montreal Neurological Institute of McGill University in Montreal, Canada. He is one of the world's leading probers of the brain with electrodes. The brain probers have now identified, for instance, the location of various memory banks. Dr. Penfield says, "It is much easier to explain all the data we have regarding the brain if we assume an additional phenomenon 'mind,' than it is to explain all the data if we assume only the existence of the brain." Why? Because they have found, so to speak, the telephone sets of the brain. They have found the wires connecting the telephone sets. They have found the automatic message-answering service and the storage systems; but, a great deal goes on in the conversations over the wires that is not explicable by the physical brain's feed-back. I have submitted what I am saying to you to leading neurologists and they have not found fault with it.

We have a phenomenon that we speak about as a generalization. In science, a generalization is very different from a liter-ary generalization. Generalization, in a lit-erary sense, means that you are trying to cover too much territory with some state-ment. The scientific meaning is precise; it means the discovery and statement of a principle that holds true without excep-tions. I will give you an example. I am going to talk to you about a special piece of rope. I could have in my hands a foot-length of three-quarter-inch manila rope. But I can also say to you, "I am going to take an imaginary piece of rope" and I, not mentioning whether of nylon or manila, im-mediately generalize a rope concept from our mutual experiences. I am going to pull on that piece of rope and as I pull on it very hard, it contracts in its girth. As it gets tauter, it gets tighter. This means that it goes into compression in its girth in planes at ninety degrees to the axis of the pull. I find experimentally, as I mentioned before in speaking about wood, that tension can be operative only when compression is also present. A cigar-shaped vertical compres-sion member that is loaded on its neutral axis tries to "squash." This means that its girth tries to get bigger, which means also that its girth expands and is tensed. So I find that compression is never innocent of tension but that they are cooperative in axes arranged at ninety degrees to one an-other. Sometimes I find tension at what we might call "high tide" or a highly visible as-pect and compression at "low tide" or at almost invisible aspect and vice versa. We have here a generalization. We have found by experiment that tension and compres-sion only coexist. That is quite an advance over the first generalization which said, "I

take a piece of rope and pull it," which was a second-degree generalization, and it is a third-degree generalization when I say ten-sion and compression only coexist.

A system subdivides the universe into all the system that is outside the system and all of the system inside the system. Every system that viewed from inside is concave is viewed from outside as convex. Concave and convex only coexist. Concave and con-vex are very different from one another. Convex diffuses energies by increasing wave lengths and widening angles. Con-cave concentrates energies by decreasing wave lengths and reducing angles. Al-though not the same and not exactly oppo-site, concave and convex only coexist.

In addition to tension and compression and convex and concave, I can give you a number of other such coexistences. This brings us then to another and further de-gree of generalization, wherein we say that there is a plurality of coexistent behaviors in nature which are complementary behav-iors. That caused the mathematicians to generalize further. They developed the word "functions." Functions cannot exist by themselves. Functions only coexist with other functions. They are sometimes covari-ables. When I say functions can only coex-ist, I have gone a little further than the spe-cial cases of concave and convex or of tension and compression, which were themselves already highly generalized. Then I'll go further still and say unity is plural and at minimum two, which is the generalization that greatly helped quantum physics. We may go a little further in gen-eralization as did Einstein when he gave us relativity. You can't have relativity without a plurality of cofunctions.

Now I will give you another progression of events. You have all seen a dog tugging at one end of a belt. He tenses it as he grips it compressionally with the concave and convex surfaces of his teeth. I am sure that you will agree that the little dog will never say "tension and compression only coexist," even though his brain automatically coordinates them. The dog will not say "concave and convex, tension and compression are similar cases of coexistence of functions." I think the neurologists go along with me in saying that what we mean by mind—in contradistinction to the brain of the animal or of man—is man's ability to generalize.

We have seen how an enormous amount of special case experiences finally led to a progression of generalizations. In this example, there were six degrees of progressive generalizations. As we went from the one case to another and to higher degrees, it was accomplished with fewer and fewer words. We finally came to just one word, relativity. This orderly simplification happens to be exactly the opposite of the mathematicians' law of increase of the random elements. What I have given you is the decrease of the random element. Generalization is the law of progressive orderliness.

The mind of man seems to be the most advanced phase of antientropy we can witness in the universe, and if there is an expanding universe, there is logically a contracting universe. Possibly man's mind and his generalizations, which weigh nothing, operate at the most exquisite stage of universe contraction. Metaphysics balances physics. The physical portion of the universe expands entropically. The metaphysical contracts antientropically. So now we have found a function for man in the universe, which was our objective. Man seems essential to the complementary functioning of the universe. Therefore the probability of humanity annihilating itself and thus eliminating the antientropic function from the universe is approximately zero.

This does not, however, mean that man on earth may not eliminate himself. It suggests that there are—as the Cambridge University astronomer Hoyle suggests—hundreds of millions of other planets in the universe with men living on them. This brings us to the observation also that to keep her ecological balance intact, when nature finds the conditions are becoming unfavorable for any of the "cogwheel" species necessary to the system, she introduces many more starts of that species. She makes enormous numbers of babies, enormous numbers of seeds of this and that tree, when she sees that such trees are not going to prosper. The seeds multiply in number, float off in the wind, randomly distributed in order to increase the probability of an adequate number surviving to keep the system in balance.

Man is beginning to change from being utterly helpless and only subconsciously coordinate with important evolutionary events. We have gotten ourselves into a lot of trouble, but at the critical transformation stage we are getting to a point where we are beginning to make some measurements —beginning to know a little something. We are probably coming to the first period of man's direct, consciously assumed responsibility in the universe.

I have pointed to the great challenge of our day. I showed that it is no longer true as had seemed true throughout all history, that man was born purposefully to be a failure in all but one case in a thousand—with the latter semisuccess occurring only as an "exception that proved the rule." Science says that the design-science revolution could make possible all of humanity's enjoying all of our spherical space-vehicle earth without anyone interfering with another and without any individual having advantages at the expense of another, but that this cannot be accomplished while maintaining the protective trade restraints behind the boundaries of the sovereign nations. Youth will learn that the design-science revolution requires universal integrity of intellectual formulations and unbiased cerebral coordination which youth will inevitably come to discover and cultivate, because integrity is innate and has been frustrated in the past only postnatally and then only by the inertial paralysis of once excellent, but later obsolete, "good customs" of yesterday, that had originally been adopted under conditions of overwhelming ignorance and deep-seated mortal fears, if not for self then for one's helpless dependents.

I was asked recently to visit Rockford, Illinois. I wrote an article in the *Saturday Review* called "Geosocial Revolution" and to my amazement the young people around the world have all seemed to have read that. I'm used to older people's interest in my work. But the Rockford, Illinois students had read my article and asked their principal to have me come and talk. I arrived there and found a clarity of awareness in these seventeen-year-old students that was displayed by their complete and sublime confidence of intellect in addressing the world. They were not at all dismayed by society's old inertias. Today's young world is revolting intuitively against all the old worlds' arbitrary positions. One such rejected position is the obsolete lines of irresponsibly lethal competition over ways to "earn a living"—to earn exemption from the negative assumption that average man is born to be a failure and only the exceptional ones can merit living. "Survival of the fittest" was Darwin's dictum. The young find that the old are short sightedly preoccupied with their own miniscule space-time environmental events, that they exhaust and pollute the resource reserves of all generations to come. The present oldsters are utterly unaware that all of humanity could be made successful and that we can amply afford to render them so.

Sensing otherwise but not having as yet discovered in critical mass degree the po-

tentially successful fulfillment of their idealistic dreams of a warless world which could be realized exclusively by the design-science revolution, the young world is blindly determined to do something—almost anything—which might lead toward their ideals. This unaimed, blind urge is often exploited by those with less well informed and less idealistically inspired motives, even by those with vindictive biases.

It seems implicit, however, despite all the ambiguities and incoherence of the vigorous breaks with tradition that youth everywhere are making, that their intuition is manifesting that evolution is intent upon humanity's becoming a comprehensive success aboard our space-vehicle earth and that the Almighty has ordained that this be accomplished invisibly and with dispatch. Suddenly it will be realized that it has "come to pass" that the meek have inherited the earth and that the earth is good. That is what the intuitions of youth seem to be trying to say.

PART IV
Wood as a
Material

The authors of this section represent research, engineering, and production; they are agreed that wood still maintains a high potential for contributions to our way of life. However, they point out, as Koch did, that a material as versatile as wood may find keen competition in a particular use because some new, single-purpose material has been developed. This fact underlines the necessity to find ways of improving wood's individual properties and so increase its ability to fulfill certain particular uses.

This section demonstrates that despite this obvious need the wood-products industries, with a few conspicuous exceptions, do not support research and development. It takes only a few minutes examination of the appropriate government statistics to document the fact that the wood industries are not independent when it comes to research. They turn to other than wood-industry sources, particularly the US Forest Products Laboratory, together with the so-called suppliers to the industry, for this most important key to their future. Whether they can continue to follow this course successfully may be debatable, but certainly it is hazardous, particularly in view of the strong support competitive industries give to research and development.

The authors are agreed that there are several urgent fields for research in wood. Fire is the ever-present hazard. Even though wood can be chemically treated against fire, such treatments create gluing and finishing problems and are expensive. The shrinkage and swelling of wood due to changes in moisture content can create loose joints in furniture, sticking in windows, as well as some other annoying problems. Effective treatments to completely control dimensional stability are available but are too expensive for general use.

The necessity to correlate and simplify

the grading of structural lumber needs emphasis. There have been so many grade segregations for structural lumber that they have constituted a veritable maze for the designer and architect. This maze has tended to discourage specification of wood construction materials. However, the wood industry recognizes the problem and has moved toward grade simplification and is even introducing mechanical stress-grading devices.

The idea is also examined that design of wood structures should be considered in terms of a system and not in terms of each piece of wood in the system. For example, Hoyle draws attention to a study in which plywood fastened to floor joists raised performance by one-third. Partitions contributed over 20 percent in stiffening effect. He calls such reactions "togetherness."

Seidl wants to maintain an equilibrium among function, aesthetics, and cost. He believes they are always in some dynamic balance, but cost, in the end, is the determining factor and limits demand for a given product. He suggests that possibly cost limitations may be overcome by designing so well aesthetically that the customer willingly pays a higher price.

Marra believes that the performance attributes of wood have not changed, but "the framework of material values from forest to factory to housewife, have changed and will continue to change." Wood must be made to meet these changes. This will require extensive research to alter its properties and to design better structures that take into account its special characteristics. He views wood as a series of structural elements, decreasing in size and modified by their geometry, that can be manipulated to increase the formability of wood.

Dietz points out that the other construction materials have their disadvantages—softening of steel in fire, combustibility of plastics, brittleness of concrete—but that research is solving these and can do the same for wood. Reconciliation of wood with other materials, especially plastics, in composites is a fruitful field. Plastics already provide the adhesives and finishes used with wood. The vigorous competition between wood and plastics in furniture is well known. Here the best mix is still a subject for study.

The electronic computer has become invaluable to the design and analysis of systems of all sorts. Vitagliano capsulizes the history of this instrument and calls attention to special applications, such as preparation of a perspective view and its examination from other vantage points. Cathode-ray display of electronically produced drawings and time-sharing of expensive computers by compact instrumentation placed on the designer's desk are accomplished facts. All of these capabilities are just as available and useful to the designers of wood as to those who use other materials.

Behind the more technical viewpoints of this section lies a general concern already expressed. The future of wood, in spite of inroads by its competitors, should not be underestimated. Wood is still the only renewable construction raw material available to man. It requires less energy for conversion to products and its renewal in the forest not only replenishes the earth's energy supply but also improves the environment. It is, for practical purposes, universally available. It occurs in a wide variety of qualities and properties which may be altered to suit a great variety of needs.

Wood in the Competition
of Materials

ALBERT G. H. DIETZ
Professor of Building Engineering
Massachusetts Institute of Technology
Cambridge, Massachusetts

Albert Dietz was educated at Miami University and MIT receiving his Sc. D. at the latter institution. He has been director of the Plastics Research Laboratory at MIT and is a past chairman, BRAB Materials Advisory Board Committee for the Department of Defense. He is a member of the National Academy of Sciences—National Research Council. He has been a Marburg Lecturer and has received a number of awards, among them the Richard Templin Award; the Award of Merit from American Society for Testing and Materials; and the Desmond Fitzgerald Medal, Boston Society of Civil Engineers. He is a Fellow of the American Academy of Arts and Sciences, of American Association for the Advancement of Science, and of the New York Academy of Sciences. He has been a director of ASTM and of the Building Research Institute.

This paper might also justifiably be called "Wood in Combination with Other Materials," because it seems altogether likely that in the future, especially in such areas as house construction, we shall not be thinking essentially of one material but of many materials, each contributing its best attributes to the whole.

I must confess to a bias in favor of wood. I grew up in my father's woodworking shop and was originally a carpenter. My doctoral thesis had to do with the mechanical properties of wood. The first course that I taught was about wood as a material and my first research was in this area, for it involved split-ring connectors, plywood, laminated timber, and adhesives. I cannot therefore be said to be unprejudiced. Nevertheless, I will attempt to take an objective attitude toward all materials as they are compared and contrasted.

Advantages. From the aesthetic standpoint, there is nothing that can quite compare with wood. The many imitations on the market merely emphasize the aesthetic qualities and the widespread public acceptance of wood as a beautiful material. It does have beauty; it has texture, pattern, and color which cannot be matched elsewhere. It can be bold or subtle, and it is amenable to manipulation by the artist and the artisan. Technically, it is easy to work, and the necessary skills are widespread for either field or factory fabrication. Commercially, it is universally available through numerous established outlets.

Wood is strong, especially on a weight basis; it is tough and resilient; it has good thermal insulating qualities compared with many other building materials; and it is durable when properly handled.

Limitations. All of these desirable attributes indicate a continuing important place for wood in construction and in other fields. However, we must not ignore the well-known disabilities that wood possesses. Being a natural material, growing under widely diverse conditions, it is extremely variable in its properties. Although an attempt is made to overcome this variability by grading into various categories of quality, it must be recognized that grading does not completely overcome variability. A serious drawback of wood, with which we are all familiar, is its dimensional instability with changes in moisture. Doors and windows that rattle at some times and stick at others are painful evidence of this drawback, sometimes structurally serious, sometimes merely annoying. Although wood is extremely durable when properly handled, under improper conditions it can deteriorate rapidly; it is readily attacked by decay and many animal organisms. That wood will burn is all too evident from the numerous fires in buildings. Wood, like all materials, has its limitations and must be used in the light of both its advantages and its deficiencies.

The principal competitors of wood, both ancient and modern, include masonry, concrete, steel, and more recently aluminum, plastics, and derivatives or composites of these and other materials.

Concrete

Concrete is hard, strong, fire-resistant, generally durable, and, being a plastic material, can be cast into a great variety of shapes. On the other hand, its tensile strength is low and requires reinforcing; it is heavy, brittle, nonresilient, and a poor insulator. In a building, it is not uncommon for the dead weight of a reinforced concrete building to exceed by far the useful live load, thereby calling for heavy supporting framework and foundation. Nevertheless, reinforced concrete, with its rapidly developing technology, has seriously challenged structural steel for buildings of considerable height and has rudely jolted the former preeminence of masonry as the facing material for most nonresidential construction. The strength of concrete can be varied over a considerable range; there are various cements available for different purposes, and, like wood, it is essentially universally available. The techniques for handling it are well known and the skills are widespread. Many finishes are available, and sculptured or decorative surface features can be obtained by the proper fabrication of molds and forms. The rapidly developing techniques for precasting small to large, plain to intricate, sections is increasing the versatility and usefulness of concrete. Prestressing greatly extends its usefulness and overcomes its former limitations to relatively short spans.

Expansive cements may help to overcome the shrinkage of concrete which leads to cracking. Latex additions may assist in reducing brittleness and improving tensile strength. Cellular aggregates and foamed concretes provide lighter weight, and the numerous additives for concrete are helping to overcome such problems as deterioration by freezing and thawing, surface wear, and moisture penetration. Nevertheless, in spite of its evident advantages and the progress being made in reducing its inherent limitations, concrete cannot be considered the universal material.

Steel

The advantages of steel in construction are well known. It is strong, tough, and stiff, that is, it has a high modulus of elasticity, the highest of all construction materials, and it is available in a multiplicity of carefully designed efficient structural shapes such as I, wide-flange, H, channel, angle, and Zee, as well as pipe, sheet, and bars. Recently square hollow columns have been added. The designer and constructor can choose from many usable forms.

The drawbacks of steel are equally well known. It is heavy, it rusts, and, although it does not burn, it is susceptible to fire and will lose most of its strength at about 1000° F., a temperature easily attained in a building fire. Consequently, it has to be protected against fire, and this greatly increases the cost and inconvenience of using the material. In the opinion of many, it cannot compare aesthetically with the variety of colors, textures, and patterns available in wood.

Because of its tendency to rust, steel normally has to be protected by paint, enamel, or other finishes. Recently, however, advantage is being taken of the ability of some low-alloy steels to form a tenacious rust film which protects the steel underneath and consequently eliminates the need for protective coatings. Whether the brown color of the rusted steel is pleasing depends on individual preferences and the given application, but these rusted steels are being used, exposed to the weather. As is evident, they must be used where protection against fire is unnecessary. Furthermore, there is some tendency for the rust to wash off during its formative period, and it may therefore stain adjacent materials during this time.

Where positive resistance to rusting is necessary, accompanied by minimum change in appearance, the high-alloy or stainless steels are employed. They are far too expensive to be used structurally, except under unusual conditions, and are therefore normally employed for nonstructural decorative or protective purposes, such as the surfacing of buildings, trim, and sometimes flashing. Here they compete with wood which might be employed for the same purposes. Generally, however, stainless steel trim and surfacing are used where building codes require incombustible materials and the competition with wood, therefore, although it exists, is minimal.

Until recently, structural steel, at least for building purposes, was largely of one grade. This led to inefficient use of steel in many instances where maximum stresses occurred only in limited places, and it often resulted, for example, in changing column sizes in buildings from bottom to top, necessitating in turn changes in girder lengths and connections. Within the past few years, several structural grades have been introduced having higher strength and higher allowable stresses than the "normal" structural steel. This makes it possible to use smaller sizes of higher strength material in those places where stresses are maximum and, for example, has permitted tall buildings to be constructed with the same column size from bottom to top, thereby simplifying design and construction throughout.

The advent of welding, both in the shop and in the field, has increased the efficiency of joints in structural steel and has simplified details, at the same time providing clean, aesthetically pleasing joints. Welding has been accompanied by the advent of high stress bolts to take the place of rivets. Bolts are equally strong, but are more quickly and more efficiently applied with fewer men, with less noise, and less hazard from flying, red-hot rivets.

A recent development, more commonly employed in bridges, but beginning to be employed in buildings, is composite structures of steel and concrete, in which a concrete slab deck, for example, is made to act structurally with the steel supporting beams or girders thereby providing more efficient structural behavior than in the older method in which the slabs were simply dead load to be carried by beams. Intensive research and development are underway to find other ways of improving the design of steel and thereby to recapture some of the market lost to reinforced concrete. Activity is therefore directed toward finding quick and efficient methods of fireproofing steel to supplant the older, heavy, and slow process of encasing steel in concrete or masonry. This can be a major factor in recapturing markets lost to concrete.

The development of efficient low-cost means of fireproofing steel could provide real competition for large, laminated, structural timbers where the two are used for similar purposes, such as the arches supporting vaulted buildings or the beams spanning such spaces as gymnasiums and churches. Here exposed laminated timber generally has an aesthetic advantage over steel.

The susceptibility of unprotected steel framing to rapid loss of strength in fires has been attested by several large-scale building collapses in the past few years, of which McCormick Place in Chicago is only the most recent and most spectacular. When fire destroyed the household exhibit, the intense heat generated caused the massive unprotected roof trusses to collapse in a matter of minutes.

Aluminum

In buildings and in structures generally, aluminum is primarily employed for nonstructural purposes. Although its strength is adequate for many structural applications and its light weight is attractive, the cost is generally prohibitive.

Aluminum provides real and important competition for wood in such places as windows, doors, and trim, including the exterior facings of buildings in which aluminum, flat sheet and simulated wood, lapsiding, are making serious inroads in traditional markets for wood. With a factory-applied finish, aluminum can claim that no repainting is needed, at least for long periods of time, and this is a major factor to the householder, faced with high repainting costs every few years. The house with masonry finish and aluminum trim can claim to require no painting.

Although aluminum has no insulating value against conducted heat, the bright-surfaced metal is an excellent reflector and a poor emitter of radiated heat. For this reason, when it is employed as free-standing, bright-surfaced foil in cavities of building walls, it is an efficient insulator and competes with bulk insulators, including those based on wood fiber.

Aluminum, of course, has its drawbacks, as has any material. A ball or pebble, thrown against an aluminum surface, is likely to cause a dent which at best is difficult to remove. To a degree, this can be reduced by using a backer board behind the aluminum, but it cannot be overcome completely. Furthermore, even though the house may not require repainting, the householder may wish to change the color, and the repainting cost, therefore, still occurs. Unless the aluminum facing of a building allows for ventilation behind the impervious aluminum sheet, serious condensation may occur on the inner face and this can lead to deterioration of the structure.

A serious drawback to any metal window is its high heat conductivity, leading to cold inner surfaces of sash and frames, which may result in annoying condensation and puddles or frozen water on the inside. Although this can be overcome by the proper design of frames and sash with heat-flow interrupters, many aluminum windows and doors do not have this feature.

Aluminum, like steel, is inherently a material of uniform and, to many people, uninteresting appearance. It does not have the basic aesthetic appeal of wood, but of course, when wood is painted, it loses that appeal also. Factory-applied colors overcome the uniform grey of aluminum in addition to providing protection against the elements.

Aluminum is a real competitor in many applications traditionally associated with wood.

Masonry

The principal competition between wood and masonry is in the structure and facing of walls and, to a much lesser extent, partitions. There have not been many notable advances in masonry construction, but a few of these do offer challenges to wood, in addition to the long-standing competition for wall construction.

Recently, burnt clay units have been developed in which the core is cellular and lightweight but surrounded by an outer facing of normal, dense, hard, burnt clay. These units not only reduce the weight of brick but increase its thermal insulating value, which has been a drawback of standard, hard, high-conductivity burnt clay products. The manufacturing process increases precision and reduces irregularities, leading to the possibility of thin mortar joints which may effectively employ the new high-strength mortars based upon synthetic resins.

Careful research into bricklaying techniques has led to the development of more efficient packaging, delivery, and bricklaying procedures, allowing for greater productivity per man per day, without an increase in fatigue. Acceptance by the labor unions is a factor, but it has been forthcoming in a number of places where the unions realize that otherwise they might lose out anyway.

New modular shapes and sizes allow brick to fit modular windows and doors thereby reducing the expense of cutting and fitting around such features.

High-strength mortars were mentioned above. Some of these, for example, have made it possible to build two-story houses of brick, only one brick in thickness, and in other instances have allowed brick panels to be prelayed under favorable shop conditions, and then hoisted into place as a unit. To a moderate degree, the strong mortars have allowed brick panels to withstand tension and bending stresses.

From the engineering design standpoint, the proper integration of monolithic concrete floor slabs, acting as giant diaphragms, with masonry walls and partitions, has greatly increased the structural efficiency of high-rise buildings, with the consequence that buildings as much as fifteen to twenty stories high have been built with masonry walls as little as six to eight inches thick.

So here, too, there are implications for greater competition between thin, strong, bearing walls of masonry versus framed wood construction.

Plastics

In many ways plastics provide the greatest opportunities for competition and cooperation with wood. Although the volume of plastics currently used in building is still relatively small, these materials are coming up fast and are already both challenging and assisting wood in building applications.

Plastics applications in buildings may be classified as 1. structural and semistructural, 2. nonstructural, and 3. auxiliaries to other materials. Like wood, they are organic but generally nonrotting, or at least highly resistant to decay, and resistant but not proof to most destructive animal organisms, to which they may be relatively indifferent, neither attractive nor repellent. They are fire-susceptible, although some are self-extinguishing, and all of them can be destroyed by fire.

The mechanical and other properties probably range over as wide a field, within their own limits, as the metals. By copolymerization, or judicious mixing and addition of fillers and other modifiers, their properties can be almost infinitely varied within the broad bounds set by their organic nature.

For structural and semistructural purposes most plastics are too weak and lacking in stiffness to be useful. Very few of them, for example, have a modulus of elasticity as high as that of common species of wood parallel to the grain, and most are well below this figure. Strength properties of unmodified plastics are in many instances comparable to those of wood in bending or compression. It is as composites, combined with high-strength fiber, particularly glass fiber, that plastics come into their own as structural and semistructural materials. The glass fibers provide the strength, but by themselves would be useless because they could not retain their shape. The plastic acts as the matrix or binder to hold the fibers in place under stress. The two together, therefore, provide synergistic behavior in that the properties of the combination far transcend the properties of either constituent acting by itself. High strength and moderately good stiffness are achievable under these circumstances. These reinforced plastics have both advantages and limitations for structural and semistructural applications. Some of the advantages are:

1. *Formability.* Since the liquid resins and the mass of glass fibers have no inherent shape of their own, they have to be molded to final shape, and it is therefore possible to select structural forms which are inherently efficient. Three-dimensional curves are particularly good for this material; these are the very shapes that are difficult to make in traditional structural materials such as wood, steel, and concrete, although concrete lends itself better to these than either steel or wood.

2. *Lightness and toughness.* On a weight-to-strength ratio basis, reinforced plastics can be among the strongest available materials. At the same time, they are tough, and consequently can be made very thin, sometimes as little as one-sixteenth to one-eighth inch thick. This reduces the weight of the component and of any supporting structure needed to carry it.

3. *Light transmission.* As thin shells, these materials may be highly translucent. Consequently they can provide a unique combination of structure, enclosure, and light transmission.

Among the major limitations are:

1. *Low stiffness.* The modulus of elasticity is low, and in the form of random chopped glass fiber in a plastic matrix, may

well be less than that of wood parallel to the grain. In other forms the modulus of elasticity may well be higher. Consequently it is necessary to use inherently stiff shapes such as sandwiches and three-dimensional shells.

2. *Cost.* On a per-pound basis these materials cost considerably more than the traditional structural materials such as steel, wood, and concrete. Consequently they must be designed to make every pound go as far as possible.

3. *Uncertain durability.* Since these materials are new, their behavior over long periods of time is relatively unknown. Probably the oldest structural or semistructural applications are twelve to fifteen years old, although boat hulls are reported to be as much as twenty to twenty-five years old and still in good shape.

4. *Fire.* The fact that all plastics, including reinforced plastics, can be destroyed by fire limits their applications in building. Nevertheless, in particular areas, especially those of semistructural application, such as shells, components of wall panels, and so forth, they represent real potential competition for wood-based materials such as plywood and building boards.

Nonstructural uses. These are the most numerous and account for the greatest volume of plastics in building. It is impossible to mention them all, but a few may be used to indicate the trends.

Flooring based mainly on vinyl plastics is now standard along with asphalt tile, which today contains little asphalt. These flooring materials, sometimes backed with a thin layer of plastic foam for resilience, constitute a serious challenge to wood flooring, which is generally more expensive to install. The appearance is entirely different, though attempts are made to simulate the appearance of wood grain, generally with little success. On the other hand, plastic flooring is evolving with patterns and textures that utilize the unique inherent properties of plastics.

A second challenge to wood is posed by plastic wall coverings, based mainly on vinyl chloride and the high-pressure decorative laminates. The latter are widely used as table and counter tops, in which they challenge wood, especially now that the wood veneer that formerly was used in these materials has been almost completely replaced by printed paper which simulates wood grain, often requiring close inspection to detect the difference. On the other hand, the same decorative laminates are commonly bonded to a wood base such as plywood or particle board, thereby constituting an example of cooperation rather than competition between the materials.

Windows have recently appeared in which vinyl overlay is applied to a wood skeleton for frames and sash. An attempt is made to obtain the best qualities of both materials by retaining the strength and rigidity of wood, combining the low conductivity of both materials, and obtaining the surface protection and appearance plus durability of the plastic overlay. Other windows, of a largely experimental nature, eliminate wood altogether by making the frame and sash completely of plastic, or combining a high-strength reinforced plastic overlay with a foam core. In other instances, the plastic overlay is on a steel spine and in still others, metal windows use plastics as heat interrupters.

Foam insulation, either prefoamed or foamed in place, competes with other bulk insulating materials including those based on wood fiber.

In other fields, plastics offer little or no competition with wood. Among them are vapor barriers; hardware; many aspects, natural and artificial, of illumination; mechanical equipment; electrical equipment; and plumbing.

Auxiliaries. It is as auxiliaries to other materials that major cooperation between plastics and wood is to be found. This is mainly as adhesives and protective or decorative coatings.

Waterproof plywood and laminated timber for severe exposures would be impossible except for the high-strength-engineering synthetic-resin adhesives based upon phenolics, resorcinol, melamine, urea, epoxy, and others. Here wood is the dominant material, but the adhesive is vital to the success of the component.

Protective and decorative coatings for wood are experiencing a considerable revolution because of synthetic resins in liquid or film form. Fast-drying, durable finishes, applied in the field or the shop, with greatly extended durability and protective or decorative qualities are offered by plastics-based paints, lacquers, enamels, and combinations. Durable films can be laminated as overlays on plywood or other wood-based products to provide protective finishes heretofore unavailable. These finishes enhance the ability of wood to compete with other materials such as metals and synthetic boards.

Conclusion. From the foregoing brief description, it can be seen that plastics offer both real competition for, and cooperation with, wood and wood-derived products. Both aspects of this relationship may be expected to grow in the future.

In the continuing competition between wood and other materials, research and development have to be carried on to overcome the limitations of wood, to utilize fully its advantages, and to find ways of combining wood and other materials into composites able to perform tasks that none of the constituents can perform by itself. Of many directions in which research and development could profitably be pursued, the following are suggested examples:

1. Impregnation and polymerization of synthetic materials in place. Over the years experimentation with a variety of polymeric materials has demonstrated, or at least indicated, that increases in mechanical properties, inherent protective finish, and enhanced dimensional stabilization are possible. A better understanding of how monomers penetrating into the fine structure of wood combine with cellulose and lignin to achieve new properties may lead to improved treatments to lessen the limitations of wood.

2. Intensive research into wood derivatives such as particleboard and hardboard may show new ways of combining woody tissue with other materials, either organic or inorganic, to provide superior composites for building, furniture, and other products.

3. Adhesives and binders have already made a great difference in the utilization of wood, but there are still many problems remaining. Among them are good gap-filling adhesives; fast-setting adhesives such as, for example, might be almost instantaneously cured by tapping or other mechanical or electrical treatment; gluing of rough, irregular, or possibly contaminated surfaces; and successful end-grain gluing.

4. Further development of already-successful laminating and joining techniques should be pursued. For example, fast and less wasteful methods of finger jointing, continuous application of overlays, and the better utilization not only of mixed grades, but of mixed species, could lead to enhanced utilization of wood.

5. Prefinishing in general, including not only overlays but sprayed-on, rolled-on, or otherwise applied finishes under controlled shop conditions, can increase the utilization of wood in building, furniture, and other applications.

6. The emerging techniques of machine grading promise better utilization of lumber

in the future and should be pursued. It seems that a better understanding of the relationship between stiffness and strength is necessary here. In this connection the unfortunate internal squabbles within the industry respecting grading and dimensions of green versus seasoned lumber have not helped the industry. Neither has it been helped by the doubtful quality of grading sometimes evident. This is particularly unfortunate when the material is used for structural purposes such as trusses, in which failures have occurred because of low-quality members in critical places. When coupled with borderline design, borderline materials can lead to failures which in turn do little to allay doubts about the ability of wood to meet structural demands.

7. Whereas in some instances serious doubts are expressed respecting wood's ability to carry loads, in others it is not being asked to do enough. For example, we build strong, rigid, frame walls for houses employing plywood and other strong sheet materials to provide walls capable of carrying considerable loads, and then we support the walls continuously as if they had no inherent strength at all. It is suggested that walls and partitions of this type could be called upon to carry more load than they do, and thereby reduce the cost of other parts of the structure, such as foundations. Similarly, we often do not make full use of the strong, stiff diaphragm behavior of floors and roofs built of large sheets of materials such as plywood rigidly connected to joists, rafters, and other framing members.

8. Composites. The combined use of wood with other materials has already been touched upon. More work could be done in this direction. For example, plywood faced with high strength reinforced plastics already finds use in large shipping containers. Particleboard faced with high-pressure laminates provides superior panel stock for furniture and other applications. Impregnation with plastics has already been mentioned. There are many others. This is an area that should be vigorously explored, so that the best attributes of different materials can be combined.

Wood is indeed being subjected to intense competition from other materials and that competition will increase. Unless bold and imaginative steps are taken to meet it, applications for wood can be expected to slip away. However, by taking advantage of wood's distinctive properties, and marrying these with the properties of other materials, cooperation among them can enhance the applications for all.

Designing with Wood to Meet Construction Requirements

ROBERT J. HOYLE, JR.
Professor of Civil Engineering
Research Division, College of Engineering
Washington State University,
Pullman, Washington

A graduate in mechanical engineering at Cornell, Robert J. Hoyle, Jr. studied wood technology at State University of New York College of Environmental Science and Forestry, where he served as a member of the faculty. While director of wood products research at Potlatch Forests, Inc., Lewiston, Idaho, he developed a system of structural grading of lumber by mechanical means. He has been president of the Society for Wood Science and Technology; chairman of the Division of Wood Engineering of the Forest Products Research Society; member of Committee D-7, Wood, of American Society for Testing and Materials; and has served on committees of the National Forest Products Association and the American Plywood Association. He received ASTM's Charles B. Dudley Medal in 1965.

Introduction

Wood and its applied use in construction have been a part of the growing technology of the twentieth century. Wood technology, the materials science for wood, has developed as an essential base for building research on wood structures. Interest in the application of good property information to structural practice has become especially intensive in recent years. The association of wood technology with agricultural and forestry educational institutions has been natural because those branches of technology have nurtured the timber resource.

At the same time this has had an obscuring effect where engineers and architects are concerned. They have not always been conscious of the sources of information on wood research and technology. In fact the fundamental language of wood technology, in its botanical aspects particularly, has probably been distracting to many designers, who may have concluded that wood technology is irrelevant. Be that as it may, designers, in their search for practical answers to old and enduring problems are generally quite prepared to switch on fresh light. Perhaps we can point to the direction signs if not to the actual destinations. It is my own feeling that we have not really reduced to practice anywhere near the amount of information we have at our disposal about wood.

I will call attention to some of the new tools and techniques available for wood design and try to encourage ventures into new ranges with perhaps broader horizons.

Construction Requirements

Structural integrity is the fundamental engineering requirement of a design. Accomplishing that within the constraints of aesthetics can be simple or complex depending largely on the suitability of the construction material to the design. Advances in materials technology and design procedure offer opportunities for new aesthetic treatments which account for much of the vitality of modern building design. In wood we have had a number of such advances and there is good reason to expect these developments to continue.

Under the heading of structural integrity the designer has three principal axes along which he can move to obtain economy in design.

Material strength and related properties
Performance criteria
Design methods

All three of these factors are susceptible to control by the designer to the extent of his skills, knowledge, and perhaps most important, his design budget. Since we are concerned with possibilities for designers, perhaps it is best to remove design cost from this particular discussion to avoid unwanted limitations. In this way we can expose opportunities that each designer can

exploit to the limit of his design budget as he sees it.

The designer's role in developing the mechanical character of a structure is taken for granted. He also exerts an influence on durability and finish that is fairly specific in the case of wood. He can do this through his choice of species, quality, chemical treatment, or skill in detailing, singly or in combination. It is quite possible for a designer to destroy inherently good durability and finish features of a material, and he has a substantial responsibility in this facet of his work.

Construction requirements impose a host of cost considerations that permeate the design atmosphere. I mention this more out of a wish to recognize them than to develop any useful comments about them. Most designers are acutely conscious of such essentials and can be depended upon to give them their due regard.

Design Properties of Wood

Timber design specialists generally will be well posted on the state of the science in terms of structural properties of wood. Everyone who has opportunities to design in timber will not be a specialist however, and those who produce wood building materials would like to see engineers as a group considerably more familiar with the subject. Our interest stems not so much from a desire to impose complex design tasks on the engineer, as to enable him to evaluate and apply the wood-product developments of our day with confidence.

Some years ago an extensive program of tree sampling was undertaken by the US Forest Service and the lumber and plywood industry. This produced much new information about the properties of the more common commerical softwood species. It added meaning and reliability to older information on wood strength and shifted the position of some species in the spectrum of strength properties. This systematic and thorough coverage of the commercial timber stands, coupled with the use of evaluation methods that had not been developed when earlier strength studies were made, lend stature to the results. The study will be continued, probably on a perpetual schedule, to enlarge the number of species covered and maintain a continuing status report on wood quality. Reports are available describing these studies and ASTM Standard D2555 summarizes the current information on clear wood strength. Plywood and lumber manufacturers' associations are incorporating these findings into their most recent manuals for design.

An interesting corollary study of the properties of Douglas fir obtained from samples collected at producing mills has thrown light upon the effectiveness of standing timber sampling for product properties. The mill-sampling results, which were based on a very carefully developed plan to insure product representation, showed remarkable agreement with tree sampling. The fact that the mill sampling of clear sections of lumber agreed so well with tree sampling greatly reduces speculative concern that strength information from forest tree sampling might be substantially different. Further the reasonable agreement between substantial bodies of quite old data with the newer information shows that basically our forest resource does not display any great change in clear wood strength with time, even though we generally recognize the attrition in volume of available material in larger sizes of the clearer grades. This means that systems of grade classification based on clear wood strength and the physical size of knots, for example, have remained valid over a period of at least thirty-five years of fairly intensive stress-graded lumber grading.

My discussion of these studies is aimed, of course, at the common speculation that plywood and lumber resources may be uniquely different, and that lumber and plywood grades must, per se, be changing in some unknown fashion. The best information I can find does not support either of these contentions.

Recent activity in the sampling and testing of lumber in all its commerical structural grades should certainly interest the designer. This rather sensible procedure was made possible by scientific approaches to sampling methods and the design of experiments and equipment for testing. Until recently the vision of enormous research costs had deterred wood scientists from proposing such a procedure. Investigators in several widely separated countries have been evaluating commercial structural lumber with renewed intensity for many years. Out of this work has come the improvement of quality-control techniques for wood, more exacting measurement of wood-density effects on strength, and improved knowledge of the grade influence on elastic properties.

Testing of full-size commercial-grade pieces has produced a better understanding of how overloaded members actually behave. The chain of events that could lead to failure, being better understood, gives rise to improved grading methods and rules for design. Size effects are better understood and changes have been introduced into recommended design practice. The testing of seasoned commercial grades enlarged the basis for understanding seasoning effects on strength. The latest revision of ASTM D245 on visual stress grading covers many of these new findings.

It has been a custom to develop definitive rules for the grade inspection of structural lumber and until very recently the same rules were used for the several different wood species, at least within any one geographical region. Under this system there would be three to four grades, each with its own characteristic knot size, allowable check or small split or slope of grain. Applying these rules to several species of basically different clear wood strength, the individual grades would have different strengths for each of the species. As a result three grades of six species would give rise to eighteen specifications of structural strength. This was convenient for a production unit, but awkward for the designer. In recognition of this problem, the variety of these strength classes is being reduced, creating a degree of interchangeability between species that should be helpful to the designing consumer. One grading system uses nine levels of strength to embrace seven species. No one of these species will yield more than about four strength classes. The fundamentally stronger species will furnish grades toward the high end of the nine levels, and the lower-density, lower-strength species will give grades near the lower end of the spectrum. Several of the grades will be available in several species, giving the designer some needed latitude in exploiting their aesthetic characteristics without the need to rework the design in each case.

In several countries nondestructive testing is gaining favor as a basis for classifying wood by strength. These techniques are somewhat more discriminating than other methods. Their particular value appears to be in improving the availability of higher-strength structural lumber than the designer is accustomed to having. In fact one of today's principal problems for the producer of mechanically stress-rated lumber is the absence of demand for his available good grades. A few manufacturers of proprietary wood structural products have used these better grades to good advantage, but the designers are not yet sufficiently aware of this potentially useful development. It may well be that these grades

will find a home in the factory-produced structures rather than the custom designs. I would hope however that architects and engineers will become more familiar with this new way to meet structural needs in the execution of their conceptions.

Structural plywood and lumber are not going to be easily displaced by the wood-base composites, but it would be wrong to dismiss the composites in a summary manner. We know that strong, high density forms capable of structural behavior are entirely feasible. Some of the hardboards can probably be incorporated into fabricated load-bearing systems. As designers become more venturesome by involving more of the framing systems in the structural function, they will need to use the strength and stiffness properties of medium- and high-density fiber and particleboards. Some of the highly durable and attractive high-density chip and flakeboards developed in the research laboratories would be grossly misused if we do not work their structural capability into our designs.

Reconstituted wood products may eventually displace much of the medium- and low-grade softwood lumber, simply because the manufacturing processes use that part of the resource to better advantage. Structural lumber and plywood are a little more difficult to improve upon in this way. Design methods and design practices must play a crucial role in drawing the more expensive but technically feasible structural product forms into the orbit of construction methodology.

While on the subject of materials properties, a word about adhesives is desirable. We have to learn to design with and for adhesives. So far, most of our designs for glued products rest on the usually reliable idea that the adhesives are as strong as the wood. This is a basically accepted idea in plywood and laminated-timber design. It is admirable that we can depend on this. There is only one thing wrong with it. Product design with adhesives is being confined to the rigid high-strength glues. Entire families of elastomeric adhesives are denied to us as designers. Yet these are entirely adequate for a host of engineered-wood and plywood uses, and they have special characteristics that fit them for field use, which the housing industry must have to implement some of the design methods and building practices to be mentioned later.

Design Methods *No need,*

Techniques for designing wood structures have shared a place with materials properties in the attention of research engineers. This is a rewarding phase of construction technology for the investigator because so many new tools of engineering and research have come to him in the past thirty years. Electronic data-processing equipment has greatly extended our capabilities to inquire and experiment. New instruments for measuring stress and strain enable us to examine the behavior of loaded structures to verify theory and move rapidly from the art to the science of structural engineering design. Concepts of probability permit us to look at reliability in a new and more certain light, to get away from broad generalizations about safety, and to feel considerable confidence in the use of the new methods, with both old and new materials. A lot of the drudgery of design can be put aside and the designer can turn his attention to thinking about real solutions to problems he once needed to avoid or embed in a cushion of judgment factors and conservative assumptions.

We have had the curious experience of discovering that old combinations of materials-property knowledge and design technique that were proven in practice contained errors which compensated for one another. Out of this we found the two wrongs did indeed sometimes make a right. The "sometimes" was the problem and it was necessary to proceed with extreme caution in transferring what we learned from the prototype testing of one design to the theoretical development of another. The pool of experience is deepening and our ability to store and retrieve information increases the utility of properly recorded data from well-designed research. Designers at large have not really been able to recognize and apply this information, but we should expect to see rapid changes in this situation. We are increasingly aware of the continuing education programs to upgrade design skills so we will not become professionally obsolete. These programs are becoming essential for keeping abreast of modern design methods.

At this particular point in time it is more appropriate to speculate on new methods for designing with wood than to survey recent trends. Certainly there is ample evidence of opportunity to apply new engineering methods to wood, because the increased basic research on properties is yielding new forms of information to plug into the design approaches that are being adopted for use with other materials. Probably a little of each is called for.

Residential construction accounts for most of the market for structural lumber. The selection of grades and sizes is generally accomplished by reference to simplified load-and-span tables, which are designed to promote safety and avoid conflict with existing regulatory considerations. Most of the people who use these tables are not skilled in structural design, although structural designers do find them useful and practical for the more simple problems. They embody all three of the elements of structural integrity. They are based on traditional performance criteria, developed from broadly acceptable design methods using the strength properties of easily manufactured and commonly available grades of lumber. The data is easy to use and the commodity products they present are convenient to manufacture and distribute competitively.

Simplified tabular engineering data has become available in recent years for laminated timber and a variety of wood structural specialties. Some of the technical brochures currently available offer a variety of support arrangements so the user can match them more closely to his design than simple span tables allow. The attention of the organized architectural profession to the subject of sales literature has been very helpful in defining the fundamental requirements of an effective technical-product presentation.

With a few exceptions classical handbook information on wood structural design is too obsolete for the serious design professional. Principal exceptions are the "Timber Construction Manual" of the American Institute of Timber Construction, the National Forest Products Association's "National Design Specification for Stress-Grade Lumber," and "Plywood" by Nelson Perkins.

Beyond these basic works the designer begins to step into the "outer space" of design with wood. His design conclusions tend now to be his own and he finds the men who talk his brand of timber design a smaller and considerably more select group. Projects that justify this kind of skill are outside the ordinary residential design field. The people whom we find in this group are the practicing professionals with commissions to do truly creative design jobs, and those in structural wood product research, and in development work in building research.

There are some excellent opportunities to apply new design approaches to residential work and designers could establish a whole new set of principles. Indeed they have already begun to do so, but building practices in general change slowly and in residential construction the sledding is especially tough. Agricultural building practice is more susceptible to change and agricultural building research engineers are striking directly at tradition and having a real influence on design and construction practice.

What are some of the techniques designers can call out to implement their aesthetic concepts and meet construction requirements?

The involvement of every part of a functional element in the carrying of load is the most obvious consideration, and that covers a great deal of territory. The materials used in a wood structure have undergone progressive and often subtle change since design practices became fixed. My great grandfather built many of the houses in my home town during the last ten years of the 1800s. Finished lumber was coming on the market then, but of course plywood was still twenty years or more away. Each floor- and roof-framing member of those structures was sized to carry its contiguous load, by itself. The subflooring and wall- and roof-sheathing materials could not participate in the basic structural function of a building frame the way plywood can function. Most of today's designs still follow this line of thinking.

Careful measurements of the behavior of building elements reveal that plywood fastened to floor joists raised the performance by one-third. Partitions, instead of imposing added weight and calling for doubled joists to carry this weight, really contributed over 20 percent stiffening effect, and continuity of joists over supports added another one-third to floor stiffness. This merely indicates the opportunity for developing structural support from the combined action that the elements of the conventionally nailed components have.

Several years ago elastomeric adhesives were used to field-fabricate quite a large number of residential floor systems. Racking tests on nailed and adhesive bonded sections of these floor systems, performed annually over the past five years, demonstrated that a fourfold increase in rigidity over conventional nailed construction existed shortly after fabrication and did not deteriorate as the years passed by.

Plywood-research engineers have developed and tested design procedures for wall and roof diaphragms, giving architects and engineers a practical working method that has become known and accepted. Diaphragm design with wood decking has never been well developed and most simple lumber diaphragms are an enigma as far as rigorous procedures for design are concerned. Recently however, lumber diaphragms, field-glued with elastomeric adhesives, have demonstrated lateral stiffness well within the requirements for building construction.

In 1965 during a development program, the designer of a series of research houses incorporated some of these "togetherness" principles into the floor system with the result that 55 percent of the support structure normally used for this particular size of building produced the specified performance. Prototype tests and field experience verified this and the dynamic behavior of the structures has proven equal to the traditional type of floor construction. Satisfied owners occupy these houses.

The stressed-skin principle has been used in aircraft design (even wood aircraft design) at least since 1930 and in the last ten or fifteen years aircraft have relied on adhesives for a part of their structural integrity. The design tools to produce such structures are, on the whole, available and their use has become quite respectable in structural engineering outside the housing field.

The role of judgment in engineering designs, at least in building construction, has been quite significant, especially to the older generation of designers. Elementary structural engineering courses present only the simplest of fundamentals. Much structural design work in timber is produced out of that background and with the most rudimentary conception of wood as a material. A good example of this is the reliance upon pin-connected joint assumptions for analysis of stresses in trusses with continuous chord members and rigid or semirigid joint connections. Any effort to refine this technique quickly exceeds the time a practicing designer can give to the task. Concerns about fastener behavior, joint rigidity, frictional restraints, and homogeneity of the wood raise speculation in the designer's mind which quickly overpower him and bring on the judgment.

We have here a very common timber-design problem faced many times every day by many designers. During the past twenty years at least two dozen people have been fashioning the parts of a solution to this particular problem and at the present moment we have some practical design techniques which take much of the indeterminancy out of the analysis of this type of indeterminate structure. The design method involves calculations that fit so well the capabilities of our new computer tools. It is conceivable that you can expect to be able to obtain these services by telephone or teletype very soon. The designer will still want to understand the procedure so he can appreciate its significance and use it with confidence. Once having done this, he will greatly expand the volume of work he can do, and do it better. And for the architect, there can be fewer frustrations of his aesthetic endeavors, for the opportunities to examine alternatives are expanded, and the analyses themselves have greater precision and reliability than has heretofor been possible.

The example of the indeterminate truss is only one application, albeit a particularly rewarding one. Timber designers face profound problems in the simple task of decking design, which again they are forced to resolve by conservative estimating or extrapolations from handbook information that only approximate the answer to their problem. The interest in roof overhangs is very common, for both aesthetic and functional purposes. With it goes the need to consider nonuniform bay or support spacing. I do not know of any computer programs for these design problems, but I do know they can be easily written and probably will be in the very near future. Some of the handbook tables on this design problem were prepared using electronic computer aid. These are only one step away from taking the problem right to the machine.

Until the time when practicing designers have ready access to computer facilities, tabular presentations of information generated from computer solutions using the more complex design methods can be made available to definite advantage for the designer.

The inclusion of a place for building-materials cost information in the computer program will generate some of the financial fuel that makes these things economically possible.

I view these design tools as quite practical and capable of being put at the disposal of practically all designers. This certainly doesn't mean that the design task can be passed down to the less qualified, for the input statement requires skill and judgment unhampered by the absence of good theory and computer capability.

I wish to stay away from the subject of new structural products. However, in developing new products it is usually necessary to formulate more elaborate design methods than those generally used by practicing engineers. Further, it is very common for these to be verified by test. Many design ideas reported in the literature are of this type. The practicing designer will probably think in terms of his usual design habits in evaluating something new. Unless he takes the time to study the background for a new product he may harbor reservations over aspects of design that differ from usual practice. Any progress in design with wood is going to involve the acceptance of many new and unfamiliar constructions. There is a common need for the consumer's design engineer or architect and the manufacturer's product-development technologist to understand one another. There is room for improvement in the lines of communication between these groups.

Design methodology must extend beyond the basic wood materials like lumber, plywood, laminated timber, fiber composites and include the complementary materials which are not forest products. Proprietary products that can be fabricated to the designer's specifications offer some interesting ways to pursue aesthetic considerations.

While it has not been very evident in the United States, factory fabrication of building components on a much grander scale is not far down on the road. The architectural profession can achieve their aesthetic and functional objectives by closer liaison with the manufacturing people. In England a rather good liaison has developed between certain architects concerned with public housing and a large group of building-component producers. The result has been some very attractive housing, profitably manufactured and competitively priced, which incorporates the principle of total involvement of the individual elements in the structural consideration of the design.

Performance Requirements

There is one facet of designing for structural integrity that the designer accepts with every job he undertakes. As a starting point he lays down criteria about dynamic and static loads and deformations.

In a country as large as the United States, load considerations are enormously varied. This is where an intimate knowledge of local conditions has great value. These kinds of data are difficult to obtain from the literature, although design handbooks and building codes offer guidance of a general nature. Historical records of weather and seismic activity form the principal basis for establishing the design loads that the external environment requires.

Within a structure, loads relate closely to the function of the structure, the expected kinds of occupancy, and the sort of static and dynamic behavior needed for the structure's purpose. Usually the designer is expected to make the final decisions about performance criteria, for he is charged with the satisfactory behavior of the finished product. Generally the owner of the structure is very dependent on the designer for good advice on performance specifications.

We now begin to deal in probabilities. Weather forecasters frequently couch their predictions in terms of probabilities. The public is becoming accustomed to this phraseology and its use certainly helps the weather scientist with the almost impossible task of making promises about events which are very difficult to predict. This is also a useful concept for the designer.

The ratio in cost between a structure which has a 5 percent chance of some minor failure in a twenty-year period and one with a $1/10$ percent chance could be two or three. The kind of failure that would occur in either case is another consideration. Probability of a structural overload causing repairable damage, not dangerous to human life, is often much greater than the probability of total collapse. The type of structural arrangement bears a strong relationship to these two degrees of safety.

A structure composed of small joists on sixteen-inch centers supporting a roof may be more susceptible to total collapse than one using large, widely spaced beams. A structure with some type of continuous roof sheathing may be less likely to dump its load on to a weak member, than one with single-span panels. An extra thickness of decking may greatly diminish the chance that the yielding of a weak member will trigger a catastrophe. The added cost may be readily justified. It is the task of the designer to consider these alternative ideas. It is the task of the research engineer to establish the procedure. Certainly laminated beams exhibit less properties variability than their individual laminae and can safely be used on wider spacing. The choice however between simple-span and multi-span decking, between solid lumber and purlin-supported plywood sheathing of different thicknesses affects the safety of the structures in very definite ways. To assist in arriving at decisions of this type more design information may come to be presented in terms of mean strength and some measure of variability.

Our techniques for analyzing the probabilities associated with these alternatives are crude at the best, but some of the building research activity of our time is directed at this topic. We do expect to consider these problems in a scientific way that will produce a new basis for setting forth performance criteria. These criteria need not be static and fixed in a given locality, rather the designer should be able to shape them according to the disposition of elements in different types of structures.

With the introduction of new design methods and new products, the designer should be prepared to reexamine the performance criteria he customarily uses. Floor and roof systems are ready for such reexamination now. Deflection criteria handed down from an era when plaster integrity pervaded design thinking are quite obsolete. Structures so designed are stiffer than the criteria suggest. If the consumer has become accustomed to stiffer systems, will he accept a return to the old behavior standards that will accompany the use of improved design methods and materials-property data? Probably not, and we should be prepared to reconsider the performance criteria. Likewise the design of structures for human habitation can satisfy older concepts of static deflection under uniform load and still produce questionable living platforms in terms of their dynamic response to the concentrated moving live loads that people actually impose. In this matter of performance criteria, there is probably some new middle ground that needs to be defined.

The requirements of rigidity for wind and earthquake loading of timber structures are quite difficult to identify. There are two good opportunities for design freeboard. One is the establishment of criteria for the permissible flexure of timber wall structures and another is the conception of arrangements of structural elements, other than deck sheathing, to resist lateral force. This latter possibility could generate some interesting architectural styling, while at the same time providing very adequate performance.

Attention to performance criteria goes beyond the work of the architect and design engineer. In the development of products an understanding of the requirements of adhesives and fasteners of all kinds would hasten the acceptance of good products and serve as an effective barrier against poor ones. Designers employed by consumers and producers are interested in developing these criteria, because they will serve as points of reference and clarify the many questions that must occur over and over again as each new building-product concept spreads to new users and specifiers. We are not entirely without these criteria, but those we have are still quite narrow in their coverage.

Good designers can have a strong influence on performance criteria. Reputable engineers and architects are the people most able to introduce changes at the grass roots of the traditional performance structure laid down for the commercial builders of plan-book designs. In the mass housing field, the advent of factory fabrication of complete structural units brings technical skill into the designs. The ability to realize labor and materials economy should justify the designers' interest in breaching the ramparts of custom to worthwhile advantage. And of course, the product developers have their sphere of activity in moving toward warrantable change and growth.

Conclusion

We see then that the effort of a large number of research workers has been devoted to wood as an engineering material. Their work exposes new ways to design and build with wood. While there is room for much more research work in timber design, and there always will be, it is time to turn our attention toward the incorporation of these new methods into design practice. That is why I have called on the designer to recognize the progress and take advantage of it in solving his problems. This is a tall order because it means substantial departure from tradition. It is not something the designer can accomplish alone, but neither can it come to pass without the designer's participation.

Lumber, plywood, and laminated timber manufacturers associations can play a key role in realizing the objective. The fact is, these groups are already aware of the research activity and have shared in some of it. They are the source of reference for rank-and-file designers working with timber, and for manufacturers. They are revising and enlarging their technical manuals to include some of the new information.

However the various advances have seldom been viewed together in their mutually complementary relationship. In the United States it is customary for basic materials manufacturers to perform this organizing function. They function by pooling their technical resources and they need to be individually perceptive of the opportunities and give them support.

Certain agencies of the government have goals that can be served by understanding support of a new wood building technology. It appears that this is a growing role which may have great influence on the character of industrialized building in the years ahead. The thinking of the designers, engineers, and scientists in these agencies will be crucial in developing the changes in design practice suggested in this paper.

We should have a sense of urgency about organizing the many good pieces of individual research into an improved and applicable design practice. There is reason for a very positive encouraging outlook, for we have a new generation of professional people coming on the scene who have the skills to make it come to pass. It is up to many of us to make sure they have the chance to exercise those skills.

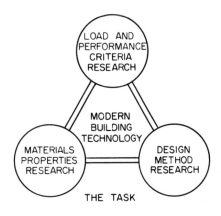

THE TASK

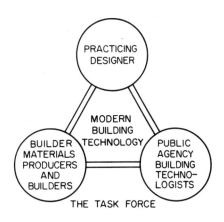

THE TASK FORCE

Bibliography

——— 1967, Agricultural Construction Literature Index, American Plywood Association, Tacoma, Washington.

——— 1967, Box Beams, Plywood Fabricator Service, Inc., Tacoma, Washington.

——— 1967, Cured Panels, Plywood Fabricator Service, Inc., Tacoma, Washington.

——— 1967, General Construction Literature Index, American Plywood Association, Tacoma, Washington.

——— 1967, Industrial Literature Index, American Plywood Association, Tacoma, Washington.

———— 1967, Residential Construction Literature Index, American Plywood Association, Tacoma, Washington.

———— 1967, Stressed Skin Panels, Plywood Fabricator Service, Inc., Tacoma, Washington.

———— 1967, Technical Literature on Plywood, American Plywood Association, Tacoma, Washington.

———— 1966, Guide to Plywood Components, Plywood Fabricator Service, Inc., Tacoma, Washington.

———— 1966, Plywood Design Specification, American Plywood Association, Tacoma, Washington.

———— 1966, Softwood Plywood - PS 1-66, American Plywood Association, Tacoma, Washington.

———— 1966, Timber Construction Manual (American Institute of Timber Construction) John Wiley and Sons, Inc. New York.

———— 1965, Western Wood Density Survey Report Number 1, FPL-27 U. S. Forest Products Laboratory, Madison, Wisconsin.

———— 1962, National Design Specification for Stress Grade Lumber, National Forest Products Association, Washington, D. C. (New edition to be published.)

Carney, J. M. 1966, Hurricane-Resistant Plywood Construction, American Plywood Association, Tacoma, Washington.

Hoyle, R. J., Jr. 1965, Annual Review of Wood Engineering, Forest Products Journal 15 (10):413, Madison, Wisconsin.

Hoyle, R. J., Jr. 1964, Annual Review in Wood Engineering, Forest Products Journal, 14(9):393, Madison, Wisconsin.

McKean, H. B. and R. J. Hoyle, Jr. 1962, Stress-grading Method for Dimension Lumber, Special Technical Publication No. 353 (Symposium on Timber) American Society for Testing and Materials. Philadelphia, Pa.

Percival, D. H. 1965, Present Status of Mechanical Fasteners, Forest Products Journal 15(1):42, Madison, Wisconsin.

Perkins, N. S. 1962, Plywood, Properties, Design and Construction, American Plywood Association, Tacoma, Washington. Out of print

Schniewind, A. P. 1967, Wood Engineering Review, Forest Products Journal 17(6):27, Madison, Wisconsin.

Schniewind, A. P. 1962, A Look at Wood Engineering Forest Products Journal 12(8):343, Madison, Wisconsin.

Schniewind, A. P. 1963, Bright Future for Wood Engineering, Forest Products Journal 13(8):323, Madison, Wisconsin.

Suddarth, S. K. and F. E. Goodrick 1967, Future Importance of Computers in Wood Engineering, Forest Products Journal, 17(6):49–54.

Suddarth, S. K., F. E. Goodrick and P. E. Dress 1964, A Digital Computer Program for Analysis of Member Stresses in Symmetric W Trusses, Research Bulletin No. 783, Purdue University Agricultural Experiment Station, Lafayette, Indiana.

Suddarth, S. K. 1961, The Design of Glued Joints for Wood Trusses and Frames, Research Bulletin No. 727. Purdue University Agricultural Experiment Station, Lafayette, Indiana.

Suddarth, S. K. 1961, Determination of Member Stresses in Wood Trusses with Rigid Joints, Research Bulletin No. 714. Purdue University Agricultural Experiment Station, Lafayette, Indiana.

Wood Products in the Future
—A Technological Extrapolation

ALAN A. MARRA
Professor, Department of Architecture
College of Architecture and Design
University of Michigan, Ann Arbor,
Michigan

A graduate of State University of New York College of Environmental Science and Forestry, Alan A. Marra received his doctorate from the University of Michigan. He has served as technical director of Pluswood, Inc., Oshkosh, Wisconsin; supervisor, Sales Service Laboratory, Monsanto Chemical Company, Adhesives Division, Lockport, New York; and also as a consultant to the wood-products industries. He has been a visiting scientist for the Society for Wood Science and Technology and received the "Adhesives Award" of the American Society for Testing and Materials. Previously on the faculty of the School of Natural Resources, he is now with the School of Architecture at the University of Michigan.

In industrial materials, as in human events, it is a common practice to use the past as a gauge for the future, speculating from what was or might have been to what might be. Since materials are easier to measure and record than people, predicting their future would seem to be a considerably more reliable process than predicting the course of human events. If this is generally so, wood qualifies as an exception. There are many reasons for this, the more illuminating being the fact that the use of wood is intertwined closely with the everyday existence of people and hence partakes of many of the vagaries associated with people. Superimposed upon this is the biological origin of wood which confers upon it properties and variabilities difficult to contend with in modern industrial operations. Moreover, wood does not have a good history of responding to technological change, as have, for example, plastics or even that age-old material, glass.

It seems logical that the lack of technological response is due to the rich endowment wood possesses in basic characteristics useful to man. With such an endowment there is little compelling need for technological intervention. Since there has always been easy-to-utilize, good timber, and wood more than any other material in all recorded history has served many of the most basic needs of people, the demand for wood is fairly well ingrained (at least through the present generation). With such a history, one would predict that wood consumption should be directly related to population increases.

Actually, although there has been considerable mechanization and modification or refinement of standard products and processes with some shift toward more panelized or sheet products, total consumption of wood has remained fairly constant for many years. This means a downward trend in per capita consumption and suggests that this old material requires new approaches in order to extract in the future the benefits for which it is noted. These approaches should take into account the nature and distribution of the forest resources. They should reduce to design parameters the anticipated functional needs people have, and they should consider the technology which can satisfy these needs economically from the timber that exists. The future then may see wood previously considered unfit for consumption, converted by processes as yet undreamed of into products still hidden in the imaginations of designers and architects.

It is a purpose of this presentation to explore the total system in the context of which wood must function and thus to derive a fresh insight to future wood products not obtainable by a study of history alone. A number of concepts are traced on the prior assumption that they must converge into a common potentiality for producing useful wood articles economically. These concepts include:

The forest resource of the future

Performance of wood
Improved wood properties
The basic functionality of products
Functionality dependence on formability, and the controlling properties of wood
The primary wood products that can be derived from the forest
The role of geometry in converting primary forest products to functional consumer products
Concepts in design
Conciliation of design with material properties
A common denominator for conversion processes

The Future Forest Resource

Forest utilization, like the utilization of other resources, is by nature a degrading process in respect to the resource itself. This is not only because of the economic necessity to take the good material and leave the poor, but also because of the ecological response of the resource to major disturbances in its composition. Such disturbances, if severe enough, can set back the plant-succession calendar for centuries, during which time little value ensues from the land in the form of marketable timber.

Fortunately the science and technology of forestry provide means for revitalizing and otherwise restoring the values of harvested areas at a rate faster than natural cycles would permit. This speed-up in regeneration of forest values, however, does not take place without substantial investment of funds, of faith in the future of the resource, and of patience to wait out the still long period before a new harvest can be made.

At the present time a greater part of United States forest resources is in transition; it is recovering its value after the catastrophic harvesting of virgin timber during the last century. The values associated with forests today, however, include others beside those of a wood source. More and more forests of today are expected to satisfy recognized needs for watershed control, recreation, fish and wildlife habitat, grazing, and climate control. Thus, not only are the forests in transition, but their sometimes incompatible functions are changing as well.

One of the great problems in the forest-products industries of the future is contending with the transitional aspects of the utilized forest. Cost of raw material seems bound to increase while at the same time its quality in terms of present conversion technology will be lower. Consequently, costs of manufactured articles may rise disproportionately. It is generally recognized among people concerned with benefits dependent upon forests that new utilization technologies are needed to ensure profits and to assure a continuous flow of the benefits. The new technologies, as a broad, far-reaching objective, should permit the utilization of any tree irrespective of its form, size, species, or quantity. With such a capability, forests could produce a perpetual supply of low-cost wood, even though the forest was being managed for other purposes. Equally important, the forest-management process would have a chance of turning profits at shorter intervals on a given piece of land.

A primary constraint on the future of wood products thus arises directly from the source, the forest; this constraint cannot be avoided but must be dealt with. In dealing with the forest end of the problem, perhaps the most important need, pending the new technologies, is inventory and regeneration information. A reliable catalogue of quantities, qualities, distribution, delivery, and continuity of supply would aid the utilization decision-making process.

A second constraint resides in wood itself as a material for fabricating useful articles for which dollars are exchanged and profits generated. While wood is regarded as easy to fabricate, efficiency of fabrication is not as great as is needed in competitive situations.

A third constraint derives from structural designs which impose a heavy burden upon the weaker properties of wood and thus demand measures for creating additional strength at various points.

These constraints beckon interest in three directions:
Aggregation processes
Fabrication processes
Design of structures

Each constraint has ramifications which carry into many phases of biological, technical, social, and economic interactions; and they may appear to present an insuperable barrier of disconnected pieces of needed information. However, an interim resolution may be made along fairly fundamental lines, revealing clearly some of the more potent approaches to improved wood utilization.

Performance of Wood

It seems safe to say that if wood is to have a viable future, it must perform as a material competing with other materials in terms of cost and worth. Performance has many meanings, but it may be partitioned into two distinct spheres of concern. On the one hand, performance may be regarded as the ability to satisfy needs or serve a purpose in a product such as a house or piece of furniture. The worth of wood is directly related to this aspect of performance.

On the other hand, performance can also mean the ability to be *processed* into the house or piece of furniture. This aspect of performance directly influences the cost of wood articles.

The performance of wood in products has a long history of successful contribution which has resulted in an almost instinctive and universal desire to have it as a part of our living environment. Process performance has also been singularly acceptable not only for the craftsman, but also for the do-it-yourselfer.

These performance attributes of wood have not changed. However, the entire framework of material values from forest to factory to housewife, have changed and will continue to change in such a manner as to make some of these old attributes less negotiable. Improving the negotiability of wood will involve both performance aspects. Current demands include better paint holding, more fire resistance, more decay resistance, more dimension and shape stability, less splitting and grain raising, larger sizes, and lower costs. These have to be provided with a timber resource which is declining in purity of quality and must be converted in an industrial system which is increasing in mechanization and automation.

A first-order consideration, therefore, seems to be the improvement of inherent wood properties. However, it should be noted that improved wood properties do not necessarily contribute to the solution of process or fabrication problems. Hence they assume a necessary but a secondary role in the total scheme of wood utilization. Since nearly all the worth of wood resides in the finished article and since more than half the cost of the finished article resides in the aggregation and assembly stages, this analysis emphasizes the fabrication potential of wood while briefly reviewing the improvable properties which would enhance the performance of wood articles.

Improved Wood Properties

A listing of the inherent properties of wood presents a fairly convincing argument that it is truly the miracle material. It does not corrode; does not burn unless heated to 450° F. or more, does not decay at moisture content below 18 percent. It is more heat stable than metal or plastics, and weight for weight it is stronger than steel. Moisture changes due to atmospheric humidity cause no changes in longitudinal dimensions, and changes of only a few percent in cross dimensions of properly seasoned wood. It has been estimated that unprotected wood weathers at the rate of one-quarter inch per century. Japanese temples are in existence today which were built more than a thousand years ago.

One might easily predict that a single board suspended in space would last for centuries. However, if a second board were placed on top of the first board, the two might become useless in less than a decade. The difference in performance would lie in the area between the boards. Capillary action causes this space to act as a rainwater trap, raising the moisture content above 18 percent for long periods of time and allowing decay to occur. This situation suggests dramatically that performance of wood per se might be quite different than performance in a structure where wood interacts with wood to change the environment. Hence performance becomes an element of design where the architect must either avoid such conditions or specify treatments to increase the decay resistance of the wood. It is probable that a majority of instances where wood has not given satisfactory performance was due to the existence of moisture traps of one kind or another.

When wood is placed in contact with the ground, a similar action takes place, since the ground is a good source of moisture and moreover harbors decay organisms. In this case preservative treatment of the wood is the only solution and should be specified in all cases except where the natural durability of some species, such as redwood and cedar, will give the prescribed service life. The preservative treatment of wood to improve its performance under decay conditions is well established.

The other important situation affecting performance is also associated with moisture content or more specifically, moisture content changes. This is the problem of dimensional stability across the grain. The dimension changes that normally occur with well-seasoned wood in the usual ambient conditions are not great, approximately 1 percent for each 3 or 4 percent in moisture content change, where the total moisture change in service might be plus or minus 6 percent. However, in the design of a structure these small changes can become accumulative and excessive, or they can be dispersed harmlessly throughout the system. Doors and windows offer a special challenge in requiring good workmanship as well as good design for best performance.

The use of mechanical fasteners to hold wood members together tends also to compound the dimension change effects. The familiar "nail popping" or bolt loosening is a consequence of dimension change due to moisture-content change. Here the best recourse is wood seasoned to the *average* moisture content it will achieve in service.

The probability of wood being heated to temperatures above 450° F. in a structure, and consequently burning, is reflected in insurance rates. Not reflected is the long time required for a heavy timber to burn before it loses its load-carrying capability. On the other hand, small wood members burn faster owing to the larger surface-to-volume ratio and consequently to their ability to generate their own combustion temperature. While design plays an important part in the fire performance of a wood structure, the contents of a building are mainly responsible for the origin and early development of a fire. To the extent these are beyond the control of builders' interests, it seems prudent to diminish as much as possible the contribution wood might have to the destruction of property.

Processes are well established for treating wood at reasonable cost so that it does not support combustion when heated to temperatures above 450° F., and as mentioned, does not decay under high moisture conditions or in contact with the ground. The development of nonleachable treatments means that exterior structures or surfaces may also be protected from fire.

The dimensional stabilization of wood is also a commercial practice, although the cost is higher than can be justified for many uses if the problem can be overcome through design changes. There are many approaches to improving the stability of wood products toward moisture and each will undoubtedly receive attention in the future as the search continues for lower-cost treatments. There are six generic approaches to dimensional stabilization, each attacking the problem in different ways and with varying costs and degrees of success:

Continuous films which exclude moisture from the wood.

Discontinuous films which reduce wettability of wood surfaces and hence reduce the rate of water absorption.

Occlusion of pores or cell cavities with resins, slowing the rate of water absorption.

Filling or bulking of the fine, submicroscopic cell walls in the swollen state so they cannot shrink with moisture loss.

Cross-linking or otherwise bonding the submicroscopic cell wall capillaries in the shrunken state so they cannot swell in the presence of moisture.

Reducing the basic hygroscopicity of wood.

Of the six approaches, only bulking of the cell wall has produced truly stabilized wood on a commercial scale. Wood impregnated with heat-converted, water-soluble resins first became available during World War II for aircraft propellers. Subsequently resin-treated wood has been used principally for die stock, cutlery handles, and chopping blocks. In general, stabilized wood has been too expensive for any but highly specialized uses.

It would appear doubtful that this approach for improving the performance of wood could become sufficiently low in cost to permit its use in windows, doors, and floors, where stability is a problem, since the amount of resin required and the process of impregnation exceed the cost of the wood. High cost also confronts the use of resins to fill the coarse capillaries (pores), unless some other needed property is also improved. Filling pores with methylmethacrylate resin serves the additional purposes of increasing hardness, creating an *in situ* finish, and imparting color to wood.

Since resin treatments are high in cost, the most common method of achieving some stability is with the use of surface coatings. Paints, varnishes, and other film-formers reduce the absorption of moisture during short contacts with water, as in a rain. However, prolonged exposure to water will result in the normal swelling of the wood with the possible failure of the film and danger to the wood through decay. One of the most likely developments in the future of wood products will be film-forming materials which are more durable and more protective with respect to moisture. Already in common use are films which are first cast and then applied to wood as overlays. They provide a high level of protection while serving a decorative function as well.

Perhaps the greatest stability need of wood, short of complete resistance to moisture change, is to reduce the rate of moisture absorption, particularly on end-grain surfaces. There the take-up and loss of water is very rapid, producing uneven dimension changes which result in surface-checking, and end-checking, and splitting. Controlling the rate of moisture change in contrast to reducing or eliminating moisture change, is a relatively simple and low-cost process. In most cases dipping the wood or preferably the assembled product in a water repellent preservative will reduce substantially many problems associated with water absorption. The treatment leaves the wood clean and free for subsequent finishing. Vacuum and pressure treatments are also available for wood to be used under more severe conditions.

For the long-range future it seems that the greatest potential for low-cost dimensional stabilization of wood may lie in developing workable cross-linking agents or hygroscopicity-reducing treatments. These are essentially chemical processes and the chemical industry can be counted on to come up with a solution if properly motivated.

Such chemical treatments may eventually resolve most of the adverse properties of wood as a substance. For wood as a structurizing material, other sources of improvement exist which have a more direct bearing upon its worth in satisfying human needs. This is the other side of the performance coin dealing with fabrication potential.

The Basic Functionality of Products

A material derives usefulness, and hence value and marketability, through the functions it can perform economically. Functions are performed mainly through the sizes and shapes into which the material can be converted.

Structural shapes performing functions of

enclosure, exclosure, support, or appearance, comprise by far the major use of all materials, including wood. With closure as a central point of attention, certain characteristics may be identified which affect the adaptability of wood.

The closure function may be served by a number of shapes: cylinders, spheres, cubes, and polyhedra, but perhaps the one of greatest applicability may be called simply a box. The box with modifications in size, angles, and openings, represents containers, houses, barns, factories, churches, stores. With further cut-outs, the box also represents furniture: tables, chairs, chests, cabinets. (Figure 1b)

Reduced to elemental considerations, a box is essentially a system of intersecting planes, produced by panels meeting at corners. While design and detail of boxes can vary infinitely, the fabrication of panels and corners is common to all. How to efficiently convert the timber resource into panels and corners, therefore, appears to be one of the prime problems affecting the utilization of wood.

As discussed in the following section however, the formability of wood is limited by some of its basic properties. With such a basic limitation in the material, solutions must be sought in the design of structures or in a strategic combination of wood with other materials to minimize the cornering problem. Post-and-panel construction, surface structures, and metal gusset plates are examples of such solutions.

Boxes may be considered to be of two distinct types. One is comprised of a rigid frame to which are attached various kinds of panels. In this case the frame contributes strength or support and the panels contribute appearance and closure. The other type has no frame; the panels serving the entire function. Between these two, apparently narrow extremes, lies a large and growing number of structural combinations which can utilize a wide variety of material properties. The proper relationship of structure with properties and these with function can lead to the utilization of materials that would be impossible under conventional systems. This accords with the general thesis being developed here, since wood is really many materials, depending upon the geometry of its use and the species from which it comes. Its weakest properties as well as the widely recognized strong properties, might, under proper design, permit the easy fabrication of useful shapes where total functional strength is then achieved by a unified load-distributing structure.

Out of such considerations must come new methods of forming structure with wood. An era of modular construction and component parts is already well established. Yet a new era can be foreseen in which more freedom of form is necessary. Adapting to such new forms represents a major challenge for wood.

Functionality Dependence on Formability: The Problem for Wood

Materials are converted to shapes which perform desired functions through several distinct processes which invoke what may be called the formability properties of the material:

1. Machining 5. Bending
2. Extruding 6. Rolling
3. Molding   7. Troweling
4. Stamping 8. Fastening

In the conversion of timber, two generic operations are involved:

1. Breakdown of the tree to manageable elements: poles, beams, lumber, veneer, particles, fibers, chemical derivatives.
2. Assembly of these elements into the

shapes and sizes prescribed by the function of the ultimate object.

These two operations bring into play only two of the above forming processes. Because of lack of ductility, almost all of the formability of wood arises through machining and fastening, with molding and bending being used to a minor degree for specialty articles. Machining and fastening, as represented by the saw and the hammer, have produced remarkably useful and desired shapes from wood. The increasing use of adhesive fasteners has further broadened the formability of wood. However, competing materials—metal, plastics, concrete—use various combinations of the fabrication processes with great efficiency. It would appear that the future of wood utilization must include attempts to employ other forms of shape formation, modifying properties, wherever necessary, to do so.

The structuring or fabrication efficiency of wood in general rests upon two major attributes:

The size and form of the tree or the wood elements derived from it.

The anisotropic properties common to all wood.

Size and form of the raw material seriously affect the paneling process. Anisotropy adversely affects the cornering process because this property denies strength in two directions.

Since most wood occurs in small size and is poorly formed, it would appear that a first-order consideration of its utilization, apart from possible accumulation problems, is an efficient means of aggregation into useful components, e.g., panels or beams.

The problems associated with anisotropy are more deep-seated, since this property is an advantage as well as a disadvantage. The phenomenal load-carrying efficiency of wood is due largely to its anisotropy as a result of which strength is concentrated in

one direction. In the manufacture of plywood, particleboard, and paper, anisotropy is redistributed so as to be more or less equalized in two directions. This improves structural properties in two dimensions but does nothing for the third dimension needed in cornered structures. Hence a basic shortcoming in material properties requires further circumvention in order to achieve efficient fabrication.

In this world of the box and the free-form in which function is primarily that of an enclosure, in which beauty can be acceptably conferred by paint, decals, and design, in which warmth can be provided by fuel and insulation, and particularly, in which strength or rigidity can be achieved by clever structural engineering of otherwise weak materials, how can wood contribute to a greater degree if other materials can conform more easily, cheaply, and perhaps even better? Specifically, how can the convertability of wood be up-dated into the context of modern needs and modern methods?

As mentioned previously, a great advantage and a great disadvantage in wood is its anisotropy, i.e., having properties which are different longitudinally, radially, and tangentially. (Figure 1a) Anisotropy is an advantage when loads are to be carried along the grain as in a beam or a post; it is a disadvantage when loading occurs in any of the perpendicular directions, since box-type structures involve stressing in perpendicular directions. It is inevitable that a weakness in the material will be encountered somewhere. (Figure 1c) The place weak directional properties come into greatest play is where loads must be transferred from one wood element to another. In boxes this occurs most crucially at corners.

In the free-form enclosure, the anisotropic properties of wood again appear disadvantageously. Simple, mild curvatures can be

**Figure 1. Anisotropy and the Rectangular Nature of
Tertiary Wood Products**

(a)

L direction is <u>20</u> times stronger than X
or T directions—and <u>20</u> times more stable.

(b)

Most wood products are cornered structures:

The weaker properties of wood are
always in contention at corners

(c)

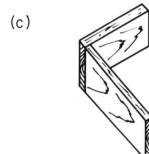 

made, although with serious process difficulties compared to other materials. But compound curves introduce in addition, technical difficulties associated with the weaker directions of wood. Wood cannot be formed in two directions simultaneously without almost prohibitively great effort to prevent splitting.

There are two main escapes from the restrictions of anisotropy. One is to design useful structures in which only the strongest properties come into play or in which loads do not accumulate or concentrate. Another is to homogenize or otherwise destroy the anisotropy. A study of various wood elements and representative structures will suggest how these escapes may be exploited.

Wood Elements:
The Primary Forest Products

Wood elements may be visualized as subdivisions of the original tree varying only in their shape and size. They may be created in a number of ways: by sawing, slicing, grinding, dissolving (chemical breakdown), or combinations of these methods, but the main consideration is that most elements of interest structurally possess a distinct geometry. A complete series of wood elements may be represented as in Table I, though some are not of structural interest except indirectly. In descending order, the elements of this series become smaller and smaller in at least one dimension. With decreasing size, something is lost and something is gained as far as enclosure performance is concerned. From the viewpoint of the resource, there is less dependence upon quality of tree and perhaps, with suitable technology, species of tree. These losses and gains can be rationalized through anisotropic effects to suggest a utilization philosophy which is projectible into new concepts.

The Role of Geometry

If anisotropy can be considered a technologically controllable variable, as well as an inherent material property, it could have possible nominal values of one, two, and three. In this sequence, one would represent no anisotropy, i.e., the properties being the same in all three directions (isotropy); two would represent the situation where the properties are different in two directions (diotropy) or the same in two directions; and three would be the normal situation where the properties are different in each direction (triotropy).

It can be seen from the list of wood elements that the third level of anisotropy is represented by the first three: poles, timber and lumber. Veneer, flakes, splinters, fiber bundles and fibers yield products having two-directional properties, perhaps varying in homogeneity. Anisotropy disappears, condition one, i.e., complete isotropy, is achieved, only after wood is reduced to chemical elements. Several consequences follow the changes in anisotropy, and these seem to pivot at the point in the series of elements represented by the flake; they coincide with the first breakup of continuity along the grain (neglecting the chip as a structural material).

1. With progressive reduction in wood-element dimensions there is a corresponding increase in formability. Lumber can be formed into simple curves, veneer into mild compound curves, although with difficulty since splitting occurs, but flakes should be formable into any shape. The formability of cellulose and lignin as plastics is well known.

2. When wood elements are aggregated into secondary products, there is opportunity for considerable trade-off of directional-strength properties for formability. For elements smaller than the flake the aggre-

Table 1. The Primary Wood Elements

1. **Poles**	Essentially the original tree trunk.
2. **Timbers**	Squared or rectangular heavy elements usually greater than two inches in thickness, eight inches or more in width.
3. **Lumber**	Rectangular elements one-half to two inches in thickness, two to twelve inches in width and indefinite in length.
4. **Veneer**	Sheet-like elements less than one-half inch in thickness, indefinite in length and width.
5. **Chips**	Small, essentially rectangular chunks of wood, approximately one-half by three-quarters by one to two inches.
6. **Flakes**	Essentially a thin piece of veneer reduced in length and width to e.g., three inches by one inch, respectively.
7. **Splinters**	Flakes reduced in width to, or slightly greater than, their thickness.
8. **Fiber Bundle**	Clumps of elemental wood fibers no longer recognizable as wood to the unaided eye.
9. **Fibers**	Individual elongated cells or parts thereof composing a major part of wood substance.
10. **Cellulose**	The major chemical component of fibers, which can be dissolved or modified to produce plastics.
11. **Lignin and Polyols**	The original amorphous binder holding cells together in wood, and the hydroxyl-rich derivatives in wood.

gated product usually suffers a net loss in strength, compared to lumber.

3. Secondary products also show a general increase in density for a given strength as wood-element dimensions decrease. Strength and density are directly related within an aggregate system and often can be manipulated as a process variable.

4. While varying degrees of mechanization are applicable throughout the series of wood elements, automation begins with the flake.

5. The flake also represents the point where wood begins to lose one of its most important characteristics: beauty of grain. From the flake on, aesthetic qualities must be conferred the same as for other materials.

6. The flake begins a major break away from traditional concepts of timber values.

Theoretically, any woody stem irrespective of form, size, or species should be reducible to a flake or any of the subsequent elements.

The above reasoning leads to a general technological guide with respect to the utilization of the various wood elements.

Assuming that the main functions of wood as a material are support, closure, and appearance, the best fundamental contribution of each wood element is approximately as follows:

Poles, posts, beams, and lumber serve their most appropriate function when used as axial stress-carrying members of a structure, since their anisotropic properties are at maximum advantage. Conversely, they are not used to maximum advantage when serving a panel function. Veneer most readily serves a closure and aesthetic function because of its sheet form and its display of grain patterns. The remaining wood elements can only serve an unadorned closure function, since they are aggregated mainly into secondary products having little textural detail. Generally these smaller wood elements are assembled into sheet products for subsequent fabrication and beautification.

It is axiomatic, however, that very few materials can compete in the modern business of enclosing space on the basis of serving only one function, unless it is extremely low in cost. The greatest value of wood as a material lies in its potential ability to serve all three functions (support, closure, and appearance) at the same time. Analysis of the various elements indicates that the one having the best opportunity of being trifunctional is veneer. However, with a small trade-off of strength for formability, flakes should also produce architecturally interesting structures.

Summarizing the above we deduce that :

1. Size and shape of the wood elements, compounded by the anisotropy of wood, are the chief determinants of convertability to useful products.

2. In a given situation where formability, strength, and weight of the material can be controlled but are in conflict, the structure itself must also be researched in order to reconcile at the most logical point material with design.

3. Technologically, two primary approaches present themselves:

    a. Developing new means of panelizing or componentizing (secondary products), together with new cornering or assembly systems. These are essentially two-stage conversion processes applicable to the utilization of the larger wood elements: poles, lumber, and veneer as well as the smaller particles and fibers.

    b. Developing molded products in which panel and corner functions are achieved simultaneously in appropriately designed structures applicable to the smaller wood elements:

        particles, fibers, chemical derivatives, and to a limited degree, veneer.

The Secondary Product Spectrum

If the sequence of wood elements shown in Table I is arranged so that they form the boundaries of a quadrant with poles at the origin, the result, Figure 2, can be used to suggest the large number of secondary products that can be assembled from them. By establishing a grid system connecting each element with each other element, the total number of possible panelized composite products is identified in generic categories. Only those products are represented which utilize one, two, or three different elements. For example, veneer glued to veneer, one element, makes plywood shown in the bottom plane. Plywood overlayed with paper or prefinished with a cellulose lacquer adds a second element raising it vertically to another grid intercepted by the paper or cellulose plane. Lumber-core plywood with a lacquer finish, three different elements, would be in the same plane but in a nearby grid.

The grids representing all the generic combinations possible with these ten elements predict that a thousand different secondary products might exist. Poles and timbers, however, may not combine readily enough to count them as producing secondary products, and this reduces the total proportionately. Nevertheless, within each generic combination there exist possibilities for endless variation in sizes of elements and their organization within the product, thereby creating special proper-

Figure 2. Secondary Wood Products Quadrant

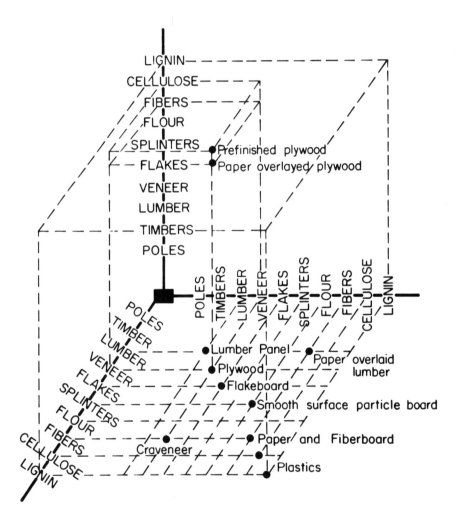

ties or economies, which enter the market as distinct articles.

The extension of the quadrant by addition of other materials which may be combined with wood—metals, plastics, cements, ceramics—produces a total spectrum of products that challenges the imagination. In the present market many of these products may be found. However, when the products are reduced to basic differences, the possibilities are barely tapped. The future will certainly fill in many of the quadrant vacancies and produce an abundance of composite products.

Thus, the problem of producing secondary products from the forest has limitless possibilities from a technological point of view. However, while many aggregated wood products lessen the constraints due to wood's anisotropic properties and thus improve fabrication performance in final structure, the overall problem of contriving useful closure shapes requires further consideration. This involves the assembly of panels and the general problem of cornering. The possible contributions of design principles offer interesting alternatives.

Concepts in Design

To one who has never tried to design houses, it may come as a surprise that homes are more difficult to design than airplanes. One reason is that in the case of airplanes the options lie between machines and materials to maximize lift, speed, and safety, all quantifiable, while in homes the options lie between materials and people where the parameters are not so easily quantified and where, moreover, fabrication costs assume a greater controlling position.

A layman might draw a less perceptive but perhaps more cogent distinction by observing merely that airplanes are never rectangular and houses never rounded. While aerodynamics is the dominant con-

sideration in airplanes, it is also true that the rounded structure is the most efficient means of enclosing space from a materials and strength standpoint. However, from a fabrication and utility standpoint, rounded structures are less efficient for present building technology and interior furnishings.

Drawing again from the perceptions of the layman, it can be noted that nature subscribes strongly to rounded structures, e.g., atoms, plants, bones, the earth itself and other planets. From this it may be deduced that the rounded structure could become a more acceptable part of our living environment than the rectangular structures dictated by traditional building practices.

If such a design motivation exists deep down in the genes of life, it would seem probable that it would come to the surface with greater force once the enabling technology appeared. Unfortunately it is difficult to justify the spending of time and money developing something for a need which is not openly recognizable. This lack of visibility (if that is all it is) means that progress may have to wait through a sequence of farsighted failures until technology and demand equilibrate satisfactorily.

This whole course of thought is illustrated by the constraints on efficient construction imposed by wood and its design limitations: the round raw material, the box-type house, the cutting and fitting operations, the cornering problems, the circumvention of anisotropic behavior of wood using members to support each other in different directions.

The progression toward simplification or "cleaning up" the structure to exploit the special capabilities of each component begins with the post-and-beam structure, where the anisotropy of wood is in full use for the supporting function and panels attached to the frame perform only the closure function. It is rectangular however, and many of the joints and corners responsible for rigidity display the weaker and less stable properties of wood. Nevertheless, it is a most efficient type of structure.

The conventional A-frame structure reduces the system of supporting members and panels to a triangular configuration, thereby gaining rigidity through structural design rather than through strength of materials and theoretically reducing the rigidity required of the materials. This concept is carried to a logical extreme in the folded-plate structure, where triangularization with the panels themselves makes framing unnecessary. While the folded-plate structure is "cleaner"—being composed of a single element—it is dependent upon the formation and sealing of a multitude of joints. This problem is partially resolved by Buckminster Fuller's all-plywood structure, in which the plates are interleaved and form themselves into a dome shape. In this case, stresses are always in the plane of the plates and are not subject to abrupt changes in direction which give rise to stress concentrations at points of juncture.

Architectural researchers at the University of Michigan have carried the principles of the dome and the folded plate to an extreme to illustrate how structural design can overcome low material strength. This shows how it is possible practically to trade material for structural strength by the reaggregation of certain low-strength primary wood elements into the final products.

A two-story structure formed solely of one-half-inch-thick, paper-overlaid urethane foam of approximately six pounds per cubic foot density has been designed and erected on the University of Michigan campus. While this material must be considered extremely weak in comparison to other structural materials, yet when properly deployed with respect to the stresses involved, it is capable of performing the entire support and closure function of a building. In this case, a large sheet of paper-overlaid foam was folded to create an internally braced component which was quite rigid and could be attached to neighboring elements to form the complete structure. The stresses in this structure are carried principally by the paper skin over the foam.

The spectacular Dow dome permits even the paper skin to be eliminated and a structure is formed of polystyrene foam alone, a material that would not ordinarily be considered to have structural properties. Here, design and formability have combined to create a structure from an extremely weak material.

Conciliation of Design with Material

From these concepts of structural possibilities despite material weakness could emerge a wide range of wood applications which capitalize more fully upon the formability of different elements.

In Figure 3, the wood elements are further broken down and rearranged into strata according to decreasing length. Within strata the elements are arranged in order of decreasing width and/or thickness. This display of the elements produces a two-dimensional system, the diagonal of which has significant implications with respect to the convertability to shapes of varying complexity. In general, the diagonal descending from left to right suggests increasing formability, decreasing strength-to-weight ratio, and increasing homogeneity or isotropy. While many of the elements should in reality be displaced further to the right in order to maintain correct size relationships vertically, useful deductions can be made from this more compact arrangement.

Examples from current practice confirm the general principles of the system. Poles

Figure 3. Functional Table of Primary Wood Elements

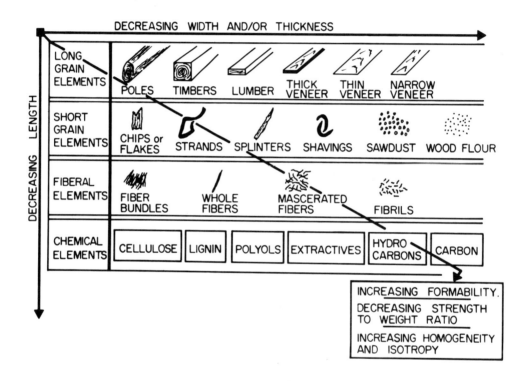

and timbers, in the upper left corner, can only produce rectangular or straight-line structures. When reduced in thickness to lumber, simple curved shapes such as laminated arches can be made. Progressive decrease in thickness allows the material to assume smaller and smaller radii of simple curvature. However, as compound curvature is desired, the width must also be decreased in order to allow deformation along contours. Thus on the extreme right is found the only element, narrow veneer, still possessing continuity along the grain and aesthetic qualities associated with it, which can be shaped to comparatively complex form such as boat hulls and the monocoque structures of airplane fusilages.

The second stratum, representing solid wood elements in which the along-the-grain direction is very short, less than three inches, theoretically should drastically improve formability. In practice this has not been widely exploited, due mainly to the difficulty of consolidation rather than to any serious difficulty of making the elements assume a desired shape. The chief commercial process producing shapes directly from these elements involve those from the extreme right. Salad bowls are molded from highly comminuted wood blended with a large proportion of resin. Flakes combined with a lower percentage of resin are also amenable to salad-bowl production. Recently, by using special consolidation techniques, other elements from this stratum have been engineered into one-piece structures. In general, however, the difficulty of consolidation to high strength has constrained these elements mainly to sheet products in which heat and pressure are more easily administered. For the same reason the elements of the third stratum also find their major form of aggregation in sheet products. Actually they are even more amenable to shaping than those in the first two strata. How amenable fiberal

elements are to shaping is dramatically illustrated by the familiar egg carton which has corners and curves of rather severe complexity. However, great strength is not required in an egg carton and this reduces the consolidation problem. Nevertheless, since fibers do conform to shape readily, they are finding increasing use in shaped products which can be die-molded.

In the lowest stratum are found the chemical compounds derivable from wood. While not all are of direct structural interest, they serve to round out the system, since they can be converted into the most intricate shapes by techniques commonly used for plastics, such as extrusion and various methods of molding.

From a study of the wood products marketed and the implications of Figure 4, it can be deduced that the potential for forming useful objects directly from primary wood elements is also virtually untapped. Technologically, the problem hinges on methods of efficient consolidation. It seems certain that since the timber resource has been liberated from many constraints, improved methods of utilizing wood by direct forming will come into being. Certainty is further strengthened by the information given in Figure 4 (taken from "The Economic Importance of Timber in the United States," US Dept. of Agriculture, Forest Service, Misc. Pub. 941). The chart shows that more than half of the twenty-four dollars it takes to bring one dollar's worth of wood in a tree to final consumer utility is required to break the tree down into elements and put these elements back together again in the shape desired. Direct fabrication into shapes, carefully designed to optimize properties, processes, and functions will enhance greatly the utility of an abundant resource and significantly reduce the cost of wood products.

This type of progress is not without its drawbacks. One of the most cherished

Figure 4.

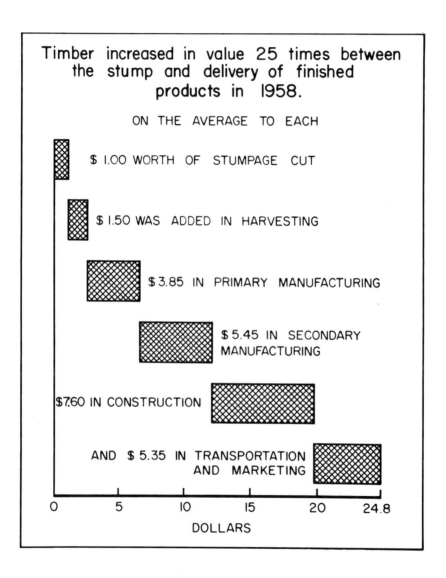

properties of wood is its beauty of grain. In most of the elements amenable to direct fabrication, beauty of grain is lost. This may seem regrettable, but on second thought wood is no worse than the materials with which it competes. They depend upon paint, films, artificial grain, and structural beauty to produce visual appeal. Wood products already resort to these methods in the majority of uses. It is conceivable that if conferred beauty leads to increasingly efficient use of low-quality wood, some cost savings may be passed along that will expand the demand for high-cost wood. The more sophisticated uses of wood which depend not only upon its inherent aesthetical properties, but also upon a high degree of craftsmanship, cannot alone support a viable forest-products industry. By broadening the utilization base, the overall system derives compounded advantages.

Throughout the above discussion attention was centered on possible new means of forming structures with wood, means which fit the forests of the future as well as the type of enclosures wanted. Although the enclosures described are not very sophisticated, perhaps more in the nature of buildings useful as second homes or cabins, the objective has been to illustrate a technological capability that seems within the realm of possibility. However, in the context of present building design and practice, there is ample room for changes of an evolutionary nature. These include improvements in the properties of wood as a substance, and in aggregation of primary wood elements into secondary products, panels, beams, components, and composites which are then used in subsequent fabrication of consumer products.

An evolutionary process can begin with any of the primary wood elements. Fiberal elements are already established as components of honeycomb panels and in corrugated assemblies, where the fiber is first formed into thin sheets, then reformed into thicker sheets and finally assembled into final shapes. Direct fabrication into relatively small structures is also established. Since fibrous materials are easily shaped, it would seem logical that progressive increase in the size of products manufactured would ensue merely as an engineering development. Some technological developments are also needed for large building components to achieve greater interfiber strength. Since individual wood fibers have been shown to have a strength of approximately 90,000 psi in axial tension, such a development could extend significantly the structural horizons for fiberal elements.

Proceeding up the scale of wood elements, the possibility of making a frameless, A-shaped structure as a system of small folded-plate plywood sections seems architecturally possible. Indeed, the formability of veneer could be exploited to produce this type of structure without a multiplicity of joints. A veneer-base material known as wave-wood, developed by Dr. Ben Bryant, seems logical for this purpose. This coarsely corrugated material is paper-overlaid, extremely rigid for its weight, and capable of long unsupported spans.

Going back still farther to poles, timbers, and lumber, the utility of these elements and particularly laminated lumber with its ability to assume simple curvature, would be enhanced by more efficient closure materials. Plywood serves this function well, as would wave-wood. However, panels derived from lower-grade trees used in combination with pole-size timber would bring a post-and-panel type building within reach of the transition forest. To arrive at a more efficient panel, all wood elements from flakes to fibers should be considered in aggregates of conventional types as well as in composites. Since the support function is borne by the posts and beams in this type of construction, the panels need to have strength only for stresses generated locally or within a panel. Hence the panelization process can attend solely to the closure function and perhaps achieve some economies in manufacture.

It is also of interest to consider the possibilities raised by the "Home of Living Light" created by the American Plywood Association and exhibited at the Seattle World's Fair in 1962. While the house was designed to provide a feeling of flowing space and natural light with maximum privacy, structurally it deemphasized the cornering problem. This it has done while still using conventional building practices of framing and sheathing. It seems but a simple step from here to the inclusion of some of the principles outlined above and achieving greater efficiency in construction.

A Common Denominator
for Wood Conversion Processes

As mentioned in an earlier section, the conversion of timber involves two generic operations, one of breakdown and one of assembly. It is the assembly stages which generate most of the costs of wood articles and confer most of their worth. When one looks at a house with its great value for comfort and shelter, one might wonder what it would be worth if all the nails were suddenly withdrawn. Or one might contemplate the value of a beautiful chest of drawers and then consider its worth if all the glue let go. It would not be fair to deduce from this that all the value of a house resides in the nails, or the worth of a bureau in the glue, any more than the total worth of a chain resides in any one link. Nevertheless, the point can be made that many products, including cars, clothes, airplanes, and others, are dependent to a disproportionate degree upon the fastening systems which hold them together.

After a tree has been reduced to appropriate elemental subdivisions, every step in the product-manufacturing process, apart from beautification operations, is concerned with fastening pieces of wood together. The fastener that through the ages has done the most in helping wood perform is the nail. With hundreds of varieties for every purpose, the nail continues to be the mainstay of the wood-construction industry. Development of special coatings or grooving to improve the holding capacity of nails and mechanization of the driving operation will assure the use of this fastening system for a long time to come.

Nails, together with screws and bolts, achieve their greatest usefulness toward the final assembly stages of a product. At the beginning of the assembly process, i.e., the first joining of primary wood elements into secondary products, some form of adhesion is the basis of the fastening system.

A wide array of adhesives is available, all specially tailored to do a prescribed job of bonding wood. Each wood element presents a different bonding task for the adhesive, even though the same wood species may be involved in each case. For example, Douglas fir lumber, veneer, and particles are bonded with three generically different adhesives. At this level of assembly, the cost and efficiency of the adhesive have a powerful bearing on the cost of the assembled product. Two considerations apply in the cost determination: first, the large surface areas that are involved in joining primary wood elements require a large amount of adhesive per unit of wood joined, and second, assuming a bond of appropriate durability, is speed with which joints can be made. Speed of curing controls the output of a gluing operation (in a well-engineered plant).

Improvements at this primary level of assembly are often sought in the price per pound of the adhesive because of the large quantities used. However, the breakthrough that will have the greatest impact on secondary products is one that will permit bonds to be made in seconds and thus enable automated, continuous aggregating processes. The use of electronic energy to cure adhesives rapidly has demonstrated the advantages of high-speed curing. When the same curing speed can be obtained on durable, high-performance adhesives without the need for supplemental energy sources, a most versatile and efficient assembly system will evolve around it.

The ability to make bonds in seconds would permit adhesives to take on a more widespread role in the final assembly stages. While adhesives are used to assemble cabinets and furniture, they have not found extensive use in assembling larger structures. Here the cost of the adhesive is minor compared to the value of the glued product, and it should be possible to spend more on the adhesive to obtain greater efficiency.

Use of adhesives in assembling larger wood structures would represent a major advance, since glued structures are more rigid than mechanically fastened structures, and certain loads can be transferred surface to surface more efficiently than through a mechanical device. In addition, surface-to-surface joining reduces some dimensional stability problems which affect mechanical fastenings. Moreover, the adhesive acts as a seal for a tighter building and the sealing action also reduces water trap effects between surfaces.

Although better primary wood products will be produced in the future through improved treating, machining, and seasoning practices, it seems logical that the forest-products industries will take advantage of new adhesive technology, thus allowing them to:

Reduce material cost by utilizing more of each tree,

Upgrade lumber and veneer by use of overlays (and prefinishing),

Reduce construction costs by increased panelization and componentizing,

Provide more efficient means for assembling primary and secondary wood products into useful shapes.

Thus in the development of new wood products it seems virtually certain that new adhesives will play a major role, for they will make possible stronger, more durable structures, and will use a forest resource of widely varying quality with greater efficiency.

Summary

This analysis has sought to tie the forest resources of varying qualities and uses with the ultimate articles into which they might be constructed. Note was made of the present state of conversion technology that Figure 4 summarizes as a somewhat inefficient or wasteful enterprise. As a means of looking beyond the status quo, the properties of wood were considered with respect to various degrees of subdivision. This produced a spectrum of wood elements which could be seen to stand between the timber resource as it exists and the market for shaped products as it might exist. Since the geometry of each wood element has a bearing upon its formability into shapes of different complexities, geometry was used as an indicator of future utility.

The formability of each wood element was considered against its strength-contributing potential and this led to suggestions as to how each might perform most efficiently as an enclosure. Improvement of wood as a substance was considered briefly. The dependence of wood on fastening systems was stressed and prediction was made that adhesives would comprise the main edge in the development of new wood products and processes.

Research, Technology, and Design in the Mass of Wood

ROBERT J. SEIDL
Vice-President for Research
Simpson Timber Company,
Seattle, Washington

A graduate from the University of Wisconsin, Robert J. Seidl was employed as a chemical engineer by Seagram-Calvert Corporation, Southern Kraft Corporation, Merrimac Paper Company, and the US Forest Products Laboratory, where he conducted research on wood products and pulp and paper manufacture. In addition to the research program at Simpson Timber, he is responsible for manufacture of resins, overlays, and pulp. He has been a Regional Board Member for the Forest Products Research Society and is active in American Paper Institute, TAPPI, National Forest Products Association, Home Manufacturers Association.

In the mass use of wood we must find the central area between what inspires pleasurable human response and what functions best physically. The equilibrium or dynamic balance point between aesthetics and function is determined by economics.

The performance of wood may be improved through research while at the same time keeping a design context in view. The raw material itself couples our interest in both design and utilization of wood, even though many divorce design from use. My thoughts are confined to mass uses for wood, with practical and not highly sophisticated approaches to aesthetics. However complicated it may be to define the relationship between aesthetics and mass use of wood, I wish to make it clear that there is, indeed, a strong common interest that must be revealed and better understood. In a sentence, we must find and maintain the best equilibrium among function, which I shall employ to denote use, aesthetics, which denotes appearance, and cost, which I shall use to denote ease and economy. I say equilibrium, because these are always in some dynamic balance, and no simple formula expresses this balance.

A few words on semantics are appropriate. Having observed the communications gap between *science* and *industry,* I would expect even more time to pass before there is much understanding of the common interest between *design* and *mass production.* At the extremes of these interests one is suspicious of the other. The classic mass producer of wood often suspects any artist who might impinge on his area. No doubt some artists view producers as "wood butchers," ignorant of the beauty in their product. An artist fashions originals with loving care, an approach understandably anathema to a manufacturer. The mass builder fears the presumed complexities and costs caused by the architect. The architect, in turn, does not welcome the abuse of aesthetics often associated with mass building; frequently he concludes he must ignore what he cannot control, and thus he loses contact with a large segment of his industry. Product managers in the wood industry may see design as the cause of product proliferation. Such a concern breeds caution if not hostility. Executives may view industrial design as one more escalation of overhead, and wonder what connection there is between design and profit. The forester in this polyglot fraternity is somewhat of a bystander, intuitively aware he is producing one of the best composites of usefulness and beauty the world has known. To cap the confusion, the aesthetic world is peopled with individualists who display no obvious common agreement among themselves. It is no wonder that understanding is slow. But there is no need to reconcile extremes, or to be distracted by them, with so much fertile ground to work in the middle area. A practical approach is to isolate and modulate the differences between aesthetic design requirements, intended use requirements, and economic requirements, and to proceed with the compromise that results.

I have been asked to comment on research needed concerning the end uses of wood. However, the end uses for wood are almost infinite in number. Its beauty is expressed in a diversity of ways—in split-rail fences, figured patterns of exotic species, a Wisconsin barn, a New England door, a sculpture, a natural redwood home, a parabolic beam, a hand-split shake roof, a tortured juniper branch, a lacquered bowl, a church steeple, a holystoned teak deck, simple driftwood, and so on and on.

I have elected to emphasize only the area of mass-produced woods for mass use such as structural members, cladding for weather surfaces, woodwork, and doors. More specifically, these are thought of in the context of industrial design and to a lesser extent architecture.

Let us examine the *need* for design in the mass use of wood. One need is human, for the natural material, wood, used well and set in a tasteful environment, offers comfort, peace, and beauty in a world increasingly filled not only with harder and colder materials, but also with synthetics, crowds, violence, and decibels. The other need is economic, simply stated as profit. People will pay more, and much more, for something that strikes a responsive chord with their senses. This is obvious, simple, and basic, but not yet properly exploited by the wood industry. The opportunity begins with the sociological needs of people, their values, and the environment they are seeking. This can be appraised and given expression through creative design. Certainly the conceptual design will suffer considerable change as it meets the realism of production and costs, but mutual respect between designer and producer is essential.

Most volume producers of wood face a difficult fight for profit. Costs have risen for land, trees, transportation, manufacturing, and distribution. Prices have certainly not kept pace. In some cases they have declined and in others one more price increase will eliminate their need completely in the face of non-wood competitive materials. Considering the millions of feet of good wood that are converted into commodity products daily by our saws and lathes, I submit that one of the few new opportunities to increase earnings is creating a situation where the consumer will gladly pay more for the fruit of our labor. Design, fully integrated with other efforts, is one key. We must find better ways to rise above the "bid and ask" pricing of so much commodity wood. We must have something to sell besides wood by the cube or the pound, period.

Wood vs. Non-wood Materials

We are on the threshold of the fierce competition with non-wood products that has long been predicted. Lead time in the laboratories has been sufficient to release prototype generations of plastics, metals, panels, and structures aimed at taking markets from wood. As an example, the improvement in both performance and appearance of printed wood grains has clearly established a prominent position for these in relation to decorative woods; the next generation of youngsters may not really know the difference. The poundage of metal and plastic per house has steadily increased. The increase in high-rise buildings in relation to single-family houses works to the great advantage of non-wood products. The popular mobile home is usually clad in metal. Use of wood has declined in school buildings because we have not solved fire problems, and also because we have been unwilling to undertake the complete systems method of building. Although we are slowly becoming *product-oriented,* we are not yet as *systems-oriented* as our competitors. Concrete has taken wood markets because of its econ-

omy, new structural techniques, and versatility for free-form shapes. Mineral fibers have become so low in cost as to threaten wood-fiber building boards. There is no doubt at all that we must reappraise our opportunities in the light of these threats.

In the contemporary period, the emergence of architectural concrete among the competitors of wood is worthy of special mention. Concrete has made a new marriage of form and function. Its stress-carrying ability has been increased while its surface has been made more pleasing. Happily, there is a good place for wood products in the forming of so much concrete.

Wood in Combination with Nonwood Products

Composite products including wood present somewhat the inverse of my previous point; this is viewing the glass as half full rather than half empty. The opportunities with composite materials are very great and lend themselves well to design and function. The wood patterns mentioned before are usually printed on a wood derivative, paper. The combinations of wood and resins yield products with a durability and performance that is unusual. Because of these we can make wood work harder, as with plywood and beams. With resins or plastic films as overlays we can overcome traditional problems with surface performance and obtain functional and decorative products of many varieties. With special resins we bond metals and plastics to wood for aircraft pallets or house walls. At long last, by use of overlays, we can provide exterior panels with twenty-year durability. The charm of wood can also be enhanced by its use in conjunction with other materials in a structure. For example, wood may well appear to better advantage when used in a tasteful manner with concrete or stone. The list of opportunities is long and encouraging, for wood can emerge as a most useful part of these composites.

Research, Technology, and Design

The technical research needed to serve a design approach is not greatly different from research needed without a design approach. For example, a laminated beam to perform well has strict requirements of glue bonds, treatments, finishes, and connectors. It will serve the function with or without aesthetic considerations. One ton of wood, converted to a privacy fence, may with equal use of technology be a graceful line on the landscape or an "eyesore." Thus, we must reconcile the simple elements of performance and the end-product shapes and textures that might solicit a happy response from a viewer. All manmade objects are in fact "designed," but certainly not all are designed well.

As a sweeping generalization, the trouble at the present time with industrial design on most mass uses of wood is that it almost doesn't exist. Technical research, on the other hand, has been put to use for many years. Although the problems and needs for research may sound all too familiar to you, it is appropriate to outline some of them here, with the hope that it will increase understanding and promote intelligent use of wood. Some examples follow:

Bonding and gluing of wood—For years we have been able to bond wood permanently and well beyond its own inherent strength. One is impressed by the potential for wood utilization and superior products that the chemical industry has given us in the form of resin glues. Yet we are only at the beginning. We need glues that will give more rapid joints at lower temperatures, do a better job of gap-filling of rough surfaces, and give permanent bonds with roll-pressure applications only. We need special adhesives that will instantly bond wood end to end in a process analogous to metal-welding. Such glues would beget new processes that would reduce product cost and enable designers to develop product potential more fully.

Among bonded products, surely laminated beams have an exciting future for designers. Small pieces of wood, properly assembled, give expression to combinations of structure, performance, and aesthetics which were never possible from the finest old trees in history. Processes must be improved to bond wood end to end and side by side to remove the curse of random sizes that has plagued the industry. One refreshing new approach to end-bonding has been to impress rather than to cut a "finger joint." This offers a precision joint and a high strength. As an example, long two-by-four members thus bonded and pulled in tension are not likely to break at the joint. Better mass-production techniques must be evolved to produce mullions, posts, and small beams in the sizes and strengths needed. The adhesives must accommodate treated wood, so that fire and preservative chemicals can also be introduced. No other single area holds more promise both to end product and utilization than that of resin-bonding wood.

Of course plywood and its new partner and rival, particleboard, are also immensely important products that owe their existence to adhesives. In the interest of brevity, perhaps it is enough to say that the conversion of a log to sheet products, as distinguished from board products, has an impact on both end use and utilization that is akin in importance, to the conversion of wood to paper. The principal research problems with structural plywood have been chiefly related to process and economics and these lend themselves to straight-forward solution. However, if these mass-produced sheets are ever to produce high profits, we must find ways to increase their value to the consumer. A design approach is one possibility. I look forward to more sophisticated development of plywood and believe that the particleboard field, which has grown at a prodigious rate in recent years, is just beginning to demonstrate its capacity. The next technical landmark in particleboard will be when the product is accepted widely for external use. This will require improved binders and the solution of problems of swelling and weathering, to meet technical needs, and this must be coupled with good design and systems to permit reasonable prices and earnings.

Coatings and finishings—A continuing need with most wood products is for better surface performance. Poor surface appearance after weathering has resulted in steady loss of markets, and progress to overcome it has been all too slow. However, there are now many resins and coatings designed to meet the challenge. These represent costly developments by plastics and chemical companies, and the wood industry need only engage in adaptive research to share the rewards. The products divide into interior and exterior types and again into clear or pigmented finishes. Various process combinations are available for coating, drying, or curing, including rapid cure by radiation, without application of heat. For most uses today there is a combination of coating and process that will perform, but the technical work needed to adapt these to the raw material and product is substantial. A related research area of first importance is to find better ways to predict performance, since the pace of today's development of new chemicals is such that full durability exposure has lost much of its usefulness.

Impregnation of wood with chemicals—There is much inducement to penetrate

wood in depth with chemicals that impart special attributes. Basic processes involve pressure treatment with chemicals that provide fire resistance or resistance to decay. The basic need is to have treated wood that can be glued and finished and that is free of extraneous odor or color. One process of recent years employs a liquefied gas as the carrying agent for preservatives. This facilitates removal of the carrier and yields a clean workable end product. Another interesting effort has been the treatment of wood with monomeric resins which are then cured in situ by means of radiation. The resulting product can be very hard and durable. This is an extension of the products produced earlier by pressure treatment of wood with resin, followed by heat curing, yielding the familiar "compreg" used for golf club heads, knife handles, and the like.

Of interest to those who would carve and fashion wood into special shapes is the treatment with a "bulking chemical," such as polyethylene glycol. Such chemicals fill the wood fiber cell walls and hold the wood in a swollen condition. This is one solution to the old problem of making wood more dimensionally stable.

One problem with both new and old methods is the difficulty of forcing liquids into wood to any great depth. While it is done in large volume daily, one might hope that research will uncover easier methods. One approach is to treat thinner pieces and to laminate them to the desired size, but this has its own complexities.

Fire and preservative treatments—These are often grouped because they attack two major enemies of wood. Of all the shortcomings of wood, its propensity to burn keeps it continually on the defensive for large-scale use. The problem is not yet major in residential construction, but it is dominant in multifamily building construction. It is a difficult problem to penetrate wood with the proper chemical, at low cost, without damage to the wood. The problem lends itself to more basic research on the pyrolysis reaction itself. Preservative-treated wood has, in my opinion, more potential than is realized by today's designers and architects. Such treatment makes it quite practical to design low structures with wood members on or in the soil. One innovative structure designed at Washington State University has treated studs emerging directly from the ground, while above ground the studs are end-glued to untreated ones in the interest of economy. This method lends itself to interesting design effects, especially for recreation houses. Still another possibility, again for recreation houses, is to "hang" the structure from a few strong, treated poles.

Acoustics—There is little doubt that an understanding of acoustics is of increasing importance in research on wood. Competence in acoustics is basic in research that deals with structures for human habitation. It is another area not yet "overploughed" in wood research. However, acoustics is a technology that deals chiefly with systems and wood research should reflect this need. Instrumentation and acoustic chamber design are available from a variety of sources and do not need reinvention by our industry. The wood industry must probe acoustics in much greater depth than has been evident thus far.

Engineering and Strength of Wood—We are witnessing new approaches on this subject; they are sorely needed and are a good omen. For years it has been necessary to test clear specimens laboriously, make adjustments for natural defects, and sort wood by visual means into various "strength" categories. I put "strength" in quotation marks to indicate doubts about any quantified relationship between appear-

ance and strength. Useful as this work has been, it is, in my opinion, out of phase with modern engineering concepts. The endless tables of species, grades, moisture variations, and span have lost the attention of engineers and architects. The minds of our real customers have wandered, understandably, from our solutions to the problem. Among major structural materials only wood is subject to so much rationalization and complex evaluation procedures. In addition, much excess material is often used in construction so that the weakest piece can be accommodated. This does violence both to economics and to logic.

New methods of testing strength, board by board, at low cost are near at hand. They promise to elevate wood to the position of structural dignity that it deserves. Each piece can have a measured stress value. For good utilization of applications such as beams, the strongest pieces can be isolated for the outside members, and the weaker relegated to the center. Practical devices for testing wood today are mechanical, or electromechanical, but interesting prospects are ahead for making similar measurements by methods based on sonics or piezo-electric effects. It is a good area for research and requires such disciplines as physics, electronics and acoustics.

Formability of wood—One of the so-called facts about wood is its easy workability, but this has sharp reservations. While it is easy to saw and cut, it is also very reluctant to assume compound curvatures or exhibit any plasticity. Unfortunately, it is not so easy to form as some other materials, although it does achieve some graceful and complex forms in the hands of designers and artists, through carving or bending. Wood can be softened chemically so that it has pliability, but only with considerable effort and cost. For larger structures especially, the bending and bonding of thin laminations permits beautiful forms to be created.

The Function of Industrial Design

I would like now to digress from the elements of technology to the realm of industrial design. I have been dubious of proceeding so far without definition of terms. The title of the symposium is "Design and Aesthetics in Wood," and I believe the meaning of aesthetics is clear enough. However, in my experience design really has no commonly understood meaning. To some it appears that only engineers "design" such things as a wall bracket, a long span, or a cantilever. Airplanes are apparently so complicated that one "configurates," rather than designs. Design clearly has an engineering connotation. On the other hand, we speak of "designing" fabrics, letterheads, doors, and even houses, so it also has a visual connotation. In short, all man-made objects are designed. For present purposes I have chosen to view design from the industrial design point of view; I describe it as the art of bringing *sensitivity* to a structure or a product, of contributing equally to aesthetics and performance with apologies for neither. I do not characterize it as pure engineering or pure art but as a blend of both.

The difference between pure art and design is that art depends on spontaneous visual or physical effects, but design depends more on achieving the appearance of spontaneity under controlled conditions. Industrial design, to which I direct your attention, is frankly directed at practical aspects of products; it acts as a catalyst upon raw materials, manufacturing, markets, and economics. Employing artistic measures industrial design operates under supercontrolled conditions, liable to all the yardsticks of commerce; thus it attempts to give an appearance of visual spontaneity

within a fixed environment. Perhaps it might be said to provide a controlled response without a technical or scientific foundation. It measures the "aesthetic pulse" in an ordered way. Industrial design is a profession; it combines a body of knowledge, special skills, and basic disciplines. The design approach opens interesting potentials with wood. The greatest asset of wood is really the unpredictable character of its natural formation. Along with split rock, the surface of water, and a few other items, the surface of wood is universally accepted as beautiful. Man should not try to make it too uniform. Yet here is a contradiction to all concepts of mass production. Paradoxically, wood is both a commodity and a visually marketable product. Where we treat it as a commodity only, our industry is insensitive to its visual aspects, and we might well expect this to be reflected in a low product price. My repeated theme is that we can and should upgrade the commodity by a disciplined approach to aesthetics.

Let us consider one or two very elementary examples of a design approach, coupled with technical research, as it affects a mass product, plywood. One can make plywood siding for houses with large knotholes in the surface veneer and can predict with certainty that the product will change hands for a very low price. One can patch the veneer with a circular "cookie" patch, but the unsightly appearance of the circle after weathering grossly limits the upgrading. One can use a "boat" patch, and make an incremental gain in appearance, but not much. With some species the knots stay in place, which gives a tolerable appearance, but just barely, and the knots usually do not weather well. If on the other hand one is willing to accept the discipline of industrial design, a planned face appearance can be created using, for example, thin shim patches or sled patches and chemically filled knotholes which give an excellent appearance after weathering, especially if the surface is saw-textured. The design approach carefully limits the size and length and distribution of the defect corrections in such a manner that the end product gives the illusion of the pleasing and random natural characteristics of wood.

Anyone who has ever tried to create a "random" surface, such as the random holes in acoustical tile, soon learns that the process is anything but random, rather it requires a painstakingly planned placement of holes. A so-called "natural random" item, mass-produced and exposed side by side, exhibits strong patterns, which are not usually pleasing. However, Industrial design can overcome the problems of knotholes or drilled holes and create a pleasing and apparently natural appearance.

The principles of design which apply to a piece of lumber or plywood also apply to a component, or to a system, or to a structure, such as a house. Perhaps it is only a matter of scale and specific relation to habitable structures that distinguish architecture from design. At any rate, both designers and architects follow a noble calling, for they have the charter to shape so much of our visual environment and to bring it into balance with our basic needs.

Pertinent to our theme is the relationship among culture, luxury, social posture, and engineered quality in the mass use of wood for shelter. Not surprisingly, guaranteed strength, durability, and lower maintenance have the lesser impact on the house-buyer. A home is a tangible symbol of prestige, position, and taste. Certainly not enough of this reality is factored into present-day research on wood.

With respect to larger structures, I have been fascinated by the ferment and change in church construction. One would expect the mass opinion of a congregation to be conservative in matters of tradition. Yet churches have shown a remarkable acceptance of innovation in design, which in turn has led to interesting structural concepts and therefore new product uses.

In summary, I have been compelled to admit that technical research needed on wood does not differ much whether industrial design is embraced or ignored, and I have outlined some areas of research and technology that invite a design approach. Also, I have tried to identify a gap that exists between the requirements for mass manufacture of wood on the one hand and the opportunities to capitalize on the non-repetitive nature of wood on the other. I have viewed industrial design as a vital agent in the adaptation of our raw material to our customers' needs, and as a catalyst that can bring about useful and profitable reaction between inherently different positions. Finally, in the mass use of wood we must find the central area between what inspires pleasurable human response and what functions best physically. The equilibrium or dynamic balance point between aesthetics and function is determined by economics.

Computer Aided Design
—Past, Present, Future

VINCENT J. VITAGLIANO
Manager, Advanced Engineering
Applications
New York Scientific Center
International Business Machines,
New York City

After receiving a degree in civil engineering at Manhattan College, Vincent J. Vitagliano did advanced study at Virginia Polytechnic Institute and New York University, receiving his doctorate degree at the latter institution. Prior to joining IBM he practiced engineering in industry, as a consulting engineer and as a faculty member at Manhattan College. He has been licensed as a professional engineer in New York and New Jersey.

As a professional engineer, I view design in a framework of problem-solving, which includes all the aspects that may be found from the conception of an idea to its fulfillment in reality. It embodies phases of planning, analysis, synthesis (or design in a narrow sense), and implementation. Having practiced as a consulting engineer, who dealt frequently with architects, I am also aware of the importance that both the aesthetic and functional aspects of design have. Now, as a computer-oriented engineer, I am continually looking for new areas of application in design for a device which has been both feared and held in awe and more frequently than not—misunderstood.

Therefore, I will attempt to put the electronic computer into a proper perspective for the designer—be he engineer, architect, or artist. I will begin by tracing some significant historic facts that led to its development. This will be followed by a brief discussion of what the computer is and what might be done with it; and how we communicate with it to get it to accomplish meaningful tasks. I will then illustrate, in relation to design, how it was used in the past, its use at the present time, and what I envision for its future.

Much of the business of computing revolves around the concept of counting. And I imagine it may have all started with prehistoric man trying to keep track of things, in the course of which he associated digits on his fingers and toes with the units being counted. No doubt this was followed by shepherds in the fields having to count beyond the ten fingers and ten toes, who then used pebbles and stones to record the number of sheep. It was not until the ancient Egyptians came along that a more sophisticated counting device was created—the abacus—where beads on strings were used as the counting medium and where the concept of carry-over became possible. Amazingly enough the abacus is still used in some far eastern countries where it proves to be most useful. In fact, even in today's schools—where youngsters are introduced to so-called "modern math" —we find the abacus being used to teach the counting concept.

It was not until the seventeenth century that a Frenchman, Blaise Pascal, invented a machine that had the ability of doing addition. A significant aspect of this device was that it included a carry-over feature. In 1801 another Frenchman by the name of Joseph Jaquard developed an automatic weaving loom, where punched cards or paper tape were used to control the pattern of a weave; much the same concept was used in the old player piano. In 1823 an Englishman named Charles Babbage conceived the idea of a "difference engine." The interesting aspect of this device was that it contained all the elements of the digital computer. Unfortunately the technology of that day was just not capable of producing it. In 1879 a nineteen-year-old youth, Herman Hollorith, was working in the census office of the United States Department of Interior. Observing that it took seven and a half years to complete the 1880 census, he conceived the idea of the punch-card concept where holes in a coded form were used to indicate a person's education, income, age, etc. The net

result was completion of the 1890 census in just two and a half years. This led to the development of an extended line of electrical and mechanical equipment which made use of the unit-record concept. This made it possible to process the information on the punched card, a unit record, by a variety of different pieces of equipment. In 1937 the idea was conceived for the development of a more versatile computer. Professor Howard H. Aiken at Harvard University put together seventy-eight adding machines and desk calculators which were controlled by instructions on a paper tape. Aiken's device was completed in 1944 and was named the automatic-sequence-control calculator. It had the ability to perform three additions per second. In 1946 the first electronic computer came into being at the University of Pennsylvania. Two men, Doctor J. Presper Eckert, Jr., and Dr. John W. Mauchly, developed a device called the ENIAC (electronic numerical integrator and calculator) that consisted of over five hundred thousand soldered connections linking eighteen thousand vacuum tubes together. Life hasn't been the same since, for the ENIAC could perform five thousand additions per second. In 1950 the first Univac was delivered to the census bureau. In 1953 IBM introduced its first electronic computer, the 701, to the marketplace. This computer was capable of performing 14,000 additions per second. Since that time we have passed through two complete generations of computers and are already well into the third generation. The first computers were designed with vacuum-tube circuitry. Their processing speeds were in a millisecond range. In the late 1950s transistorized circuitry was introduced. This resulted in much more reliable computers and still faster processing speeds in the microsecond range. In 1963 we entered the third generation of computing, where the concept of microelectronics was introduced and where processing speeds are in the very low microsecond range and even in the nanosecond range.

The acceptance of the computer by engineers and scientists in general was not immediate. Although it did find its place in the aerospace and atomic-energy fields and to limited extents in large corporations and universities, primarily it was used for the repetitive commercial applications of business.

The explanation is apparent when one considers how much first-generation computers cost and how tedious and time consuming communication with them was. Yet things have changed drastically, and today a revolution towards the computer has taken place among professionals. A simple comparison can illustrate the dynamic changes that have brought this about. The vacuum-tube 701 weighed ten tons, required ten to twenty tons of airconditioning, eighty KVA of electric power, and extensive floor area. By contrast the third generation 1130 is desk size, requires no airconditioning, and operates with about two KVA. Although their memory storage capacities are nearly identical, the 1130 is more than three times faster than the 701. The older 701 rented for twenty thousand dollars per month compared with approximately one thousand per month for the 1130.

Well, just what is this device we call a computer. We call it a digital computer, from the word "digit," for very simply it is a device that manipulates digits. The digits may be numbers if we are solving problems; letters of the alphabet if we are manipulating words as in commercial applications; and even special symbols like dollar signs, parentheses, commas.

As a problem solver, however, I view the computer as a calculator—it does arithmetic, it adds, subtracts, multiplies, and divides. In addition, however, we can teach it to evaluate logarithms and square roots,

trigonometric functions, and raise numbers to power.

The computer is more than a calculator in that it possesses a memory. The memory consists of addressable locations where digits are stored. The digits represent meaningful information such as data and instructions. Now because instructions are stored, it means that the computer must have at least one other attribute; namely, the ability to follow these instructions. There are instructions for doing arithmetic —adding, subtracting, multiplying, instructions for getting information into and out of the computer's memory—input, output instructions, instructions for controlling the computer's operations—control instructions, and instructions for moving information around within the computer's memory —transfer-type instructions. When the computer operates, it does so in a systematic, orderly way. It operates in a cycle, first accessing an instruction, analyzing it, and finally executing it. So, basically the electronic computer is a calculator with a memory in which data and instructions are stored and with the ability to follow instructions. And, finally, as it does this, it also checks all of its operations.

Now, let us explore the manner in which we communicate with these devices. The first computers were programmed using what are called machine languages—in fact, these are the only languages they understand. They are languages of numbers, which are both tedious and time-consuming to use. They are not tremendously difficult to learn, but for the most part, the professional just cannot be bothered with them except for special cases. In the past, therefore, with first-generation computers, the professional communicated with a programmer, who in turn communicated with the machine. There were difficulties in this arrangement in that the programmer did not always understand the problem being solved and as a result the time involved before meaningful results were obtained was significant. To make the job easier then, symbolic languages were developed, where symbols replaced the numbers. To a great extent, such languages are still in use today particularly for commercial applications. They too, however, involve a significant degree of tedium when being used.

In the late fifties, programming languages were developed. Many exist today—FORTRAN, COBOL, RPG, and others. These eliminate the earlier tedium, for they are easily learned and easily used. As an example, with a language like FORTRAN, one can learn to use it in as little as six to ten hours.

My main point is that there are no mysteries about computers and programming. But computers are to be used by and for the benefit of humans, so without men to instruct them, they are of little or no value. The barrier that often exists between man and the machines should not be there and can be broken down with remarkably little effort.

Now, let's look at how computers have been used in the past. Because of the time and expense involved, the first computers were used to solve problems that were repetitive in nature so that the programming investment cost could be written off over some period of time. In addition, they were used to solve the problems that required exorbitant amounts of calculating—the problems in research environments—those that would have required a lifetime if solved manually. Frequently, they were used to generate design tables and standards which were duplicated and then distributed to design engineers to serve as supplements to the handbooks already on hand. In other cases, engineers were told to fill out input forms with data for certain standardized types of problems; these were turned over to the computer personnel, and subsequently particular answers could be returned for specific problems.

Then with the development of programming languages like FORTRAN, which were a simplified means of communicating with the machine, understood by more people, the solution of problems became more direct. The user no longer had to deal with a programmer but was able to communicate with the computer directly. Not only that, the overall time from problem definition to the obtaining of meaningful results was cut drastically. The net result is that it is now economically feasible to use computers for problems that will be solved only once. To generalize, any problem which is solved by manual means may be programmed and solved by machine. Problems that involve large amounts of computation and minimum amounts of thinking—ones where engineers spend hours pushing a slide rule or punching keys on a desk calculator—these should definitely be solved by machine. On the other hand, there is that class of problems involving a maximum amount of thinking and a minimum of calculating which very definitely should not be solved by machines, but are better handled manually. Finally there are those problems in between, where only experience and good judgment can dictate whether a manual or machine route would be the best.

In terms of specific problem areas where computers have been used—in relation to design and more specifically to architectural design where wood and wood products are used—there are a number of applications that may be mentioned. First, problems concerning geometry where arithmetic precision is a factor and where logarithms or desk calculators might be required are most amenable to computer solutions. Second, in the structural design area, the analysis of structures can be easily undertaken regardless of whether the structure is plane or complex, trussed or rigid. Specifically, in the area of building, I know of one firm that has been successful in automating large portions of their design work from the determination and tabulation of column loads, to the sizing up of the columns regardless of the design material, to the design of footings be they square, rectangular, or pile-supported. Third, in the planning and implementation phases of design, much has been done with computers in connection with job scheduling and control, including the whole concept of critical-path scheduling. More recently computers have also been used by some firms for specification preparation. These are just a few areas that can be mentioned. Many others exist in a wide variety of disciplines in which design takes place.

To make the communication between man and machine even easier and to facilitate computer usage, higher level languages have been developed that are called problem-oriented languages. Here, with minimum instruction and ease, one familiar with a problem area can obtain computer solutions easily. Many languages of this type exist, such as COGO for coordinate geometry, STRESS for structural engineering systems solver, SEPOL for soils engineering problem-oriented language; and STRUDEL for structural design language.

To provide users with a convenient computer facility, the concepts of time-sharing and remote-computing have come into being. With time-sharing, one computer is shared jointly by a varying number of users, who use it simultaneously. The sophistication of present-day hardware allows such systems to exist. Synonymous with the concept of time-sharing in problem-solving is the concept of remote computing, where desk-top terminals, much like typewriter keyboards are used to communicate with computers at remote locations. The terminals tie into a central computer by means of telephone or teletypewriter hookup. In this manner, a designer may use the computer at his own desk whenever he needs it.

Much has already been done in the graphics area. Here the computer, in addition to providing numerical solutions to problems, can also produce solutions in the form of graphic drawings. Mechanical plotters can produce machine-made drawings from coordinates worked out automatically by the computer. Samples of such drawings are contour maps, highway cross-sections, structural framing plans, mechanical drawings, and electrical circuits.

Because mechanical plotting is relatively slow, cathode-ray displays have also been developed to produce drawings electronically. These drawings can be generated in two ways—either by conventional programming, when mathematical models generate the points to be plotted, or by a light pen manually traced on an oscilloscope screen by a designer.

Still another area where computers are proving to be of value is in the storing, retrieval, and dissemination of information. Such applications are common to all types of information systems. Information, whether current or dated, is essential to the successful implementation of any plan, project, or business. An automated system is particularly desirable when the quantities of information dealt with are large and subject to changes and particularly where results are sensitive to correct information at any point in time. Many such systems are in existence today.

In effect then, computer uses at the present time cover a wide range. For the most part the primary applications in design are found first in analysis phases, second in the synthesis (or design in its narrow sense) phase, and last in the areas of planning and implementation.

Looking to the future, it would be foolish to try to predict what will happen. The computer has had so dynamic and dramatic an influence to date that there is no telling what new applications it will have, particularly as the professionals—engineers, architects, scientists—learn to make even more effective use of computers as a matter of routine.

Certainly we can expect to see many more developments in computer-aided design. In the area of graphics alone, a tremendous amount can be expected. For example, it is already possible to develop a perspective view automatically from basic plans and elevation information and then observe this view from a variety of vantage points. Even the possibility of making changes in a perspective and then automatically producing revised plans and elevations does not stretch the imagination too far. In addition, where computer graphics applications were very costly not too many years ago, we find that now such costs are beginning to work their way down to more realistic levels.

Information-system applications also have a significant potential in the design area. The creation of information banks containing generalized specification information or even product information as well as design information can be conceived. One could then keep this information current and have it readily available to be retrieved at random by a large number of users. The primary determinant for when such systems are implemented is economics.

The fact, however, that we are embarking on a time-sharing era in computer usage leads one to believe that some of the more sophisticated computer applications will be made practical much sooner than we think. While we recognize that such applications more often than not require the use of the larger, more powerful, and more costly computers, the fact that a host of people can use them simultaneously places them closer to the grasp of all.

I have by no means even begun to touch all the areas of design where computers are having and will have some impact. Areas such as mathematical modeling, simulation, optimization techniques utilizing linear programming, and others are but a few that could be discussed.

Afterword

GEORGE F. EARLE
Professor of Art
School of Landscape Architecture
State University of New York College
of Environmental Science and Forestry

The symposium on which this book is based was held in the fall of 1967. Its entire concept was contemporary—the insights, criticisms, and commentary were of the moment, and although projecting into the future, we did not think of classic timelessness, for we expect that viewpoints of such contemporary currency may become quickly outdated.

In our modern world of unparalleled acceleration this is especially so. Of all the aspects of change shaping our current life, none is so radically new nor so universally agreed upon as the rate or speed of change. Taste cycles, styles of living, and group attitudes that used to last for a century or more now are dated after a couple of years—last year's ideas, like last year's product design, are already obsolete in many, many instances.

And yet, these thoughts about wood and its design, and even those more vulnerable environmental-social concerns about wood's impact on human values, seem, if anything, to have intensified in their significance. During the passing months, the moving changes that have occurred have brought these declarations of the symposium into greater bearing upon social needs. The elapsed time seems to have intensified the points expressed, they have not run down or been overtaken by developments.

The specific problems the symposium considered could be grouped as follows: the need for a renewed use of wood in design and construction where its functional characteristics have been falsely compared with, or eclipsed by, newer materials; the need for technological developments with wood to improve its functional character competitively; and the need for the aesthetic values of wood as an enrichment to an increasingly sterile and synthetic social environment. These problems, and the many subproblems related to these, are no closer to solution; in fact, the need for solution has intensified. But this problem is now more clearly recognized and the field is more ready to accept such solutions.

Even the exhibit of specific wood products and objects of art in wood remains surprisingly classic and invulnerable to fashion. Perhaps the natural organic character of wood as a material gives it a classic quality—makes it proof against time. Certainly the material itself persistently dictates its ultimate shape beyond the limits within which the artist or craftsman may mold it. And, of course, its material identity, its visible texture, and its tactile warmth, as so many papers in the symposium bring out, have always held a timeless appeal and fascination for man and been an intimate part of his environment. This very intimacy possibly makes wood as timeless in its meaning to man as other organic living forms, such as the trees themselves, animals, and the unclothed human body.

One can think of an exhibit with similar types of objects worked in other materials —ceramic, plastic, glass, cast in metal, or even chiseled of stone—being much more submissive to the will of the artist or craftsman, much less controlled by the material! Such an exhibit would seem far more subject to ephemeral fashion and the changing tastes of our accelerating world.

In any case, the message of the symposium is more alive and current than ever. The need to reintroduce warmth and human scale into a world gone cold and brutally monotonous cries out not for a return to tradition but for a reworking of those elements, materials, and forms that have always enriched life. The infinite shape-plasticity of modern technology's productions, made of materials that deny any self-identification in their total commitment to their function, are not easily related to man's experience with living. Instead, the knotty, splintery, irregularly dimensioned, warping, shrinking, swelling, directionally grained, uneven strengthened piece of wood expresses better man's grasp of the imperfect reality of life, as compared with his computed abstractions. Wood is but one of the many humanizing elements our new cultural environment requires, but as these papers have made evident, wood has unique powers of timeless service while charming with grace and elegance.